FAMILY
FORTUNES

FAMILY FORTUNES

*How to Build Family Wealth
and Hold Onto It for 100 Years*

BILL BONNER
WILL BONNER

WILEY
John Wiley & Sons, Inc.

Published by John Wiley & Sons, Inc., Hoboken, New Jersey.
Published simultaneously in Canada.

For general information on our other products and services or for technical support, please contact our Customer Care Department within the United States at (800) 762-2974, outside the United States at (317) 572-3993 or fax (317) 572-4002.

Wiley also publishes its books in a variety of electronic formats. Some content that appears in print may not be available in electronic books. For more information about Wiley products, visit our web site at www.wiley.com.

Library of Congress Cataloging-in-Publication Data:

Bonner, William, 1948–
    Family fortunes : how to build family wealth and hold onto it for 100 years / Bill Bonner and Will Bonner.—1st ed.
        p.   cm.—(Agora series ; 77)
    Includes index.
    ISBN 978-1-118-17141-7 (Cloth); ISBN 978-1-118-23987-2 (ebk);
    ISBN 978-1-118-26451-5 (ebk); ISBN 978-1-118-22684-1 (ebk)
        1. Families. 2. Wealth. 3. Financial security. I. Bonner, Will, 1978– II. Title.
HQ734.B688   2012
306.85—dc23
                                                                          2012015373

Printed in the United States of America

10 9 8 7 6 5 4

This book is dedicated to our matriarch, Anne Bonner.
She rocked the cradles . . . and our world.

CONTENTS

PREFACE

What separates the rich from the rest of us?

Hemingway claimed it was the fact that they had more money.

Recently, we drove through a working-class neighborhood of Baltimore, called Dundalk. It is an area of simple one- and two-story wooden houses on small lots. Fifty years ago, it was where Baltimore's industrial labor force lived. The residents worked in heavy industries for companies such as Bethlehem Steel, General Motors, and the B&O Railroad and at the busy harbor.

Today, those high-wage industries are mostly silent and rusting. Some sites along the water have been converted into loft apartments for Baltimore's young professionals. And some of the children and grandchildren of the older residents have moved away—to the suburbs or to other cities.

But most of them are still there. Their parents and grandparents earned a good living. But few got rich. And now, few of their descendants are rich, either.

Across town, in the rich "old" northern suburbs of Roland Park and Ruxton, the people are different. The rich left the city many years ago. But in these green suburbs, they remain. Some richer. Some poorer. But by and large, they're the same people whose parents were there 50 years ago.

What accounts for it? How come some families stay rich generation after generation, while others never have a nickel?

"Culture," you will say. "Education," perhaps. You won't be wrong. But what, specifically, about culture and education is it that makes such a big difference in outcomes?

The secret is simply this: The rich take the long view.

Let me ask you something. If you thought you'd live forever, would you do anything differently? Wouldn't your attitude toward your money change a little? Wouldn't you slow down, realizing that you're not in such a hurry to make money? And wouldn't you reduce your spending, too, knowing that your money would have to last you a long, long time?

If you look carefully, almost all Old Money secrets can be traced to a single source: a longer-term outlook. The truly wealthy are careful to spend their money on things that hold their values over time.

It's why they do not trade in and out of investments. Instead, they find a few positions and stick with them—for decades.

It's also why they prepare their families, over the course of many, many years, so that they will be prepared for the challenges of managing and enlarging the family wealth.

It's why they invest in education and training. And why they make sure family members add to their collective wealth, rather than subtracting from it.

It's why they try to guide their children to suitable spouses. They know that a rotten apple will spoil the barrel.

It's why they spend time and money on lawyers and accountants, too, making sure that the structures are in place to pass along wealth and protect it.

It's why they prefer deep-value assets over momentum investing. Over time, value rises to the top. Momentum slows.

It's why they will wait a long time—many, many years—for the right investment at the right price.

It's why they like investments with long-term payoffs, such as timber, mining, and infrastructure. And it's how they are able to benefit from compound growth, letting relatively modest gains grow over several generations.

It's why they are almost fanatical about eliminating costs: taxes, investment charges, and unrewarding living expenses. They know that wear and tear, over time, will wreck their family fortunes.

It's why they develop long-lasting partnerships with the professionals they need to make sure their interests are protected and their plans are carried out.

It is all a matter of time. They have money. But they expect to have it for a long time. So they work hard, investing in education and professional advice, to make sure they have the personal resources they need.

As you will see in the pages that follow, the long view comes into play in almost everything. But it's one thing to talk about the "long view" and quite another to take it. What it usually means is something that most people don't want to do: give up something today for something tomorrow.

Psychologists have done some work on this subject. What they have found is what you'd expect. People who can forgo immediate rewards in favor of longer-term goals are more successful.

In one study, for example, children were offered marshmallows. But they were given a choice. They could have one marshmallow right away. Or if they were willing to wait, they could have two later on. The children were then filmed. They fidgeted. They fussed. They struggled to resist taking the candy, because they knew that two would be more satisfying than just one.

In the study, the average child held out for a bit short of three minutes. But about 30 percent of them held out for 15 minutes and were given two marshmallows.[1]

The chief researcher in these studies, Walter Mischel, had tested the friends of his own young daughters and was therefore able to keep an eye on his subjects throughout the years. As they grew up, he began to notice a link between his marshmallow tests and the girls' subsequent performances in school. Curious, he followed up with a serious inquiry into how his marshmallow tests corresponded to other areas of performance. What he found was that, generally, the children who could not wait often found themselves in difficulty later on . . . either with behavioral or academic problems. They had lower SAT scores. They had trouble paying attention. Even their friendships were weak.

On average, the kids who could wait 15 minutes had SAT scores more than 200 points higher than those who could wait only 30 seconds.

In another study, researchers offered teenagers $1 immediately . . . or $2 a week later. They found the results were far better indicators of academic success than IQ tests.

But the researchers didn't stop there. The kids grew up, with the psychologists looking over their shoulders. The low self-discipline children became—surprise!—fat, unsuccessful adults.

In his testing, Mischel found something interesting and a little disturbing. Children as young as 19 months old could be tested, reliably, to see if they could delay gratification. If they could, they seemed destined for success. If they couldn't, they were surely going to end up in prison or the poorhouse. This made it appear to be a genetic matter. Either you were "born that way" or you weren't. But Mischel says it's more complicated that that. It's like learning to use a computer. You won't do it if you don't have access to a computer.[2]

Broadly, from our point of view, we interpret that to mean that you won't develop the capacity for forbearance unless you have a reason to.

If there is one thing that marks families with money over the long term it is this: delayed gratification.

There are psychologists who believe that the performance of different cultures can be largely explained by this single point. Those who look ahead to the future and those that plan for it—surprise, surprise!—have better futures.

There are even some geo-theorists who believe that the relative outperformance of certain ethnic groups of people can be explained in the same way. How come Europe grew rich while Africa remained poor? How come North America is relatively rich, while South America is relatively poor? (However, this was a better question a few years ago, when the differences were more obvious.) How come, generally, colder countries are more successful than warmer ones?

The reason, they believe, is that colder climates force a longer-term view.

Believe it or not, there are still groups of primitive hunter-gatherers living on the African savannah. Anthropologists studying them have found little sense of the future. They do not prepare for it because they don't need to. One day's hunt is much like the next. One day's nuts and berries differ little from those of the day before. No need to think much about the future or to plan for it.

Presumably, people very similar to these primitive tribes spread into Europe and Asia, and there they encountered new challenges. Thirty thousand years ago, there were human tribes following the caribou along the face of Europe's continental glacier.

Near our house in France there is a cave that provides evidence. For thousands of years, a group of hunters made the cave a stopping point. But it was only a stopping point. They followed the herds of caribou that ranged over Europe at the time. As the weather changed, so did their lifestyle. They had to change their living patterns—and their living places—to keep up with the weather.

In cold climates, you need to stock food, clothing . . . and prepare shelter . . . in anticipation of bad weather. In some places, growing seasons are only a few months long. People had to work night and day in order to put aside enough for the long, cold season ahead. Whether this brought about a change in the habits of mind that cause a person to think about the future—or whether the harsh climate merely eliminated people who could not prepare for it—we don't know. But somehow the idea took . . . and became more than an idea; it became a cultural rule.

No doubt, the notion that thinking ahead pays off was reinforced by the introduction of agriculture. It was one thing to gather wild grains. It was quite another to plant them. Planting required prepared land, seed and, in the warm, dry climates of Mesopotamia and Egypt, irrigation. All of these things forced people to think ahead. And they required sacrifice in the present for the sake of the future.

How many families went to bed hungry rather than "eat their seed corn"? They had to sacrifice . . . to forbear . . . to discipline themselves to not eat the kernels of corn they had spared for planting, or they would not have any corn to harvest the next year. People must have also learned to save not only *some* corn, but the best corn, for those were the best seeds. So a family had to deprive itself of its best food . . . in order to have more later on.

A quick look at a map will also reveal another curiosity. Look at places that are rich. Then look at places where people are poor. Take Haiti, for example. It is one of the poorest countries on Earth. It is also one of the easiest places to grow food. Go figure. Want to find other easy places to grow food? Just look at some of the poorest countries in the world: the Democratic Republic of Congo, Burundi, and Liberia.

Now take a look at Switzerland. It is perhaps the richest country on Earth. It is also one of the hardest places to grow food. Go figure again. And look at other relatively rich countries: Sweden, Norway, Denmark, Germany, Britain.

Is it a coincidence that these are difficult places to grow food? Where, for thousands of years, people had to look ahead, plan, and prepare in order to avoid going hungry?

Of course, there's more to the story. Take West Virginia. On the surface of things, West Virginia and Switzerland are almost twins. Both are mountainous. Both are landlocked in the middle of great economies. Both are inhabited almost exclusively by people of European descent.

But the similarities end there. In terms of resources, Switzerland is poor. West Virginia is very rich. While Switzerland has little timber, little arable farmland, and few mineral resources, West Virginia has almost unlimited supplies. Its oil and gas resources, for example, could power the entire United States for more than 100 years. It doesn't have wide, flat fields, but compared with Switzerland, it has much more useful, fertile farmland; its mountains are not as high or steep. It also has timber and water resources in abundance.

Oddly, in terms of earnings and net worth, there is an even further divergence, but in the opposite sense: The people of Switzerland are the richest in the world. The people of West Virginia, however, are among America's poorest. How could that be?

We don't know. But the cultures are quite different. Switzerland evolved a forward-looking, patient, and self-sacrificing culture. Perhaps it was the long, snowy winters that exaggerated the "prepare, prepare, prepare" culture. The Swiss build houses out of concrete, stone and solid wood, according to the toughest building codes in the world. They even have to have bomb shelters . . . with food and supplies stocked up against disaster. They also have, per capita, the biggest intergenerational wealth transfers in the world.

We know West Virginia fairly well. It is perhaps our favorite state. But it is also a puzzlement. There are rocks and trees everywhere. Compared with the soft, funny-shaped rocks of Poitou, France, where we've spent years repairing stone walls, the rocks in West Virginia are a stonemason's dream. They are hard … and often rectangular. They practically lay themselves.

As for the timber, imagine the envy in a Swiss woodsman's eyes when he sees it. The old hardwood forests of Switzerland must have been cut down centuries ago. What is left is controlled growth, mostly conifers, which have nice qualities of their own, but are in no way equal to the majestic oaks, beeches, and hickories of West Virginia's green hills.

The first settlers used the trees to build log cabins, mounted on stone foundations. Later came two-by-fours, aluminum siding, and drywall. Not to mention tarpaper and mobile homes! Even in the twenty-first century, many of the houses you will see in West Virginia are shacks—architecturally disgraceful, uncomfortable, charmless, and temporary. Compared with the sturdy Swiss chalet, the common West Virginia house is little more than a hovel.

What's more, when you look at almost any house in Switzerland, what you don't see is as telling as what you do. Before your eyes, you will find a handsome building, designed to last for centuries. You will not see any of the typical lawn decorations so popular in West Virginia. There are no rusty automobiles with their hoods up and their wheels off. There are no refrigerators lying on their backs, as if killed in battle and left to lie where they fell. Nor will you see lawnmowers, tractors, cement mixers, children's toys . . . or any of the other paraphernalia that West Virginians use to fill the empty places in their parks and gardens. No one knows why this is the case, but we will put forward a hypothesis: They are victims of abundance.

In Switzerland, the approach of winter meant many months with little access to food. It required the Swiss to think ahead, to plan for the lean months. You might think the same phenomenon would shape the culture of the mountain men of West Virginia, too. But the Mountain State is a much richer place. And it was settled—at least by Europeans—after the invention of the efficient hunting rifle. The first European settlers, tough Scots-Irishmen, found plenty of game, even in winter. They were much better armed than the "Indians" who preceded them. They found it relatively easy to feed themselves.

In fact, according to some reports, the native tribes had bad habits of their own. They didn't have to work too hard to survive, either. And when the first white men learned from the natives, not only did they pick up their skills, but they took up their insouciant attitudes.

Even today, the mountain men do not seem particularly concerned with planning for the future. When the going gets tough, the tough men of the Appalachians go hunting. Just like the Indians.

As for their miserable lodges, the settlers merely picked up the habits of the migratory hunters who preceded them. There was no need to build lasting structures; they would move to the next valley . . . the next hollow . . . the next county . . . soon, anyway. And why not throw the refrigerator out the door? It was such a big wilderness . . . so rich in everything, especially land. Throw out the trash and move on. The attitude was well adapted to the place. Why go to all the trouble of building proper garages—and proper houses—if you're going to move on soon, anyway?

But it is not an attitude that encourages long-lasting wealth. We must be more like the Swiss and the Dutch than the West Virginians or the Haitians. We have to make sacrifices now, for the benefit of the future.

Unfortunately, it may be a future in which we personally cannot participate. For it is a distant future we are talking about, 20 . . . 50 years ahead.

It is only by looking ahead, into a future we may not be able to see with our own eyes, that we can build enduring wealth. And by the way, there's more to "wealth" than just money.

One thing you can see for yourself: Rome wasn't built in a day. Nor were the Jardins du Luxembourg. The architectural wealth of Europe is the result of centuries of investment and preservation. The hovels and shacks disappear. The Louvre and Versailles are still there. They are part of Europe's public wealth.

There is immense private wealth, too. You can have an ugly house. Or a pretty one. The values, from a tax—or even a market—standpoint could be the same. The pretty one takes more effort to get right. Even over generations.

We bought the Chateau d'Ouzilly for a pittance in 1994. The owners sold it to us because they could no longer afford to keep it up. We discovered that we could barely afford it, either. The correct translation of the word *chateau* is "money pit." Most people would argue that it is a wealth destroyer, not a wealth builder. Most people would say that it is a way to deprive future generations of wealth, not to save it for them.

But life is funny . . . curious . . . and full of ironies. The previous owners had bought the chateau for nothing, paying for it in revolutionary scrip during the French Revolution. The local nobility had fled France for their lives. The chateau was there for the taking.

By the 1970s, however, the lands around the chateau had been divvied up by successive generations, and the remaining fields—about 300 acres—were not enough to support the house and the family. It had to be sold.

The seller told us that the weather was always good in the summer. "It never rains in July or August," he claimed. As for the roof, "It never leaks." One day in July, soon after we bought the place, we discovered that he had lied twice.

It would surely be cheaper and easier to repair the roof of a small house in West Virginia than to fix the roof of a chateau in France. The *ardoise* (local slate) costs a fortune. But when it was done, what did we have? We had a chateau that was dry and a roof that would last for maybe five times as long as we will. It was costly. But perhaps our children and grandchildren would thank us, for we could give them a long-lasting asset.

All over France, there are relics of the "chateau age." Some are assets. Some are not. Where owners have not fixed the roofs, the chateaux are liabilities. But where the owners have kept them up, they are assets that can last for generations, assuming the French government doesn't tax them too heavily.

The same general comments could be made—with fewer "if"s, "and"s, or "but"s—regarding gardens. In Europe, too, you will find gardens that were planted to increase the wealth of future generations, not necessarily the people who planted them. At our place, for example, we put in an *allee* of plain sycamores. Alas, the trees grow slowly while their owners age quickly. They will not reach their full majestic payoff until this author's grandchildren are as old as he is.

The present generation, those who plant, are arguably as impoverished as those who replace a slate roof. But those who reap the rewards are enriched. Time has worked its magic. The future generation enjoys stately trees that took a lifetime to grow.

Again, you wouldn't plant trees unless you planned to stay around—or, more correctly, you planned that your descendants would stay around . . . or perhaps that someone would stay around who would appreciate what you had done.

Another group that has been extraordinarily effective at creating and preserving wealth is the Jews. Many Jews throughout history have worked not as farmers, but as tradesmen, merchants, doctors, teachers, and moneylenders. Frequently, if not generally, they were denied ownership of land. They couldn't plant trees. They couldn't plant anything. Often, they didn't have the need to "save the seed corn." You'd think they would be the biggest spendthrifts and "live for today" crowd on Earth. But they are not. They are careful with wealth. And extremely forward-looking. Why?

Well, one thing that comes readily to mind is that Jews are also extremely oriented toward their own history. And history is a kind of future in reverse. Perhaps it gave them the same focus on the need for preparedness.

Jewish history is a long story of disasters, one after another. Many of those disasters involved avoiding extermination by fleeing. And fleeing costs money. The Jews, perhaps more than anyone, had to think ahead. They had to be prepared. At any minute, the heavy boot of the state or the mob might come down on them. They could not plant trees. But they accumulated wealth, often in the form of gold and diamonds. It is no coincidence that they are the world's leading moneymen today.

In fact, with the Jews in mind, we might broaden our hypothesis into a general theory:

Adversity leads a people to appreciate preparedness. Wealth is preparation in negotiable form.

The first chapter of this book addresses the objection: Why would you bother? Can't we safely assume that the supply channels will keep the supermarket shelves stocked, winter and summer? Aren't the pogroms over? Isn't the desire to stockpile grain—or wealth—for generations a bit useless and anachronistic, like a prehensile tail? Besides, it would be so much more fun to spend your money now, wouldn't it?

Assuming you have jumped that hurdle, the following chapters suggest ways to do it.

Not that we, your authors, are experts on the subject. We are just learning. But we happily pass along what we think we have learned and/or figured out on our own. Whether it is correct or not—or whether it is useful or not—you will have to judge for yourself.

But the main point is worth keeping in mind: This book is not about getting something. It is about giving up something. It is for the planter. For the roofer. For the builder. For the saver. It is for the person who wishes to make a sacrifice—even if it is a relatively agreeable sacrifice—so that others may benefit from it, perhaps others whom he will never meet.

Bill Bonner

ACKNOWLEDGMENTS

Special thanks to Robert Marstrand, Chris Hunter, Kat McKerrow, Susanne Clark, and Elizabeth Bonner for their generous help in preparing this book.

INTRODUCTION

FAMILIES THAT WON'T FAIL AND MONEY THAT WON'T DIE

Much of what most people think about "Old Money" families is wrong, including much of what many Old Money families themselves think. You probably have an idea about what kinds of people they are. And you're probably not too far off. But there are too few of them, and they are too varied, to provide a meaningful stereotype. Some are smart. Some are dumb. Some show off their money; others don't. Many—perhaps most—are so discreet that we don't know who they are and what they do.

For those and other reasons that will become obvious, we have chosen prescriptivism over descriptivism. That is, we will prescribe what we might call the "ideal" Old Money. We tell you what we think Old Money ought to do, what it ought to think, and how it ought to manage its wealth.

For example, you probably imagine that serious Old Money families are very conservative with their wealth, favoring "safe" U.S.

Treasury bonds over riskier stocks and bonds. And if you have a lot of money, that is exactly what the typical investment advisor will tell you to do with it. You need to play it safe; stick to bonds.

But if you depend on wealth "professionals" to help you manage and protect your money, you are already making a big mistake. Most financial professionals are good at mixing drinks; some are excellent raconteurs. You shouldn't let them near your money. As for U.S. Treasury debt, it is probably one of the riskiest investments you can make.

In this book, we talk about Old Money not necessarily as it is but as it should be. And it should be very different from what you probably imagine.

It is commonly believed that seriously rich people should withhold money from their children in order to toughen them up, so that they will "find their own ways" or "make it on their own." Many favor giving their fortunes to charity in order to avoid corrupting their own kin.

This is nonsense, in our view. All wealth either is consumed or must be owned and managed by someone. Serious Old Money accepts the responsibility of taking care of its own money and preparing the next generation to do likewise.

Besides, most charity efforts squander wealth, and many harm the people they were meant to help.

Everyone knows, also, that you should try to give your children as much education as possible. But that, too, is wrong.

And so are Warren Buffett and the other super-rich people who think paying higher taxes will be good for the country. It won't be, and Buffett must know it.

The closer you look, the more you see that the ideas most people have about wealth—and how to hold on to it—are silly, superficial, and probably a kind of financial suicide.

Not that we claim to have the ultimate truth on the matter. But, at least, we can see that most of the ideas you find on the subject are humbug.

As you will see, family money is very different from other kinds of money—even the money of the rich. It requires different treatment, different management, different security measures—a different investment philosophy—even a different cultural bias.

There are a lot of families. And there are a lot of rich people. But there aren't many rich families, at least not for long. And there's a good reason. Keeping money and the family together over longer than a generation is tough. Statistically, it's unlikely. Practically, it's hard work. Most people don't even want to try. Because it's too hard. Or because they don't even think it is a good idea.

Real family money—Old Money—is rare; it's way out on the edge of the bell curve. And it involves sacrifice, not self-indulgence. It involves giving up, not getting. It involves more work, not more leisure.

It is a challenge, not a reward.

But if you are the sort of person to whom this challenge appeals, the rewards can be very substantial.

Let's say, for example, that you're able to put $1 million in a family trust. If you organize it correctly and get a rate of growth averaging 6 percent compounded (there are some very important tricks you need to know), your grandchildren could have $18.4 million in 50 years.

But there's much more to this than money. In fact, money is the least of it, the easiest part of the whole program. Nor is it the biggest benefit. Not by a long shot. This is not about making or preserving money. It's not about gaining fame and fortune. It's not about living the good life of luxury and ease.

It's about building the kind of family that can maintain its wealth and independence over generations. This is no easy feat. It's against the odds. It's almost against nature itself. Nature always tries to drag a family back down to the ordinary. And most ordinary people don't have any wealth to speak of. So if you're going to have wealth—and hold on to it for longer than a single generation—you're going to have to do some rather extraordinary things.

Such as?

Well, once you've made money, you might think the hard part is over. You might think you don't have to take chances or work so hard. All you have to do is to put the money into "safe" investments and kick back, right?

Wrong. The "safest" investments always turn out to be the most destructive, from a long-term perspective. And besides, you can't afford the low returns that these supposedly safe investments bring. You need investment returns *higher* than average. That means you need an entirely different investment approach.

The key to this approach is that you have to learn to use time to your advantage. Time works against almost everybody. But if you want your family to maintain wealth over several generations, you have to make time work for you or you're doomed.

Time destroys fortunes in obvious ways, and in some ways that aren't so obvious. Each year that passes imposes costs: living costs, taxes, maintenance, and so forth. There are also investment costs: fees, commissions, charges. Plus, there are inevitable setbacks: bear markets, errors, oversights, inflation, crashes, fraudsters. All cost you money, sometimes big money.

You have to limit these costs, which isn't easy, and you need to earn higher rates of return to offset them. You can do it, with a little luck, if you let time work for you.

The typical investor is betting against time. He buys a stock. He hopes the stock will go up . . . and that he will then get out before time takes it back down again.

But if you're willing to let time help you, you can wait long enough to see what direction the *market* is taking. The big trends are long-term trends. The last big bull market on Wall Street lasted 25 years. The bear market before that lasted 16 years. The bull market in bonds began in 1983 . . . and it's still going on. These are the trends that pay off. And if you listen and watch carefully, you can see them coming and going. And you can use them to limit your losses and improve your gains.

But that is not the most important thing. Time also has a devastating effect on families. People grow old. They're no longer able to do the work required to maintain a dynamic, capable family. New family members are often less able or distracted. Husbands, wives, children— every new family member comes with risks attached. And over time, one or two of those time bombs is bound to blow up.

More important than the money, the family has to be kept strong and healthy. A strong family can make money. A weak family can't even hold onto money that someone else made. A strong family can build and develop business opportunities. A weak family can only fumble and destroy them. A strong family can meet its financial, business, and other challenges. A weak family collapses under the pressure of them.

So how do you use time to make sure you have a strong family?

Well, that's the real secret of Old Money families. And it's a story that is scarcely understood by anyone. The key is that Old Money families are very, very different from regular families. And they are not at all what most people think they are.

They are not "conservative," in the usual sense. Instead, they are active and forward looking.

They may or may not live in luxury. But they always take care to live well.

They do not spend their time in idleness and leisure. Instead, they are engaged in business, investment and family activities.

They do not even rely on Old Money. They know that each generation needs to renew and rebuild its wealth—and itself.

You may find our view of Old Money surprising. In fact, a lot of people who actually have Old Money may find it surprising. For it is not merely a view of what people with multigenerational money do; after all, some are just lucky. It is not merely a sociological or financial study.

It is a manifesto for a new way of looking at both family and money.

Will Bonner

CHAPTER 1

WHO YA GONNA CALL?

We are learning the secrets of France's richest family. At least, they appear to be the richest family in France. They have businesses with annual revenues of about $70 billion—and more than a quarter of a million employees. But we'll bet you've never heard of them. And you've almost certainly never seen a picture of them. They are the Mulliez family from the north of France. Discreet. Private. Unostentatious.

They own huge discount shopping centers all over France and much of Europe. They were able to figure out how to run large-surface, low-price, rapid-turnover merchandising enterprises. Once they had the system figured out, they were able to apply it to several different retail industries.

The Mulliez family has been in business for half a century. They have managed to create one of the world's biggest and most profitable family business empires. And they have done it while also creating one of the biggest and most successful families.

From a business perspective, they followed the same three-step success formula John D. Rockefeller famously prescribed: They got to work early. They stayed late. They "struck oil" in the discount retail business.

But the really remarkable thing is the way the Mulliezes have been able to work together as a family, providing all the members—including over 520 in the extended family, not just those who happen to run the businesses—with substantial and enduring wealth.

What's their secret? We don't know. But we can guess.

First, it helps to have a big family. The disadvantage of a large family is that you have to split up the wealth among more people. But the advantage is that you have more hands to do the work. And the odds are you will have some clever people in the group.

The founding couple had 11 children. Their children almost all had children, too. Three of them had 7 children each.[1]

Second, the family decided not to split things up, but to have a system of "everything for everybody," in which all the children of the founding couple shared equally all the wealth (shares in active companies, mostly).

This was a break with tradition in a couple of respects: Usually, the people who actually build the wealth get a larger share of it. And, typically, in the north of France, although wealth may be partitioned equally, women are usually given real estate and men are given businesses (on the theory that they will take the risks and rewards of active enterprise, while women will be happy to have the solidity of real estate).

This decision, made decades ago, made a big difference. It kept the whole family focused on the family business because they were all in it together. Among the second generation, many did not play an active role in the business, but often, their children, who had as many shares in it as the children of the active siblings, did. The family could draw on three generations of talent. It still does.

Also, as new businesses were created, they were spun out from the center—with "everything for everybody" still the guiding principle.

Third, the family makes a huge effort at *affectio societatis*, the conscious reinforcement of the family's original principles and philosophies. The founders' business—and other—ideas are rehearsed, recalled, and recycled into each generation.

Fourth, they are careful not to get sidetracked by wealth or fame. They keep out of the public eye. There are few, if any, photos of the family members. The general public doesn't know who they are or what they look like.

Fifth, they do not sell. They've had many chances to "monetize" their businesses. They've rejected each one systematically. Their businesses double every seven years.

Sixth, the family requires all shareholders, who are also uncles, cousins, and other relatives, to play a role. Even if they are not active in the business, they are supposed to inform themselves about how the business is doing and to help sustain the founding principles of the enterprise.

These interested, knowledgeable, and committed shareholders permit the Mulliez businesses to take a more long-term outlook. They are not particularly concerned with quarterly results or with dividend payouts. What concerns them is the growth and health of the extended business empire of which they are all part.

This is just a guess, but we think families such as the Mulliezes are likely to be much more important in the future than they were in the recent past. Family money, in particular, is likely to be much more appreciated.

THE FAMILY VS. THE STATE

People are social animals. They need organizations, institutions, and collective arrangements that suit them. Family organizations come naturally. The family, extended to uncles, aunts, cousins, and so forth, has been the most important grouping for most of our time as humans. It used to be the family that provided most of our wants and needs—from shelter to food, clothing, entertainment, companionship—you name it. The "means of production" were controlled by the family. Production took place within the family. Only mating was, and still is, usually done outside of the family.

The Old Testament is largely a story of families. And the development of the Roman Empire, too, is a history of a small group of families on the banks of the Tiber that managed to gain control over much of the known world.

In Ireland, where we have our family office headquarters, family-based political and economic power lasted up until the time it was crushed by Oliver Cromwell's armies in the seventeenth century. Even today, the Irish parliament is known as the Fine Gael, or the "Gaelic families."

Families receded in importance with the rise of the social welfare nation-state. The promise of modern government was that it would take care of its people. And the illusion was that it didn't matter what kind of family you came from, that you would be equal to every other citizen. You would have equal access to public transportation, public education, job opportunities, and, ultimately—a good life.

Occasionally, the idea of the state as a replacement for the family was taken to extremes. Soviet-era work farms took charge of children at a very early age and raised them to be good communists. At least, that was the idea. Free from the biases, privileges, and residual bourgeois sentiments of family life, a collectively raised child was supposed to be the "new man" the Soviets thought they needed. What they got was a failed experiment and a nation of alcoholics.

Still, in modern developed countries, people are meant to owe greater allegiance to the government than to their own kin. They pledge allegiance to the flag. They register for the draft. They pay taxes. When they are in need, they visit a government assistance center. When they have a health problem, they expect a government-funded health system to take care of them. When they are unemployed, they look to the government to pay them—and to tide them over until they find another job.

If unemployment is statistically high, they expect the government to take action to fix the problem. And if there is a natural disaster, such as the flooding of New Orleans, they look to the government to look out for them.

Yet government's performance has been spotty. In fact, every study ever done concludes that the family can be far more helpful to an individual than the state. Schools with more parental involvement—in areas with "good" families—produce higher test results. People from successful families earn more money. People whose parents were happily married are more likely to be happily married themselves. Neighborhoods with stable, decent families have lower crime rates. People from good families even live longer.

People with some family money behind them are more likely to start successful businesses. Successful families help their members overcome problems. Help them get back on their feet when they fall. They help them in countless ways, most of them immeasurable.

Governments spend enormous amounts of money. Presumably, this money is intended to help people lead better lives. But there is no evidence that people are any better off. And there is strong reason to suspect that they would be better off if the money spent by the government had been left in the hands of the families it came from.

The growth in government, as a substitute for or competitor to families, coincided with a huge growth in wealth. Arguably, people accepted larger and larger government like they accept runaway bar tabs—when they can afford them.

But there is no reason to think that the trend toward centralized authority is immutable. In fact, history may be a long tale full of sound and fury, like the ravings of a lunatic. But there are patterns to it. Sometimes, credit, confidence, and centralized political authority expand. Sometimes they contract.

Sometimes centripetal forces dominate, sometimes centrifugal.

GOING BUST

The past 300 years have been marked by further and further centralization: first, the consolidation of kingdoms, duchies, and principalities of western Europe in the eighteenth century. Then, the building of the nation-states in the nineteenth century. And, finally, the creation of the European Union in the twentieth century.

The United States of America was created at the end of the eighteenth century. Its centralization was assured by the War Between the States in the middle of the following century and, later, by the imposition of a federal income tax, the direct election of senators (which ended individual states' participation in the federal government) and voluminous legislation and numerous Supreme Court decisions further enlarging the power of the central government at the expense of "states' rights."

All over the world, gradually, the local dialects, local money, local customs, and local military power disappeared. By 2007, all the major— and quite a few minor—European nations used the same currency, traded in the same goods, paid the same interest rates, and spoke a common commercial and diplomatic language: English. So, too, did the entire world come to practice modern credit-enhanced capitalism as taught in the leading business schools worldwide.

Why these things happened, we don't know. Was it just because, with the availability of modern communications, it was possible for the first time? Was it because technology had enabled further elaboration of the division of labor, in which each region could do what it did best and depend on the others for what it lacked?

Was it because offensive weapons had achieved supremacy? With the invention of modern artillery, there was no standing behind castle walls to protect a local fiefdom.

Or was it because modern centralized, enlightened government—combined with free trade, free elections, citizen soldiers, and guided capitalism—was simply a better, more productive system? We don't know.

But now we know something. The political/economic model used by European and American nation-states for the last 150 years is going bust.

They can't continue to pay for lifestyle enhancements with debt. Every major developed country in the world now has total debt-to-GDP (gross domestic product) of more than 250 percent. Britain and Japan are near 500 percent. You can do a simple calculation to figure out why that level of debt is unsustainable and why, as we write, Europe is on the verge of a crisis. With debt equal to five times GDP, interest payments take up a large part of output. At zero interest rate, the situation is manageable. But when interest rates move up, which they inevitably do, the debtor can't keep up. Imagine an "ordinary" rate of interest of 5 percent. Five percent of 500 percent is 25 percent.

There is no way a society can afford to use a quarter of its output just to pay for things it has already put into service—and much of which has been fully consumed! As debt payments, the money for past spending, increase, there is less and less money available for the here and now and the future. The economy slumps. As the economy goes down, revenues decline, making less money available for debt repayment. It is an obvious trap—so obvious that the whole system "blows up" soon after you head in that direction.

A centralized, united Europe is not a sure thing. Europe's leaders are fighting to stay in the footsteps of Louis XIV, Napoleon, Hitler, and Monnet: toward a unified Europe. They believe the debt problem can be hidden under the rug of a larger, more centralized political union. But the forces pulling apart the union may be greater than those bringing it together. The end of a 300-year-old trend may have finally arrived.

In America, too, the poor now threaten the rich. The middle class feels betrayed. Young men have been dubbed "Generation Jobless," with the highest unemployment rate since the Great Depression. As for the poor, they grow ever more desperate.

FROM THE BLOG *THE ECONOMIC COLLAPSE*

19 Statistics about the Poor that Will
Absolutely Astound You

1. According to the U.S. Census Bureau, the percentage of "very poor" rose in 300 out of the 360 largest metropolitan areas during 2010.
2. [In 2010], 2.6 million more Americans descended into poverty. That was the largest increase that we have seen since the U.S. government began keeping statistics on this back in 1959.
3. It isn't just the ranks of the "very poor" that are rising. The number of those just considered to be "poor" is rapidly increasing, as well. Back in the year 2000, 11.3 percent of all Americans were living in poverty. Today, 15.1 percent of all Americans are living in poverty.
4. The poverty rate for children living in the United States increased to 22 percent in 2010.
5. There are 314 counties in the United States where at least 30 percent of the children are facing food insecurity.
6. In Washington, D.C., the "child food insecurity rate" is 32.3 percent.
7. More than 20 million U.S. children rely on school meal programs to keep from going hungry.
8. One of every six elderly Americans now lives below the federal poverty line.
9. Today, there are over 45 million Americans on food stamps.
10. According to the *Wall Street Journal*, nearly 15 percent of all Americans are now on food stamps.
11. In 2010, 42 percent of all single mothers in the United States were on food stamps.
12. The number of Americans on food stamps has increased 74 percent since 2007.
13. We are told that the economy is recovering, but the number of Americans on food stamps has grown by another 8 percent over the past year.
14. Right now, one of every four American children is on food stamps.
15. It is being projected that approximately 50 percent of all U.S. children will be on food stamps at some point in their lives before they reach the age of 18.

(Continued)

16. More than 50 million Americans are now on Medicaid. Back in 1965, only 1 of every 50 Americans was on Medicaid. Today, approximately one out of every six Americans is on Medicaid.
17. One out of every six Americans is now enrolled in at least one government antipoverty program.
18. The number of Americans that are going to food pantries and soup kitchens has increased by 46 percent since 2006.
19. It is estimated that up to half a million children may currently be homeless in the United States.[2]

The Occupy Wall Streeters attack the government from the left. The Tea Partiers launch their assault from the right. The central authority may not hold.

But things are coming apart for a reason. Centralized control no longer works. Expanding credit no longer produces expanding output. Further government "investment" no longer produces decent returns. The whole edifice wobbles—and then collapses.

And people are better off. Belgium, which has been coming apart for years, still has one of the highest growth rates in Europe.

Since modern nations can't really afford the lifestyle goals they have set for themselves, they must cut back. That will mean that the people who counted on national health programs, free education, unemployment, welfare, pensions, and the other services provided by the government will be disappointed. They will look for alternatives.

And the alternative they will find is the one that was there all along—the one that has been the most reliable, from long before any histories were ever written up to the present: the family.

Unable to depend on the government when times are tough? Who ya gonna call? A federal bureaucrat? Or a friendly uncle?

To whom will you pledge allegiance? To the nation-state that let you down? Or the family that holds you up?

"NOBODY REALLY STARTS WITH NOTHING"

A study conducted in the early 1990s found that of those who inherited around $150,000, 20 percent left the labor force within three years.[3] This phenomenon has been confirmed by more recent research.

In *The Millionaire Next Door*, Thomas Stanley and William Danko found that children who had received family money were worth four-fifths less than those in the same professions who did not receive money from their parents.[4]

These numbers should make you worry. Give money to your children and you may ruin their lives. But is it better to ruin the lives of someone else's children?

One way or another, if you leave any surplus wealth behind, it's going to end up in someone's pocket. That person can benefit from it. Or not.

Merryn Somerset Webb, editor-in-chief of our own *MoneyWeek* magazine in the United Kingdom, says, "The great majority of entrepreneurs we write about have some money somewhere behind them."[5]

Many entrepreneurs—including the elder of your authors—are proud of the fact that they "started with nothing." But it is more a vanity than a fact. Nobody really starts with nothing. We set out from where we are. Perhaps we live at home, feeding at our parents' table while we prepare our business. Perhaps we depend on the kindness of strangers or a winning smile to help us get started. We all have something at the beginning and something at the end. The trick is to make the most of the middle.

But how?

One of Old Money's most precious secrets is time.

Here's another one: modesty.

It pays to be wary of knowledge, facts, and certainty. In business. Law. Investments. Character. Family relations. Everything connected with family money. Nobody really knows anything. It is all guesswork. The best we can hope to do is to guess well so that the space between the beginning and the end is filled well.

Be aware that you may not be able to do all you hope to do, and if you're not careful, you'll do considerable harm. Tread boldly, but carefully.

Also, be aware that almost everything you read or hear on the subject is either stupid, wrong, and/or self-serving. Very often, the professionals who offer to help keep family and money are "talking their book," encouraging you to do things that just, by coincidence, also put money in their pockets.

That is true, generally, in the investment world, too. The people who offer to make you money often have stakes in the investments they present. They sell and take commissions. They manage and take fees. They broker deals and take part of the upside.

While much of this conflict of interest is obvious, much of it isn't. Nearly all of Wall Street (that is to say, all of the financial industry) has a bias to the upside. Its "book," which is Wall Street lingo for its own financial interests, or its book of trading positions, wants you to believe that "investing" pays off. This is regarded as a matter of common knowledge. It is a "fact." Yet it often isn't true. And if you mean "investing" the way most people invest, it usually isn't true.

Regarding family money, many of the other things that people take for granted should be taken out and examined more closely. Often, we find they are absurd, incorrect, or counterproductive.

A HISTORY OF FAMILY WEALTH

But let us begin our story in the beginning. . . .

Reaching back into history, what do we find? In what institution did people most often put their faith and their money? The government? Banks? Mutual funds? Lawyers? Clubs? The Church?

People made many different arrangements, depending on what was going on at the time. But the institution that most commonly held and allocated wealth was the family. We say that without any real proof. But it seems self-evident. Most people never had much real wealth. The little they had was what they lived.

When society reached the stage at which a significant accumulation of wealth was possible, it too was naturally focused on the family. The earliest records tell the story of people who tried to pass along wealth—and often power—to children. Often, these are sad stories. Of course, that's what makes them good stories. A story needs adversity, something to overcome. And the transfer of wealth and power was fraught with trial and tribulation. Frequently, it was a tragedy, not a comedy.

Families began figuring out ways to control family wealth, and its passage from one generation to the next, as soon as they had enough to worry about. Inheritance issues are frequent sources of conflict in the Bible: Who gets what. Why. And when.

In the story of the coat of many colors, for example, Joseph's brothers were so jealous they tried to kill him. So did emperors and kings throughout history murder their rivals with tedious frequency. Being the younger brother of a successful general or a king was often dangerous.

Gradually, more peaceful methods of dividing and managing wealth were developed. Younger brothers were given dukedoms or kingdoms of their own. Successful generals were kept away from the centers of power.

Generals often captured the loyalty of their men. In the Roman Republic, for example, generals were not allowed to return to Rome with their troops.

That is, of course, why "crossing the Rubicon" was such a big deal. Caesar broke the law of the republic and turned Rome into an empire. This opened the door to another go-round of succession battles. By (now) long tradition, in modern countries military authorities are subordinate to civilian authorities.

Intrafamily institutions for managing wealth appeared at least as early as the Roman era. A family would hire an administrator, a *major domus*, who became a *major domo* in the Middle Ages, to run its financial and business affairs. While family members proliferated, heads of families and administrators realized that there was a benefit to keeping wealth intact and centrally managed.

Europe developed the *fideicomiso*, which held wealth together, even as the family expanded and dispersed. Then private bankers took on the task of looking out for a family's wealth—for a fee, of course. Trusts were developed to hold wealth, and then became an industry as well as a financial instrument.

The Industrial Revolution was a period of rapid capital accumulation. It brought a new kind of wealth that was neither directly connected to dirt nor the residue of ancient plunder.

Until the nineteenth century, most wealth was in the form of land. Most people were farmers. And most of the wealth they had was in acreage and what it would produce. This made succession an easier matter than it is today. A young man had few options. And he had a keen interest in protecting what was then the family patrimony: the land. He naturally stepped into the shoes of his father, if he could, and then left them for his own son.

This also tended to preserve family wealth, for land was not easy to dissipate. You could sell it. You could mortgage it. Otherwise, it stayed put. It passed from one generation to the next naturally and easily. Rarely was there a "liquidity event" that opened the door to lifestyle enhancements.

The advent of more portable capital—shares, bonds, partnership interests, and so forth—also brought new ways for families to hold and manage their newly created riches. Corporations evolved. So did trust arrangements. And private bankers, family offices, wealth managers, and many other service providers. These, along with stockbrokers, luxury salesmen, yacht dealers, art mongers, and other professionals, offered new opportunities to invest and/or squander family fortunes. A liquidity event (typically, selling the family enterprise after the death of its founder) brought them round like bees to a cracked watermelon. Too often, the more they helped manage the family's newfound liquid wealth, the faster it disappeared!

THE TAX "SOLUTION"

In the twentieth century, also, another type of "solution" to the problem of holding and passing along family money arose: taxes. Seeing so much wealth building up in private hands, the government found it convenient to take some of it away. In America, there were no income taxes until 1913. At first, the government was fairly restrained about it. The top marginal rate was only 7 percent when it was first imposed. And it was applied only to people who had more than $500,000 in income—or about $12 million in today's dollars.

It was a tax on only the very rich.

Once the idea of taxing the rich took hold, people became quite enthusiastic about it. Taxes on the rich in Britain, for example, rose to over 90 percent of income in the 1960s. This created the "flight of the millionaires," which saw the British film industry, for example, flee to Hollywood and the Rolling Stones decamp for the South of France.

Which shows how much things have changed. Few people would go to the South of France today for tax reasons. The French soon joined, then surpassed, the English in taxing the rich.

Tax rates on the rich almost everywhere rose to the point where they were no longer productive. As rates rose, the rich ducked. Retired. Or fled. Capital left. People stopped investing. Incomes fell, and tax collections dropped along with them.

Since then, the taxers have become craftier. Art Laffer's curve suggests that there is an optimal rate of taxation, at which point higher or lower rates would bring forth less revenue. Top marginal tax rates have fallen in most of the leading developed economies. The authorities believe they have found the highest rates that do not suppress revenues to the government.

To paraphrase seventeenth-century French economist Jean Baptiste Colbert, collecting taxes is like plucking a goose. The idea is to get the largest number of feathers with the least amount of squawk.

Now efforts are under way—particularly in Europe—to "harmonize" tax rates so that the rich cannot easily flee. This will allow them to get more feathers. There are also efforts afoot in America to raise tax rates on the rich. This is seen as such an unquestionably good thing that some of the richest men in the country have joined the chorus for it. Similar songs are being sung in Europe too—in France, Francois Hollande proposes a 75-percent top rate.

There are two parts to the argument. First, the feds need the money. Second, it is "fair."

As to the first point, most people would find nothing to dispute. The governments of almost all the developed countries are deeply in debt. As populations age and economies weaken, they will not be able to provide the health, pension, education, and security benefits that have been promised unless they can find another source of revenue.

The answer to that argument is twofold. First, as we have seen, tax rates may already be at optimal levels. Increasing taxes on the rich—the people whose money creates new businesses and new jobs—is likely to be counterproductive. Second, will the world be a better, or a worse, place if the feds get more money? Well, strictly in material terms, it will almost certainly be a worse place, not a better one. It is made a better place (again, we are talking about only material things) when resources are used wisely and well.

If resources were invested so that they produce more resources, the world would be a better place because people would then have more things—including food—to use as they please. If they were invested in a way that produces no more output—or even decreases output—the world would be poorer.

In order to believe that transferring money from the rich people to the government is a good thing, you must believe that government bureaucrats will invest it more wisely than its lawful owners. If not, higher taxes on the rich produce poverty and misery, not prosperity and happiness.

It hardly seems necessary to discuss the point further. Government is a notoriously bad capital investor. The trouble is it's hard to prove, because government operates outside of the price system. People do not get to "vote" with their money on whether they wish to send a squadron of fighter planes to Iraq or build a school. They do not get to choose what things have real value and what things do not. The feds decide for them, making choices that usually turn out to be foolish.

Today, a family that wishes to preserve its money over several generations must include taxes at the top of its list of things to worry about. But this takes us back to the most basic question: Why bother?

A STAB IN THE BACK

A letter appeared in the *Financial Times* last year. The author had just returned from a world cruise, on which he had met several elderly passengers. He was disturbed that these senior travelers were spending so much money on world cruises while their grandchildren may be struggling financially. "It is time for the elderly to step up to the plate to support the younger generation," the writer suggested.[6]

In America, each generation is expected to make it on its own. At least, that is the idea. So old people think they are quite within their rights to spend all their money on themselves, leaving little for their heirs to inherit. They do not see themselves as selfish. Many even think they are doing the next generation a favor, protecting them from sloth and dependence.

They go around with T-shirts that say, "I'm spending my kids' inheritance." Instead of taking care of grandchildren or helping their sons and daughters with the family enterprises, they retire to Florida, organizing their financial lives so their money lasts not a minute longer than they do. They grow old and lame and then expect special parking places. They spend their time playing golf, watching daytime TV, or pressuring their elected representatives to give them even more benefits.

The old have not merely abandoned the young to their own fate; they have stabbed them in the back. It's bad enough that they use up all their own money. But they don't stop there. They spend other people's money, too. And then they spend money that hasn't even been earned yet.

The biggest items in the U.S. federal budget, Social Security and Medicaid, benefit the graybeards, not the young. And the budget is so far out of whack that for every dollar of tax revenue, the feds spend $1.60. That is to say, they add 60 cents that will have to be paid sometime in the future—most likely, by their own sons, daughters and grandchildren.

How lucky the next generation is! If a lack of money breeds tough self-reliance, the young in America must be the toughest generation ever. Not only do they have to pay their own way in the world, they're also expected to shoulder a debt burden that would make break Atlas's back. Their parents and grandchildren bequeath them public debt and unfunded obligations of more than $200 trillion, according to Boston University professor Laurence Kotlikoff's estimate.[7]

Forbes publishes a list of the world's richest people. But suppose it published a list of the world's poorest people. Who would it put on this list? Surely, America's young people would lead the rankings. Each one is a slave, shackled to such a big ball and chain of debt he is lucky if he can still move.

It hardly seems fair.

Economist Robert Samuelson, writing in the *Orange County Register*, shares our opinion: "Whether our elected politicians will take back government from the AARP, the 40 million–member organization representing retirees and near retirees"[8] is the big question for the 2012 budget debate. Obama's budget proposals left Social Security and Medicaid untouched. Why? The greedy old geezers vote.

Those programs have become a form of "middle-class welfare," says Samuelson; they must be cut.

THE FAMILY OFFICE

We are not complaining. Nor do we believe in trying to change the course of history. We are not world improvers. Still, we do our best to improve our own lives and those of our heirs and descendants.

Three or four years ago, we began to think seriously about what to do with our own money. What was the plan? Spend it? Save it? Forget about it and hope for the best?

What was the plan for the children? What would become of them if something happened to their parents? Would they be able to "make it" on their own? What if something went wrong? Should they depend on the charity of the state or the planning and preparations of their own father and mother?

It was about that time that we discovered the concept of the "family office." Poor people have food stamps and bail bonds. The middle class has Social Security and Medicaid. Rich people have family offices.

When we say "rich people," we're not talking about those who win the lottery or a million-dollar contract to play football. We're talking about people who make their money the old-fashioned way and try to keep it in the family, often for several generations. They see it as an heirloom to be passed down, not used up.

Just because people are rich doesn't mean they are stupid. Old Money must have its secrets . . . its tricks . . . its wisdom, too. How do they do it? We've already revealed a couple of "secrets": time and modesty. What other aces do they have up their sleeves?

We're just finding out. We had no Old Money in our family. We inherited a few pieces of banged-up furniture from our mother, who inherited them from her father. That was it. What money we have now is so new the ink isn't even dry yet. Should we spend it all ourselves? Should we retire to Florida too and wish the family good luck?

For better or for worse, we decided to share, to prepare, to work together, to involve the whole family in our financial life, with trusts, an investment committee, a family constitution, budget goals and everything else the family office guidebooks recommend. We decided to burden the children with the fruits of our own lives. They are supposed to join in our key financial decisions, help manage family property, and partake in the family business. They're meant to help preserve and enhance the family wealth, such as it is.

Don't get the wrong idea. We're not taking the high road. We never like the high road; it makes us a little queasy. But we don't like the high life much, either. Spend our time playing golf? Fishing? Cruising around the world? Doesn't sound like much fun. And we have no interest in fancy cars or expensive clothes. We drive a Ford pick-up and wear what we get for Christmas.

So we've taken a different route. To us, it is more interesting, exciting, and challenging. And there's much less traffic.

But what's involved? What's it all about? What do you have to do?

First, let's begin with the basics. If you're going to have family money, you need two things. You need a family. And you need money.

There, that's simple enough.

But what kind of family? You'll find out more about that in the next chapter.

The other part of the formula is easier, at least in theory. Money is simple. It doesn't have contrary opinions. It doesn't talk back to you. It isn't ungrateful, spiteful, petty, envious, incompetent, moody—or any of the other things that can destroy a family. And it never goes through the teenage years. You can always work with money in a purely rational, logical way. Like an adult. No need to beat around the bush or use reverse psychology on money. It is as direct as a bullet and as simple-minded as a congressman. You can play it straight with money. You can use your left brain, just as you would if you were building a house or repairing a toaster.

Getting money ought to be easy. And it ought to be easy to hold on to it, too.

There are two main elements to human beings, said the ancient Greeks. Of course, the Greeks had their ideas. We have our own. In our view, the two parts of the human personality are roughly these: There's the part that is concerned with practical things—getting wealth, running a business, building a house, and so forth. The other side is concerned with religion, art, spiritual things, involving less tangible, less easily manipulated or measured things. Like honor, integrity, religion, beliefs, culture, feelings. Those are things that light up brain cells at family discussions.

Two parts of the brain. Two aspects of the human personality. Two elements of family money.

Looked at another way, you can say that family wealth is just the ability of family members to pursue happiness and enjoy freedom and security, thanks to the wealth racked up by previous generations. That is true, too. Money is just a means. The family—and its happiness—is the end. But you can't get the end without the means. Again, the two things are clasped together like the two halves of a deadbolt lock.

Family wealth is dependent on a family's ability to generate and hold on to money. The spirit knows what it wants; it needs the rational, goal-oriented brain to get it.

THE FAMILY BALANCE SHEET

To understand a family's ability to make and maintain a fortune, you might think in terms of a family balance sheet. Every family has a balance sheet. It has assets and liabilities.

There are four primary elements of family wealth: the human, intellectual, organizational, and financial capital that a family possesses.

Most families do not think in these terms. Whether successful Old Money does or not, we don't know. But it seems like a good way to look at it. Successful families need their capital in all four areas.

Why not just focus on the money?

If the family balance sheet is too lopsided, if it has financial capital but little else, it probably won't know how to hold on to the money for long. Or how to generate more of it.

Money that is earned too easily or too fast tends to go as quickly and as readily as it arrived. That is largely because money that is too easily made is held in contempt by those who make it. It is like a woman's heart that is too easily won or a prize that is too easily awarded. It loses value.

It also takes time to learn how to keep money. Money earned over a long time comes with valuable lessons attached. You learn how to manage it. How to invest it. How not to waste it. Often, you are loath to spend it. Failure to learn those lessons is usually fatal to a family's wealth.

That's also why "new money" tends to have such a tinny look to it. You expect it to wear out fast. Old Money, however, has a more solid look—like it might last forever.

As we will say more than once in the book, it takes more than money to be really wealthy.

Let's look in greater detail at the different forms of capital that families possess to better understand how to hold on to our wealth over the long term.

HUMAN CAPITAL

Human capital is typically described as the knowledge, ability, and experience that individual family members possess. But it's much more than that. It's also a family's emotional stability, its culture, its willingness to take risks, its willingness to work hard and to forgo immediate gratification, its ability to get along and pull together to protect itself, as well as to achieve common goals.

Focus on the attributes of the individuals in your family unit for a moment. . . . There are the physical attributes: The family members are short. They are tall. They are good looking. They are homely.

There are mental attributes: They are smart. They are dumb.

Then there are the personalities: They are honest. They are liars. They are trustworthy. They are hard working. Some are healthy; some are sickly.

The individual members of your family and their unique, or not so unique, characteristics are what make up the human capital of the family.

Much of what constitutes a family's human capital is beyond our reach. People are born with certain features. Many of them you can't do anything about. They are what they are. (Note that you can change a family's human capital, even the parts that seem immutable, by bringing other people into the family, either by marriage or adoption. More on that in the next chapter.)

Whatever raw material you find yourself with, you can generally improve it. How? Well, there are probably no secrets to this part of Old Money success. But the more you encourage, nurture, subsidize, and insist upon the characteristics you want in your family, the more likely you are to have them.

The most obvious example is education. If you want your family members to be capable of managing and preserving money, you need to make sure they have the training to do so. We are not naïve enough to think that this is as simple a matter as it appears. You might think: Oh, that's easy; we'll send our boy to college and make him take courses in economics and finance.

Yes, maybe that would do the trick. And maybe it wouldn't. Much of modern education is a sham. Much of what college professors believe about economics is wrongheaded. And much of what is taught in finance courses is theoretical, abstract, and mostly useless—if not downright dangerous. More than one family business has been ruined by a business school graduate who decides to apply the lessons he learned in school!

The best education is experience. Direct. Immediate. Real. As Nietszche once explained, there are two kinds of knowledge. The first is what you might learn in school or from reading the newspapers. The second is what you learn by actual experience. The first is useful, stimulating, interesting. But the second is much more reliable for business and investment purposes.

It is a bit like the difference between knowing that the number of old people in America is increasing rapidly and having the real experience of running an old folks home. The first might give you a clue about where to look for business and investment opportunities, but the second is much more likely to help you find one.

Whenever possible, you want to enhance your family's human capital by bringing individual family members more fully into the picture. Children should be encouraged to participate in business and investment decisions, and challenged to analyze problems in a clearheaded, thoughtful way. It is not enough to come back from business school and tell the family how to increase shareholder value in one of its holdings, for example. The new graduate must also explain why, how, when, and for what purpose the proposed undertaking will pay off.

Julius Caesar learned his trade largely at his father's side. Your family members should do the same, working alongside one another in order to spread not merely knowledge, but something more important: culture.

But we'll come back to that in another chapter. Right now, we're just talking about how to inventory your family's human capital, and what it means. You will notice that different family members can have different talents. And different talents are useful. Not everybody has to be an entrepreneur or a financial genius.

Take the case of John Davidson Rockefeller.

John D. Rockefeller Jr. did not share his father's enthusiasm for business. The old man might have been one of the greatest wealth creators of all time. But the son had talents, too. Different from his father's, those talents proved extremely useful. The younger Rockefeller focused on his family and setting up a family office structure. That structure is still in place today and has helped seven generations of Rockefellers preserve their wealth and flourish.

Many of the strategies developed by John D. Rockefeller Jr. for choosing advisers, managing the participation of family members in the family business, and philanthropy have been used as models for many other wealthy families since.

James Hughes, in his book *Family Wealth*, says, "An unrecognized part of the Rockefellers' success in long-term wealth preservation is the extraordinary act by John Davidson Rockefeller Sr. of not compelling his son to remain in the family business once he had determined that his calling lay in family governance and philanthropy."[9]

The act of letting a son go to pursue his calling was a successful strategy for developing the human capital of the Rockefeller family. This has become the standard among family wealth professionals. "Encourage young people to find their own paths in life," they say. While, superficially, it certainly sounds like a good idea, we're not sure it is good advice. While you don't want to stop a child from pursuing his own goals, in practice, most young people don't know what they want to do with their lives. Smart Old Money families guide them. (More on that in the next chapter.)

You develop human capital by fostering the growth of natural talents and the pursuit of individual happiness among family members.

Your human capital can also have liabilities, such as substance abuse, behavioral issues, medical problems, investment delusions, or disabled elderly family members.

Families must do everything they can to resolve these issues. If they can't fix them, they have to make sure they protect themselves from them. Those liabilities sit there on the family balance sheet, whether you acknowledge them or not. If the family and its wealth are not insulated against these problems, they are just waiting for trouble.

An unrecognized, or unprotected, problem is similar to an unfunded liability on a balance sheet. Sooner or later, it is going to blow up. If the family has enough positive human capital, it will survive. If not, it will be dragged down—and effectively cease to be a going concern.

That is also why successful families leverage their human capital. They know that there are always hidden liabilities, in both human capital and the other kind. They know that they will take unexpected losses. The only way to protect themselves is to grow and develop as much human capital as possible.

They do this by encouraging family members to develop the talents they have, whether or not they bear a direct relation to the immediate financial goals of the family. But they also give them as much exposure to and responsibility for the family money as possible.

NO ROOM FOR RETIREMENT

We have been speaking primarily about young people. Now let's talk about the old. Let's say you have worked all your life. Now, you are entitled to retire and spend your money, aren't you?

The idea of retirement was invented by social engineers who were trying to develop economic models for welfare/warfare societies. The idea has deep roots in the mechanical fascination that dominated nineteenth-century intellectuals. They were so impressed by machines that they began to imagine that whole economies could be designed and organized in much the same way.

There were the resources, the engines, the cogs, the screws, the belts, and the drive trains. And there were the control panels too, with levers and knobs that could be used to control the whole process. And guess whose hands were at the controls? The social engineers! Of course, they couldn't design a lawnmower or operate a power saw safely. Still, they saw themselves running an entire economy as though it were a passenger train.

And there, down where the tedious, repetitive work was done, were the poor cogs, the workers who had to be replaced as they wore out. They could "retire" when their useful work-life had been exhausted in order to make room for a new cog fresh out of trade school.

This vision of the way things ought to work was the basic template for Bismarck's social welfare state. Later, it was expanded by the Marxists, who were even more ambitious. They wanted even more control from the cradle to the grave—literally. In their great experiment in the Soviet Union, they told the cogs where to live, how to live, where to work, everything. For a while, they even took care of infants, removing them from their parents and raising them to be good Soviet citizens—that is, good cogs.

The Soviet Union went bust. It was supposed to be a workers' paradise. But in practice, it was more of a workers' inferno. It promised to increase man's material well-being. Instead, it impoverished him.

Economists are still amazed. The Soviet Union managed to take raw materials out of the ground, transport them, smelt them, mold them, press them, bolt them, drill them, hone them, attach them, screw them together, color them, take them to market, and put them on the shelves and finally into the hands of consumers. And what had the USSR accomplished? The finished products were worth less than the raw materials it started with. It was a value-subtracting business on the largest scale ever, losing money on each sale and trying to make it up on volume.

But the vision of "retirement" outlived the Soviet Union. It is now a standard feature of every major economy in the world. People look forward to their golden years—to being able to live off their savings while they spend their days walking along the beach, hand in hand, or playing golf in the sun.

In our vision of things, there is plenty of room for golf and beach perambulation, but there is no room for retirement. A person should not expect to become a leech on the rest of society just because he reaches a certain age. He should continue to use whatever skills and wisdom are available to him. When those run out completely, then and only then can he become a leech.

The typical lifetime budget of the typical household shows the accumulation of wealth until age 65 . . . and then the wealth declines as it is consumed in retirement. Fair enough. Nothing wrong with that. But in our experience, as limited as it is, both families and retirees gain when old folks, as well as young folks, continue working toward common family goals, including capital formation and preservation. Besides, it isn't as if old people have nothing to contribute.

Youth and energy may be valuable to producing wealth. But old age and cunning are essential to holding onto it. The older a man gets, the more he has seen, including the more scams and absurdities. He is better able to spot them than a younger man. And he is essential to the family's wealth management/protection plan.

Believe it or not, old people are useful in many other ways.

For decades, we lived with three generations in the same house. Never once did we notice that our mother and aunt (or grandmother and great-aunt, depending on which generation you were in) were "retired." They were always busy: fixing meals, looking after the children, cleaning up the house. They were always there, keeping the home fires burning, a plus for the household from every point of view.

Not only were they very helpful in household management, but they were a great source of calm and experience in family matters.

"Inasmuch as you are the oldest and wisest," we would say to our family matriarch, usually after a difficult conversation with a teenager of our own, "what should we do now?"

Our great-aunt died some years ago. But our mother—and grandmother—is still much in demand. She is a stable, wise, and cheerful matriarch at 90 years old. The fact that she is too frail to travel is actually a benefit. She is always at home, a warm and welcoming presence in the house 24 hours a day.

As you will see, family money depends on family culture. And family culture depends on family members, old and young. Neither is a burden on the family or its money. They are both the source of family fortunes—and the reason you have them.

FINANCIAL CAPITAL

Family money is very different from the cash that individuals have in the bank. Members of successful Old Money families think of themselves as stewards, not owners, of their financial capital. Since they are not owners of it, they don't feel they have the right to use the money for their own personal enjoyment. Instead, they are just supposed to look out for it, as if it were a piece of heirloom furniture. They might not even like the old thing. They might not particularly like being the custodian of it and regard it as more of a burden than a pleasure. Still, they do their duties.

Personal money has a purpose: to increase your quality of life. It helps you take vacations. It permits you to live in the house of your dreams (if you can afford it). It pays for your beer. It lights your house. It finances your retirement.

Personal money must feel appreciated. It is called upon almost every day to perform some errand or chore. It services the car. It buys subway tickets. It tips the waiter and provides the children with their allowances. It is ready to do almost anything . . . anytime . . . anywhere, provided it is able.

That is the trouble with personal money: There is almost no service to which it might not be put. As a result, it is often stretched too thin and worked too hard. For most people, personal money races from pillar to post, never quite getting a chance to recover its strength. Often, it gets worn out and exhausted. And sometimes, it collapses altogether.

Which is not as bad as it sounds. Personal money is personal money. It's not meant to outlast the job it is meant to perform. For most people, that job ends when they do.

But that is not what we're talking about in this book. We're talking about a different kind of money: family money. It belongs to a family, but to no one in particular. Like all institutional money, it has people who are in charge of it. It has people who are supposed to make sure that it doesn't disappear, and other people who are supposed to make sure it grows, if possible. Those people are not supposed to spend it on themselves.

The conversion of institutional money to personal money happens all the time when it is paid out in fees, salaries, dividends, and so forth. But a custodian who takes institutional money and converts it into his personal money is a poor custodian. He may even be committing a crime . . . or a sin.

While personal money gets little rest, family money gets little exercise. It gets "old" from disuse. It sits there, growing and compounding, undisturbed. It is aimless. Almost pointless. Sometimes useless.

It is no one's asset, yet it belongs to all the family. It does no one's work, yet it is at the service of the whole bunch. It increases no one's standard of living, yet it should increase the quality of life for them all.

That makes it very different from personal money. So you must think about it differently. You must treat it differently. You must also protect it differently.

However, money is money, and many things about money are the same, no matter whose money it is. And so you will need someone in your family who is "good with money."

First, of course, you need someone who is capable of getting the kind of money a family needs. We address that issue in Chapters 3, 4, and 5. Not everyone can do it. Not everyone would want to. But if you don't have someone like that in your family—preferably at the head of it—you're not likely to have "family money."

Then, you need someone who is capable of managing and preserving it. This talent is probably a little more widespread and perhaps more easily learned. But it is not insignificant. And you need more of it. You might need only one wealth creator. But you'll need a strong manager—preserver—in every generation. And they have to want to do it. Remember, they are creating and/or preserving money not for their only benefit, but for someone else's—maybe even that of someone they will never meet. It's a lot of work. It is difficult. It is a long project with uncertain results.

Why do it?

ENEMY OF THE STATE?

Over the door of the farmhouse we built as soon as we had enough money to build a proper house, we chiseled the words of Virgil: "*Hic domus, haec patria est.*"

Roughly translated: This is our home; this is our country. But when you say it, you have to put the emphasis on the second "THIS." Then it makes sense.

"This is our home" is a statement of fact.

"THIS is our country" is practically treason.

It is to the state, not the family, that people pledge allegiance. The state ministers not only to peoples' material needs, but also to their psychological and emotional desires. In the time of war, for example, a citizen puts his own interests subordinate to the interests of the state. If he is called upon to give up his life or his treasure to the war effort, he is ready to do so, content that the sacrifice was noble.

In peacetime, national elections are viewed as great contests in which the individual wins or loses, along with his candidates. When his party wins, the voter wins. He feels not only that he will get what he wants but that his enemies will get it too!

When national health care was instituted, for example, those who favored it must have walked with a bounce in their step, even though they had contributed nothing to the campaign and had no idea whether or how it would actually improve the health care of the nation. They were sure it was the right thing for themselves and others, even those who didn't approve of it.

Historians will note that modern times are much more like the imperial days of Rome than the days of the Roman Republic. In our quote, Virgil (partly to please Augustus) was still talking about the virtues of the republic, during which time families were still more important than the central government of Rome. The republic was dominated for hundreds of years by families that guarded their honor, protected and promoted their family interests, and built and maintained family fortunes.

Later, during the days of the empire, family fortunes were harder to hold on to—because emperors wanted the money. But that is a long, long story.

For our present purpose, let us just remember that the goal of anyone who wants a family fortune is partly to protect himself from the state. Families maintain their own resources largely because they don't want to have to rely on the generosity of the state. We've already seen several state-run pension systems go bust. Health care systems, notably that of Britain, are often subject to bad management, money shortages, and institutional failings. As for those who depend on the state for their sustenance, as Jefferson put it, "We should soon want bread."

But that is not the worst of it. History shows that not only is the state an unreliable helpmate, but it can turn into a family's worst enemy.

The aristocrats of France, for example, found themselves practically hunted down as the Revolution turned into the Reign of Terror. The Committee of Public Safety came under the control of Maximilien Robespierre in 1793. He sent some 16,594 people to the guillotine. Their crime? Being in the wrong place at the wrong time.

We don't have to go far to find other examples. The one that leaps to mind is the case of the Jews in Germany and Eastern Europe in the 1930s and 1940s. Government became not just a parasite that took their money, but became their mortal enemy, rounding them up, sending whole families—millions of them—to labor and extermination camps.

The early and mid-twentieth century was a heyday for murderous governments. While the Nazis were preparing their campaigns against Jews, gypsies, subscribers to various religions, homosexuals, half-wits, cripples, democrats, and other groups, the Soviet Union was doing its own ethnic cleansing.

Whole nations were put on trains and shipped east, where they posed no threat to the communist rulers. Business owners and small farmers were systematically persecuted, exiled, imprisoned, or murdered. Anyone who resisted, or might resist, the collectivization of the farms or factories was labeled a "class enemy" and marked for elimination.

The Kulaks, small farmers in the Ukraine, were tortured so they would reveal where they had hidden food. The food was confiscated and the Kulaks starved to death. Millions of them.

Communists in China were no less brutal. Again, families with independent means were singled out as class enemies. They were arrested, tortured, starved, imprisoned, and murdered. No one knows exactly how many died in these campaigns, but it was in the millions. Probably more than in the Soviet Union or Germany.

What makes these campaigns especially interesting to us is that they targeted families. Totalitarian states, of which France's Committee of Public Safety was an early trial run, insist on the full cooperation and absolute obedience of their subject peoples. They cannot bear any competition from alternate or independent sources of fidelity. Neither religious groups nor ethnic groups, nor families are allowed to compete for power, influence or allegiance with the central political power. Anyone who opposes them, even if only by preaching or pamphleteering in opposition, is eliminated.

The last great example of this kind of state-level massacre was in Cambodia, where anyone who could read or write was labeled an "intellectual" and sent to labor in the country. Since no provisions had been made for these people's lodging or nourishment, millions died on forced marches, diseases, overwork, exposure, and starvation.

What we take from these examples, as well as from the logic of the situations themselves, is that the state is often the enemy of families. In addition, the bigger the state gets and the more absurd its pretensions and promises become, the more likely it is to want to wipe out families as a source of competition.

The other thing we take from this is that you are much better off with a well-organized, well-financed family. In all of the above cases, people with family money—preferably beyond the reach of the state—were better off than those without it.

In the end, well-run families are stronger and more reliable than the state.

CHAPTER 2

———

THE FAMILY

The modern "family" won't work for our purposes. That is, you can't reconcile the need for a very long-term wealth strategy with a moveable, flexible family—at least, not usually. . . .

An example: We know several couples that never got married, but nevertheless lived together for years and had children. The children grew up and moved on and, in almost all cases we know of, the parents then decided to move on, too. In all cases that we know, this caused financial, as well as emotional havoc.

Of course, there are all sorts of "households" today. Alternative lifestyle couples. Groups of friends. Remarried parents with stepchildren from various marriages.

There was a belief common in the 1980s and 1990s that you didn't need to marry at all. People expected friends to fill the roles typically played by spouses, in-laws, and children. Popular TV shows illustrated for us how much fun it would be to live with friends, rather than with family.

A critique of lifestyle choices is far beyond the scope of this book, but as far as we know, the only likely way to build and retain wealth through more than one generation is with a traditional family. Friends tend to be transitory. Casual relationships, love affairs, and friendships come and go.

Family relationships, however, tend to endure—for better or for worse.

You might say that the real secret to a family fortune is permanence— or at least as much permanence as is possible in this transitory life.

Many things are beyond our control. It is not possible, for example, to live forever. Nor can we control the world of politics or the weather. We just have to adapt to them, such as they are. But we know what we want: permanent relationships . . . permanent strategies . . . permanent culture . . . permanent wealth.

Permanence begins at home. And family wealth fails because families fail. What we want to do is to create as much permanence as possible in those things that are within our control—first, in the family itself and then in its money.

So let's return to the old-fashioned approach, the so-called "nuclear family" or "contemporary family" model. In this approach, you get married and you do what comes naturally until something else that comes naturally comes naturally, if you know what we mean.

Most people do what most people do—they build a family randomly. They go off to school. They meet someone. They end up living somewhere. Then family life starts. They end up in a career. The children go to the local school. They might attend the local church. Then they become entrenched in the local mass culture. They get caught up in social pressure to do the same things that everyone else is doing.

The same is true of the conventional rich. They go Republican. They stay in the mold. They buy the right house, the right car. They attend certain social events. They give to the right charities. They compete with the other rich people to look successful. As their wealth grows, so does their consumption. Later, they become more wealth consumers than wealth producers.

Serious Old Money families do things differently. They create their own culture. They're relatively independent. They plan their lives purposely. And their time horizon is much longer than those of normal families. They think in terms of 20, 50, 100 years, or longer. . . .

They leverage the natural cycles of life using the talents of family members, young and old, to build the family business and the family wealth. Youth and energy may be valuable at producing wealth. But old age and wisdom are essential to holding onto it.

The young people are sources of energy, enthusiasm, and new ideas. The older members of the family are sources of experience.

These older members of the family can play the role of elders. They can:

- Mediate disputes (finding the best, most consensus-building resolution).
- Enforce the decision-making rules, but not set those rules.
- Tell the stories and history of the family.
- Carry on rituals and ceremonies and memorialize them.

Conventional, modern families do not actively leverage life stages. Instead, every generation looks out for itself. But the nuclear family model is inadequate for multigenerational wealth building.

The nuclear family is egocentric, isolated, and impermanent. These are the opposite qualities of successful multigenerational families (particularly the kind that tend to thrive in places such as Italy and Spain, where the traditional extended family model is more prominent).

In the modern nuclear family, each generation tends to focus on itself. And each generation, overall, depends on itself financially. Because financial support and responsibility are limited to a single generation, the small family of limited means tends to look to government for services. Not surprisingly, it also supports the government's transfer programs and wants more of them.

The typical modern family spends most of what it makes. The next generation has to start over again. Many modern families will go into debt to support a lifestyle they cannot really afford. Then the government goes far into debt too—for much the same reasons. Thus do government and modern families depend on each other—and both depend on debt.

The modern, nuclear family is focused on the short term. If the parents earn a decent income, they might save for retirement or for a child's college education. The rest is spent. Parents in these families are often members of the "SKI" club. They "Spend their Kids' Inheritance." They indulge themselves, rather than save for the benefit of the next generation. This short-term egocentric focus drains the financial resources of these families, even if they earn very high incomes. That's part of the reason savings rates in the United States are so low, just 3.5 percent. Each generation focuses on its own needs and wants.

When one generation does support another, it is only temporary. Children are supported until they get out of college. Elderly family members are often at their children's charge. This leads to a strange and morbid incentive. The adults can't wait until the children end their educations and the oldsters die!

IT TAKES TEAMWORK

"It takes two to tango," said an older woman friend, at a wedding reception in France.

"It's the only way a marriage can work. Each person has to dance. If one stops dancing, the other can't continue. Sure, he can look for a new dance partner, but it's not the same thing.

"There's just so much to do. People today think only of making money and spending it. But there's a lot more. You have to create a family. That's different than just having children. Creating a family means creating family life. And that takes time. And it takes both husband and wife. The wife can't be the husband too. The husband can't be the wife, either.

"It takes two to tango. Two different steps ... two different people ... but dancing together. . . ."

Creating a "family life" in a household where the patriarch is focused on wealth creation is hard. It puts a strain on families. Building a fortune requires the vast majority of the husband's (it could be the wife's—we don't care, but we're going to use husband and wife in their most traditional and stereotypical form) energy. He may not able to attend his children's sporting events or help them with their homework. Instead, he's got his own homework to do. It takes an extraordinary effort to produce extraordinary wealth. Ordinary people do ordinary things; they end up with ordinary money. Family money is unusual. It takes unusual efforts to get it and hold on to it. The energy that is put into work is often sacrificed at home.

That's why it is almost impossible for a single dad or a single mom to create family money. It's just too hard. If one spouse is going to focus on the money, the other has to focus on the family. There are, of course, exceptions. We know one wealth-building friend who is not at all in a conventional, traditional family. Instead, it's a commune with its origins in the hippie communes of the 1960s.

More often, the husband focuses on the money. The wife focuses on the family. She, too, will have to make an exceptional effort; she, too, must do something extraordinary.

This is part of what a great matriarch does. She is to be a counterweight to the lightness of her husband in the home. She bears the responsibility of turning an ordinary family into an Old Money family.

How? She shapes the family and nurtures the people in it. She helps create the "shared vision" a family needs to succeed.

LIFE ON A DUAL-INCOME TREADMILL

In most conventional, nuclear families, especially in the United States, both the husband and the wife work. At first glance, this seems like a shrewd way to build family wealth. With two family members working, you essentially double your household income. Initially. But that's true in the short run only. Over time, having both husband and wife work could actually make the family poorer.

How could that be? When both have normal jobs, working normal hours, neither will have the time to do something extraordinary. The wealth builder will not have the time it takes to succeed. Neither will the family builder. You will end up with an ordinary family, not one that can preserve wealth over generations. When both family members work, neither works hard enough at his task to succeed.

First, let's look at the money side of it. If both adult family members are working, it adds to family expenses in terms of child care, transportation, clothing for work, meals, tutoring, and other necessary expenses that come with holding two full-time jobs. We have to expect, too, that household chores are shared—in the modern fashion. This leaves each spouse working normal hours. That's the problem right there. You're not likely to earn an exceptional amount of money working normal hours. So both spouses earn normal incomes, against which they also have two-earning-household expenses.

This leaves them on a typical treadmill. They have more money than a one-wage-earner household, at least starting out. But not enough so that they are ever able to reach what we call "financial escape velocity," which we'll explain later. For now, we'll just note that they have two rather ordinary incomes.

But two rather ordinary incomes are not enough to produce a family fortune. Two wage earners pay two taxes. With all the expenses of a two-wage family, too, there is not going to be enough money left over to build real family money. We'll look more at what you need to do to get a family fortune, even if it is a modest one, in the next chapter. You'll see that one person devoted to making money can earn far more than two who are only doing it in a perfunctory way. For now, let's just note that as a strategy for building family wealth, the two-income approach doesn't work.

But the even greater failure is on the other side, the family side. The lack of focused involvement on the part of any one single parent can cost a family dearly. No one has the time to make sure the children are emotionally fulfilled. No one can closely monitor if there are subtle conflicts between siblings. No one can instill a sense of duty upon the children. No one has the time to elaborate the family culture: the attitudes, rules, and reflexes needed to sustain an Old Money family.

Even if the two wage earners were able to put together the money for a family fortune, they would be unlikely to be able to put together the family itself. Over time, many are the threats to family wealth—most of them arising from the family members themselves. These are the things that can pull the family apart and ultimately destroy the family wealth.

Raising children properly is a critical family function. It should be the focus of one parent. There are numerous studies that confirm this.

And let's take it a step further.

The presumed bargain in the "social contract" with modern government is this: Families turn over a large part of their incomes to the government; the government provides education and some health care services. The less money you have, the harder it is for you to resist. But it comes at a high price. Not just in the taxes you pay or in the imminent bankruptcy of the welfare state, but also in terms of what it does to your family. Government-provided services, typically, are (1) not very good and (2) designed to enhance the power of the government.

Not that we have much experience with this, but the logic of our argument suggests that you're better off educating the children at home. Or at least surveying their education closely. Turn them over to the government, and you'll have government-formed children. Your human capital is likely to lose value.

Education is an important part of your children's preparation. It shouldn't be left to chance or to the public school system, which has a curriculum designed to promote ideas that are often contrary to the values of successful families. Public schools teach the government's narrative, not a family's narrative. And it's the family narrative that makes up an important part of the family culture.

That doesn't mean you can't send your children to public schools. It's just that if you do, you need a parent to oversee the child's progress. You also need to provide children with more than the public schools can. Even if they do their jobs well, the schools—public or private—are providing only a small part of the training needed to succeed in life.

Remember, the real wealth of a family is not financial. The primary assets are the family members and their unique talents, knowledge, and experience. After all, if you pass along significant financial wealth without the means to manage it, it will be more of a curse than a blessing, and your family will not possess that money for long. Wealth can provide freedom, security, and opportunity for your family. Money can help family members live richer, more fulfilling lives.

But putting money into the hands of unprepared family members can have the opposite effect—it can make them less free. Instead of finding themselves with a tool they know how to use, family money can be like a chainsaw in the hands of a drunk—a danger to himself and all around him.

Family members can become dysfunctional and demotivated by receiving large amounts of unearned wealth. They can become combative and litigious. Unearned wealth often leads to strange and deleterious emotional reactions, for example, feelings of unworthiness, incompetence, and guilt.

You don't want this to happen to your children and grandchildren.

EVERYTHING REGRESSES TO THE MEAN

In virtually every culture, there is a phrase equivalent to "shirtsleeves to shirtsleeves in three generations."

That's because, statistically, there's a tendency of families over time to regress to the ordinary, in every way.

The first generation is unusually expansive, creative, and hardworking. The next generation still has enough money, and enough of a recollection of how the money was made, to avoid squandering it all.

Then, by the third generation, the family has usually become quite usual—that is to say, the unique talents, luck, circumstances, drive, and ambitions that built the family fortune have disappeared, both from the gene pool and from the family memory. What you have is a typical bunch of people dealing with an unusually large amount of money in a typical way. That is, they are spending it, wasting it and handing it over to professional managers until it is all gone.

So how do you fight generational regression?

Make no mistake, your children are under a constant barrage of ideas that dull their senses and pull them down toward the mean. That's what modern society and government do. Public schools, television, social media, mainstream news, sports, pop culture—nothing wrong with them. Most things are, by definition, ordinary. Your children are likely to be ordinary, too. In many cases, it's the best we can hope for!

But if you want to have an extraordinary family, you have to do something extraordinary.

THE ROLE OF THE MATRIARCH

Here's a surprise. You probably think the most important contribution to family money is made by the fellow who works night and day to make the money, right? Wrong! The role of the spouse—the person who, usually, doesn't "work" at all—is critical.

Trouble is, few people are aware of this person's critical role in the creation of family money. Perhaps it's because the idea of traditional roles is not politically correct, but there's very little written about the role of the matriarch in most family wealth and estate-planning books.

But the fact is that a great family fortune requires a great matriarch. (Remember, it could be "patriarch" . . . but it is typically the woman who does this job.) And only with both of them "on the case" can they hope to create a family fortune.

Both must want to do so . . . because it takes discipline, sacrifice, vision, and a lot of hard work. First, the spouses must agree not to dissipate or consume the money. Then, they must work together to build the institutions, the culture, and the people that can hold it together.

For the family to be in harmony, the husband and wife need to be. They need to agree on their vision for the family, how they'll live and the plan for succession of the next generation.

So if you want to have family wealth, you need the right sort of family, and that begins with the right spouse, the one that has the potential to be a great matriarch.

Who is she?

The matriarch of the truly wealthy family is not like the "housewives" you see on reality TV shows. She's not a big gossip or a social climber. A matriarch is not a trophy wife. She doesn't spend her time focused on herself. She's not a big "consumer" of products. Instead, she's a "producer" of capable, confident children. She focuses on her children, making sure that they are emotionally provided for, that they are well-educated, capable individuals. She instills in them a sense of duty, to themselves and to the family.

The matriarch must be able to:

- Share in the family culture and be capable of passing it along. Indeed, she must play the leading role in creating it.
- Be capable of providing a stable home environment (even when the family is on the move).
- Understand and support the wealth-building strategy.
- Support socially the family objectives (which could include entertaining customers, clients, associates; learning foreign languages; managing contacts with friends, relatives, business associates).
- Master complex tax and trust issues (not to mention subtle investment issues).
- Be emotionally mature and confident and have the depth to avoid getting distracted.

All the experts agree that someone must be in charge of the wealth. The family also needs a leader. An emotional leader. Someone in charge of the family's affective, cultural, and spiritual life. The role of the matriarch, the family manager, is absolutely critical to the development of the next generation and the family wealth. While the husband might be chief executive officer of the family business, the wife is the CEO, the chief emotional officer, of the family. She has meaningful emotional relationships with everyone in the family. The CEO can help resolve disputes between family members. She works to strengthen family bonds and maintain harmony.

THE GLUE THAT HOLDS IT ALL TOGETHER

Iphigene Ochs Sulzberger was daughter of Adolph Ochs, who acquired the *New York Times* in 1896, and the wife of Arthur Sulzberger, who published the paper following Ochs's death. Iphigene had 4 children, 14 grandchildren, and 24 great-grandchildren. One of her children said that she was "the glue that held us all together."[1]

Filling the shoes of the patriarch is no small task, but neither is taking on the mantle of the matriarch, the family "glue." While there are not many hard data to support it, failure of the matriarch to build a strong, capable family is probably the root cause for the majority of wealth transfer failures. Seventy percent of family wealth transfers fail. The majority of these failures are due to family issues. These family issues usually have their roots in emotional issues. Without a CEO, these emotional issues go unresolved and unchecked. Eventually, they boil over into conflict.

One of the most frequent causes of failure is conflict between siblings. How many times do you hear stories about successful families who turn on each other as soon as the patriarch and/or matriarch dies? Once the two key leaders are out of the picture, there's a power vacuum that often leads to trouble.

Siblings who grow up together often carry their childhood issues into adulthood. One child feels neglected. Another feels unappreciated. One enters the family business. Another becomes an artist. Often, the real problem is a dysfunctional heir who causes conflict between siblings. The tabloids find these stories immensely entertaining.

Sibling rivalries can cripple a family organization. Most family fortunes do not survive an extended conflict.

What goes wrong? Nobody really knows. Apparently, some people are doomed to have problems. But we have to believe that many problems can be avoided or resolved. But how?

Business-owning families have more fuel for the family conflict hearth. Some members of the family are likely to work in the business and have more control over the family's wealth. Those on the outside are likely to feel neglected. Often, they will resent the "perks"—cars, travel, salaries—that those in the business give themselves. Or they will disagree about how the business should be managed. Or want to get control of the business for themselves.

IN HER OWN WORDS . . .

Our family matriarch, Elizabeth, reckons it's the mother's role to recognize these problems—and to solve them. She has to use her rational brain to understand the family's trusts, business, and tax strategies. But she must also use her intuition and instinct to foresee personal issues that could lead to conflict.

Elizabeth's family history prepared her for the matriarch role. In her own words:

In my own family, there was not enough money to permit one brother to buy the other out and no daughter-in-law able to come to the rescue. My grandfather, who married very late in life, was born in 1864, after his father came home from the Civil War. He and his siblings lived in the twentieth century as though it were still the 1800s—on inherited commercial property and textile mills. And we know what happened to mills in the Northeast! They had careers as diplomats and soldiers, but they never worried about earning power.

My grandparents were no fools and saw which way the wind was blowing. They sent both sons to graduate school—my uncle to study business, and my father to train as an engineer at MIT.

My grandparents did what they could. The family was very close, and they educated their sons to be able to support themselves and a family.

Nevertheless, it was a very difficult succession. My father and his brother inherited equally the large house and land in the Hudson River Valley of New York, an estate that had remained in the family since colonial times. One of my ancestors had had the house built for his bride. That property's history was intertwined with the history of my family. But it just was not possible to share, with two wives and two sets of children, and it was painfully difficult to divide. To make matters worse, my father died suddenly during the division, and the breach never had time to heal.

(Continued)

And I know that this is far from an isolated example because I still remember my mother's father telling me about the division of *his* family property with *his* only brother. My grandfather lived to be 100 years old, yet the memory still pained him. (In his case, there was little to divide, since his parents had invested in steamship ferries in Canada and had lost just about everything! But there were books and papers and bibelots— and he came home to find that his brother was burning it all in a bonfire. And, unfortunately, behind the resentment he felt was the sense that his brother was the privileged one, the one who was sent to university while he had to go out to work.)

I never wanted those things to happen in my family.

I have tried to learn from the challenges faced by my forebears and from the failures I have observed. I have thought a lot about the subject. And though I may not be able to give a formula that will *ineluctably* protect your family from failure, I can give you three observations based on my own observations.

Only strong families keep the fortune in the family. We do not want our money to destroy our families. We don't want inheritance battles. We would like to avoid divorces and disgruntled or designing spouses. So we have to build strong families.

Well, how do we do that? I have noticed time and again that strong families are built around strong, shared values. A strong, shared identity. I'm sure most of you have heard of the Cabots and the Lodges—not at all like the Capulets and the Montagues of Shakespearean fame. The Cabots and Lodges intermarry frequently. I went to college with a boy named Cabot Lodge. There is even a little poem about them:

Boston, oh Boston, the land of the bean and the cod
Where the Cabots speak only to Lodges
And the Lodges speak only to God!

The Cabots and Lodges probably think of that as a nice little nursery rhyme for their children.

That's a family! They even have a family archives, where family papers dating back to their origins as fur traders are kept.

But, seriously, family culture makes a family strong. You see it all the time. Families that seem to succeed, generation after generation. History is full of them—think of the Borgias! One pope after another. One famous poisoner after another!

We have dear friends who are perfect examples of strong family culture—and they are so successful as a family that we can't bear to read their Christmas letters. After years of hyperachievement, one child is at Harvard, and the other, just to be different, is at Yale! Not only that, both children are regional tennis champions, and my friend, the mother, built a koi pond in the yard by herself. And she rotates the tires on the family car! Yes, I used to hear about that from my husband.

And mentioning my husband's nagging about the car, and the fact that I don't rotate the car tires and that our children—so far—have not gone to Harvard or Yale, brings me to the third point I want to share with you, which I will call very simply . . . .

"Love and happiness."

And that's not just the name of a song I heard Edward singing while we drove to school. It is so trite, yet so true: For the family to survive, it must be a source of happiness to its members. Think about it: If our children have to choose between keeping wealth in the family and the sacrifice that might entail, and taking their share and getting away from a disagreeable atmosphere—well, what would you do?

This issue of family happiness is of particular interest to us because we all know that while a family can be happy without a fortune, an unhappy family will not hold on to its fortune for long. We are talking about how to keep wealth in the family over generations.

I am not trying to say that being from an unhappy family or being unhappy in your family means you can't be extremely successful in your own life. Jacob was driven away from his family tents, and it turned out to be the best thing that could have happened to him. Cain did not do so badly, either, come to think of it.

And I am talking about more than personal happiness. Individuals are not always going to be happy in their lives. And that's probably good. We need to push out beyond our comfort zone if we are going to do something extraordinary with our lives. Even if we are going to move ahead.

But the family has to be a place where the individuals in it can refresh themselves—a sort of green pasture where you can lie down and be refreshed. Where you can let down your guard, and where you can feel good about yourself just because you are part of that family.

The matriarch has to deal with the internal conflicts in the second generation. Emotional issues such as:

- Feeling unworthy of an inheritance.
- Having difficulty finding direction in life.
- Lack of confidence.
- Being inclined to abuse drugs and alcohol.

Self-confidence, the ability to focus, and hard work are necessary skills for fortune building. Each generation needs capable wealth builders to keep the family fortune together and growing. It's a lot of work to keep everyone emotionally fulfilled. The matriarch has to be fully committed and focused.

Wealth creation is hard on a family because it requires so much of the wealth creator's time and effort away from the family. The "family creator" has to hold things together. The matriarch has to fill in for the absence of the wealth creator. And she has to pull the wealth creator into the family at times, as necessary. The family creator has to allow the wealth creator to do his thing, while building a strong family.

To build a strong family, Elizabeth believes there are three main things that you need: communication, connection, and culture.

Communication means open, honest, regular dialogue between the children and the parents, and between the children themselves. It's the matriarch who helps facilitate dialogue. She talks. And she organizes the settings that make others talk, such as regular family meals. When communication is needed, she makes a point of reaching out to family members and stimulating communication between family members.

You want to get the family together as much as possible, observe family accomplishments and events collectively, and generally feel a part of each other's lives. The matriarch schedules and manages family events. And she pushes family members to be a part of them.

Families also need to feel unified. They need to feel that they are more than a random collection of people who just happen to live together, temporarily. They need what Elizabeth calls "connection." They need to be tied together by bonds of friendship, love, mutual respect, and a shared sense of enterprise. Family life is an adventure. The family is a team of adventurers—a band of brothers and sisters—united by their own history in common purpose and common experience.

A family culture is the result of a family's history, its beliefs, its biases, its attitudes, customs, and rituals.

THE THREE "D"S

Let's look at what Elizabeth considers the primary threats the matriarch has to watch out for: the three "D"s.

Division

This is when the family divides into different factions. It could be because of a long-running disagreement. It could be because of a childhood slight or jealousy. It could be because of some sort of perceived injustice or inequality. The matriarch must be keenly aware of growing division among the children and make efforts to rectify it.

Division, of course, includes divorce. A legal divide between the matriarch and patriarch can break apart the family and is one of the most common ways for a family to lose a fortune.

Dissatisfaction

Hurt feelings can't be allowed to fester. Disappointments and sour relations between siblings or toward parents are a big danger. The matriarch must be sensitive to these sorts of feelings and make efforts to resolve them well.

Distance

Time and life changes create distance between family members, both geographic and emotional. The matriarch tries to close this distance. She keeps the lines of communication open, even when family members are far apart, organizes family reunions and meeting, and helps make sure that everyone attends. She encourages communication between family members, drawing attention to family members' accomplishments and life events.

Here are seven more family wealth traps that a matriarch can help the family avoid. . . .

SEVEN COMMON PITFALLS FOR WEALTHY FAMILIES AND HOW TO AVOID THEM

1. *Give advanced notice to heirs about what's headed their way.* This includes financial wealth and other responsibilities. Failure to inform the next generation can devastate young families.

   On her 35th birthday, Kristin was contacted by a trustee, asking where she wanted her "trust income" deposited. Unknown to her, her grandfather had put stock in a trust for her when she was born, and income distribution was to start at age 35. When she inquired into the amount of the income, the trustee told her that it was $500,000 after taxes for that year. She and her husband were comfortable earning $60k per year. At age 40, she was to receive half of the principle, and to receive the balance at age 45. Three years later, unprepared for this wealth, she and her husband divorced. The money had undermined the relationship. They were unprepared for what had happened to them. The best intentions of the grandfather ultimately proved harmful for the family.

2. *Avoid alienating family members.* All efforts should be made to engage all children in the family affairs. Everyone should have some role that they deem as "important" to the family.

   A family member was considered the "loser" of the family. He had no interest in the family business. Everyone made him feel that if "you are not a businessman or president, you are nobody." However, when the planning got to philanthropy, the heir saw possibilities to work in a different environment. He blossomed. His energy and enthusiasm for the family foundation was contagious. He plunged into it and learned how to make "good" philanthropic decisions. Eighteen months later, he was president of the family foundation and a major success, a total transformation.

   (We have mixed feelings about philanthropy. Most of it is probably a waste of money—or worse. But it appears to be a good way to keep some family members focused on a common goal.)

   Options or even obligations to participate must be created for heirs. Deliberately include all heirs; resist the tendency to exclude those who do not seem to fit in. Find roles for them to play.

3. *While striving for excellence should be encouraged, too much competition can wreak havoc on a family.*

    The Martell family had built a $200 million company and educated their sons at the best universities, with both attending first-rate business schools. Competition between the sons was encouraged; they were always trying to outperform one another. They competed in auto purchases, home building, and managing sectors of the family company. The behavior became destructive to the family business, threatening its financial stability and hurting the brothers' relationships with the family.

    The parents had to change their patterns of rewards and recognition. Once they did, proper communication was restored, trust was rebuilt, and the competition was brought down to a healthy level.

4. *Avoid mixed messages between parents; there should be a single, unified vision for the family.*

    The father was a leading European industrialist who had built a multibillion-dollar chemical manufacturing company. He did not believe in shared leadership of the family business. The mother resented the preferential treatment she felt that the father had given the eldest son. Her dream was to see all of their offspring collaborating and looking after one another's interests. She described the deep sense of shame she felt every time someone asked why the other three children did not work in the family business.

    How did they work it out? The mother and father spoke openly of their hopes and ambitions. They agreed upon a continuity program for the family business.

5. *Don't wait too long to pass on ownership and responsibility.*

    One patriarch was entering his 80s and slowing down. He had hesitated for years to turn his business over to his only daughter. But he knew she'd have to take over.

    He called her into his office to promote her to president. He was shocked when she replied, "Daddy, I'm 65 years old next week and scheduled for retirement. Maybe one of the grandkids might be interested, but one's a doctor and the other's a musician. I doubt they're interested in giving up their professional careers."

6. *Help your children choose the right spouses.*

It's a politically incorrect topic. But problematic spouses can tear a family apart. You want to engage family members as much as possible in family affairs, family plans, and family finances. If the children have a sense of what the family is and what it is trying to do, it will help them choose spouses that can help them.

7. *Make sure the family shares the vision of the succession plan.*

Succession plans have to be based on the shared vision of your family, not simply by the decree of the patriarch.

In summary, it's the job of the matriarch to strengthen the family, while the patriarch builds the wealth. There are certainly other ways to do it. But this division-of-labor model has been used by the majority of successful families for hundreds of years.

The family needs to be prepared to make collective decisions to effectively manage the family wealth after the matriarch and patriarch are gone. You can't replace them. But the family will need to replace their leadership roles. The next generation needs money leadership, as well as family leadership.

Everybody knows that you have to have a person in charge of wealth creation and protection. But the chief emotional officer is much less obvious. And a much harder role to fill.

The point of succession is typically when there is the most emotional strain. The family should orchestrate a succession long before the matriarch and patriarch are out of the picture. That way, they can help make sure it happens without a blowup. And if the CEO role is empty during and after succession, the chances of a blow-up are much higher.

THE MATRIARCH OF THE ROTHSCHILDS

My mother's love for me was so great I have worked hard to justify it.
—*Marc Chagall*

We all know how Mayer Rothschild made a lot of money in banking and how he sent his five sons all over Europe to build the family banking empire. But why were the sons willing and able to take up the burden? Turns out that the old saying "For the hand that rocks the cradle is the hand that rules the world" is true.

The matriarch of the Rothschild dynasty was a remarkable woman named Gutle Schnaper. She bore her 19 children, of whom 10 survived to maturity. She gave birth virtually every year from 1771, the year after her marriage, through the next 20 years.

She raised this prodigious family in an overcrowded alley in the Jewish ghetto of Frankfurt. Three thousand people were packed into this area, which was designed for 500, on a street called Jews' Street. The densely packed houses created a fire hazard, and the area burned down three times over.

They were second-class citizens, not allowed to leave Jews' Street after dark, on Sundays, or on Christian holidays. They were forbidden from owning land or farming, or trading in silk, wine, fruit, or weapons. They had to pay special tolls when they traveled. They weren't allowed to enter taverns, inns, or city parks.

In the 1780s, the average mortality rate among Jews was 58 percent higher than among Gentiles.

A traveler in 1795 observed how "most of the people among the Frankfurt Jews, even those who are in the blooming years of their life, look like the walking dead. . . . Their deathly pale appearance sets them apart from all the other inhabitants in the most depressing way."[2]

The 11 Rothschild children shared one tiny bedroom. The first Rothschild banking house was a back room measuring 10 square feet. Gutle cooked for her family in a small passage about four feet wide with space on the hearth for only a single pot. There was hardly any furniture, just a bench and a small chest.

Somehow, in this grim setting, Gutle created a harmonious and industrious home. She was prudent, frugal, and very religious, but also warm and loving.[3]

She worked very hard and demanded the same of her children. She, along with her husband, instilled in them a sense of duty to the family and to each other.

The family unity continued for generations. Against overwhelming odds, they have successfully grown family wealth for over 250 years.

The youngest of the children, James, as an adult remarked, "It is only the reputation, the happiness and the unity of the family which lies close to my heart, and it is as a result of our business dealings that we remain united. If one shares and receives the accounts every day, then everything will stay united, God willing."[4]

And the Rothschild brothers did stay united, even after the Vienna office imploded due to bad investments. They reorganized and went on to build the most successful network of investment banking businesses the world had ever seen.

But even as the family fortune grew and her children became powerbrokers across Europe, Gutle lived in the same old house in the ghetto for the rest of her life. She kept the family anchored in their humble beginnings.

Gutle died on May 7, 1849, at age 96, with her surviving sons at her bedside.

The loss of their mother, even at her great age, deeply affected the second generation of Rothschilds.

Gutle Rothschild played a huge role in her children's emotional lives. A great matriarch gives balance to family members by helping fulfill their emotional needs. She provides for them and makes them feel loved. And this is what builds the family side of the family wealth equation.

GROWING HUMAN CAPITAL

It's the matriarch who builds the family. She develops its human capital. This is the family's most valuable resource. A family with members who are capable of building and preserving wealth will always be able to rebuild if something goes wrong.

The Rothschild family was able to survive and grow its family wealth for 250 years. They survived numerous wars, religious/ethnic persecution, government seizures, plagues, famines—you name it. Over the years, various branches of the banking business failed. But there was always a Rothschild family member somewhere who could help the family.

Imagine if your wealth suddenly disappeared. Would your family members rally by your side to help rebuild the family fortune? Do your adult family members have what it takes to get it back? Do they have the skills or the qualities necessary to acquire the skills to start from scratch?

If the answer is no, you'll want to think carefully about how they could gain these skills. What lessons do they need to learn? Perhaps, if they're lucky, they won't need to be wealth creators. But if they lack even the potential to be wealth creators, they are unlikely to be able to preserve the family wealth for very long.

DEVELOPING YOUR FAMILY CULTURE

Successful families are those that develop their own family culture: a set of beliefs and a sense of mission, as well as a common narrative about who they are, where they came from, and what they are doing.

Without someone working on developing a strong sense of shared family culture, inheritance issues tend to become minefields and battlegrounds. Often, these battles can be traced to things that have nothing to do with money. They are "lack of culture" wars. They result from not having a shared sense of values and history.

Family money depends on family culture. And family culture depends on family members—old and young. Having a family culture that supports wealth generation and preservation is another secret of Old Money.

For example, Old Money families embrace production over consumption. This becomes part of their culture, their identity as individuals and as a family. Successful multigenerational families spend a lot of time developing a family culture that encourages production and discourages consumption. This becomes a kind of shared family value, another form of "glue" that helps hold your family together.

Of course, this culture has to be real. It can be developed and embellished. But it can't be made up. And it has to be relevant to new generations. So it must build on family traditions and be dynamic and flexible at the same time.

Another way of looking at this is that the Old Money family needs to stay as "outsiders." It has to remain apart—to some extent—from the culture of the masses, or even of the rich.

Your family's culture is not something you can easily define. But that doesn't make it unimportant. Let's look at some of the elements.

FAMILY VALUES

These are the social and moral beliefs that are important to your family (not the politicized "family values" you hear so much about). Although you may hold many such values in common with other families, there will be some that seem unique to your family. And the way you go about expressing those values may also be unique to your family.

Take, for example, the family business. If your family is involved in a business, it will be a major component of your family's culture. Your family should hold in high regard the unique skills and secrets that make it work. You should also teach these skills and insights to the next generation as a right of passage.

One thing to avoid: It is typical in modern America for people to mock or denigrate a business, its customers, and its products. The sophisticated ironicist feels uneasy with the earnest efforts required in a business—especially one that he owns. He may also be slightly embarrassed about being "in trade" or about the kind of work his family business does. He may have gotten a degree in philosophy and now may find himself far removed from the concerns of a metal recycler or chain of self-service laundries. He may regard the family business as a bit unworthy, or even unattractive. But attitudes are subtle, infectious, and insidious. The polished cynic may be able to deprecate himself and the business with which he is associated while still doing his best to make it better. But lower down—among the young, the hourly employees, and the real cynics—people will become sour, dissatisfied with themselves and their work. The business will suffer.

It is all right to joke. And it is probably a good idea not to take yourself too seriously. But work is serious. Family members should be taught to respect the source of their wealth and to be willing to do all they can to support it.

If your family is not involved in a family business, think about the common occupations your family is involved in. Maybe you come from a line of farmers, lawyers, or doctors. Or a family of blacksmiths or college professors. Whatever these common occupations are, they are an important source of family identity.

THE FAMILY BUSINESS

The family business is a huge cultural asset, as well as the most important financial asset. Its identity should be an extension of your family's identity. The more your kids or grandkids—and your cousins, nieces, and nephews—get involved on some level in the family business, the stronger that part of your family culture will be.

Like it or not, you spend a lot of your time working. Your career is a big part of who you are. A few centuries ago, people recognized this by naming themselves after their professions. Blacksmiths were given the last name "Smith." Millers were called "Miller," and so on.

But beyond that, the following are a part of the family identity:

- Niche business know-how.
- Business infrastructure developed by previous generations.
- Trusted family contacts and friends.
- Family reputation (the family brand as understood by outsiders).
- Financial resources.

Family Hobbies

Any hobbies that can be passed on from generation to generation are an opportunity to express your family's identity. Shared hobbies can strengthen family bonds and create opportunities for family to get together.

One thing my family likes to do is get together on weekends and holidays and do simple construction and other manual labor on the family properties. Your authors renovated two chateaux in France, learning how to do stone masonry, among other things. In Argentina, we built a solar-heated adobe house with vaulted ceilings and a dome roof. In Maryland, we built another house, using construction techniques that were novel and, ultimately, a little stupid. But those building experiments continue, and they are part of family lore.

Education

The type of education your family gets says a lot about your view of the world. What sort of schools do members of your family go to?

Ivy League universities? Big state universities with big athletic teams? Small liberal arts colleges? International schools?

Is there a local elementary school that your family members have always gone to? Do people in your family take a year off to do some sort of activity before going college?

Your younger author studied the classics at a small liberal arts school called St. John's College in Santa Fe. His brother went to the same college.

Some members of the second generation were home-schooled in middle school. They also followed a classical education program similar to St. John's. An education based on the great books of Western civilization is a part of our family's family culture.

Does your family have an alma mater that multiple family members have attended? Are there certain fields of study that members of your family have in common?

Try to keep those educational traditions alive and have members of the next generation aspire to follow in your footsteps.

Marriage

What sort of people do you marry? Does you family tend to marry into other wealthy, socially connected families? Or does it tend to marry into hardworking salt-of-the-earth sort of families? Will the next fiancé fit well into your family?

In our family, we have a test for prospective spouses. We call it the "Gualfin Test," after our ranch in South America. We invite him or her to come with us to the ranch. From the United States, it is a long and arduous journey culminating in five hours of rough mountain driving in a 4 × 4. Sometimes the road is washed out. Sometimes we have to turn back. When we finally get to the ranch, we are at an altitude of nearly 9,000 feet. It is very dry. Very hot in the day. Very cold at night. Typically, when we arrive, we stop for a cup of tea, and then get on horses for a four-hour ride to visit a remote valley.

How a boyfriend or a girlfriend handles the journey—and the stay at the isolated and arid ranch—tells us how he or she will fit into the family.

It used to be that successful multigenerational families would marry strategically; it was a way of social climbing. Or they would marry certain people to achieve strategic goals, such as forging a partnership with another wealthy family.

We doubt that this is advisable. People who "marry for money," as they say, earn it. Seeing that the prospective spouse will fit with the family identity is more important. A lasting, stable, happy marriage is the most desirable outcome when it comes to family wealth.

Philanthropy

In many wealthy families that no longer own or manage a family business, the family philanthropy becomes a focal point of the family activity and identity. A family foundation can be an important opportunity to contribute to the family identity. (But beware of philanthropic claptrap. More later.)

Politics

Your family's political stance and activity are important components of the family identity. In our family, we try to avoid politics altogether. We believe in remaining outsiders. We think it is dangerous to try to get on the inside. You risk becoming insiders, looking for handouts and wealth redistribution rather than wealth creation.

Family History

Your family history is a key component of your family's identity. Anything that answers the question of who you are, and what your family is and where it came from, helps build out a sense of being special and different. Just knowing your lineage and family history helps enrich the family identity.

Beyond that, the family history can also be used as a narrative that helps motivate family members. For example, a story of an ancestor overcoming some sort of obstacle can be inspiring for family members. Of course, the story can't be made up. It should be basically true. But as we all know, the truth is remarkably elastic. You should highlight stories and themes that show your family in the light you want it.

This helps you establish what is called a "family brand." It's a way of identifying your family and a simple way—like a cattle brand—of keeping track of who you are and why you are different. Branding can guide the family self-image and help family members reach their potential. But it has to be a real potential. You can't simply invent family characteristics, inclinations, and skills that don't exist. That would be counterproductive.

But there are plenty of things that you have control over that can be expressed as a part of your family brand.

Family Motto and Crest

The Rothschild family crest was created according to the rules of heraldry and includes symbolism unique to the family. There is a clenched fist with five arrows symbolizing the five sons of Mayer Rothschild and a reference to Psalm 127: "Like arrows in the hands of a warrior." There is a red shield in the middle, as the name "Rothschild" derives from the German *roten Shild* (literally, "red shield"). The family motto appears below the shield: *Concordia, Integritas, Industria* (Harmony, Integrity, Industry).

If you don't already have a family motto and crest, consider what they might be. Remember, these should reflect qualities that are unique to your family and help promote your family identity.

Family Traditions and Rituals

Family traditions are important because they are unique expressions of your family identity. They also give a sense of permanence and stability. The more unique activities you can do with family members that they enjoy and take seriously, the better.

Family rituals and celebrations for family members reaching certain milestones help strengthen family bonds and the sense of belonging. For example, when a new family member joins the Family Council, this is an opportunity for a family rite of passage.

The Jewish bar/bat mitzvah is a great example of this. In the Episcopal Church, confirmation is a similar coming-of-age ritual. You should consider having similar rituals for young people entering your Family Council and other "soft structure" institutions (more on that in Chapter 8).

Beware of allowing family members to opt out of family events. Certainly, there will be periods when individual family members need to "do their own thing." But, ideally, this should be in addition to the family activities, not a substitute for them.

Family Relationships and Reputation

Family relationships and the family reputation are critical manifestations of your family's identity. These things can take decades and sometimes generations to build up. And they can be used by multiple generations to create wealth.

Who you know can be more important than what you know when it comes to building wealth. Trusted family friends, advisers, and contacts can be invaluable for supporting family members. These are not only financial relationships, but emotional ties, also. It's very important for family members to maintain these relationships because they take a long time to build.

Family Vacations

Where does your family go on vacations? And why? Spending vacation time together is important for family bonds. Relaxing and getting away from work with family helps keep family relationships fresh and enjoyable. When you associate time with family with vacation, it's a positive association.

Family vacations are an opportunity to strengthen your family culture and identity by doing something that is unique to your family. It helps to have a place to go as a family for vacation and holidays. Keep the old family farm or beach house. Schedule events well in advance. Welcome in-laws, boyfriends, girlfriends, and new family members as warmly as possible.

Family Properties

A family property is a part of your family's portfolio that everyone understands and has an opinion about. Physical property is tangible. You can see it. You can live in it. You have friends near it. You can lie on the grass with your cousin and look at the clouds. You can listen to your favorite uncle tell war stories on the porch. You can paint the fence!

Family properties are the most familiar and often-used assets in the family portfolio. This also creates an opportunity to draw family members into the family enterprise by asking them to manage family property. Properties also hold emotional value for family members. Memories are tied to family property. For these reasons, family property should be well managed and treated carefully.

Family members will often associate themselves and the rest of the family with family property more than anything else, especially in families that do not have family businesses.

Family property is where family members most often come together. You want to keep property as a unifier, not a divider. So avoid dividing up properties among family members as much as possible. Avoid arguments about how to manage and maintain properties. Talk it out. Compromise.

Family gatherings on family property offer an excellent opportunity to strengthen family bonds. These should be held at major holidays, and preferably, there should be a gathering to celebrate an event that is completely unique to the family. Weddings. Funerals. Graduations. Use family properties to mark important family milestones.

Family Investments

What your family chooses to invest in also makes up a big part of your family's identity.

How does your family manage wealth? How will it do so in the future? What sorts of investments does your family favor and why? Who will participate in managing the family money?

These things are all expressions of your family culture. And they reflect the unique style of your family. That is why it is so important that you have a group in place to look after your family's investment decisions. When you make an investment decision, you make a statement about your family's culture.

Look on each investment you make as an opportunity to expand and enrich your family culture. You want family members to view family investments as consistent with the family culture.

Our family has a few unique traditions and rituals that help promote our family culture. As children grow up, for instance, they are invited to accompany their father on business trips. These usually take the family to far-flung places where the family has an outpost. We have been to Hong Kong, South Africa, India, China, and many other locations. We remember the trips. We learn from them, too.

Travel makes up a big part of our family's culture. We tend to travel fairly frequently. We try to make the effort to learn about different cultures and languages, especially in places where the family business is located. The first member of the third generation of our family (the younger author's son) was born in Buenos Aires, Argentina, where his family lived for three years. The older generations spent 15 years in France. Most of the second-generation children went to French schools and speak fluent French.

Another tradition of sorts we have is that, at family gatherings, a few of us play guitars and the rest of us sing along. This isn't a formal tradition of any sort. But it's something that we always do together. And that makes it a special family tradition.

All these things are manifestations of the family identity and the family culture. They reflect the unique style of the family. And they are each opportunities to expand and enrich the family identity. Family members should view these things as positive and accurate identifiers of the family. A successful family culture is one family members want to be a part of and identify themselves closely with. This holds the family together and helps maintain harmony because they have something in common that is held in high regard.

While all families have their traditions and their own cultures, one cultural feature is particular to Old Money families. They must learn the family business and/or the skills to preserve and create wealth.

Overcoming Setbacks

The Rothschild family is one of the most successful families in modern history. For over 200 years, the family has managed to stay together and preserve and grow wealth to astonishing levels. There are plenty of conspiracy theories about them. And there's much that we don't know.

However, they are a real family, also. They endure setbacks and pitfalls like the rest of us. The Parisian arm of their banking business was nationalized by the Mitterrand government in 1982. But they were able to rebuild in France, starting over from almost nothing. Because that's what Rothschilds do—they have the know-how and the connections to build successful finance businesses. We've seen it over and over again throughout history.

And not all Rothchilds are successful bankers. Lionel Walter Rothschild, 2nd Baron Rothschild, was a zoologist, born in 1868. At age 21, he reluctantly went to work for the family business. Nineteen years later, he was finally allowed out. He started a zoological museum and funded expeditions around the world. He formed the largest zoological collection ever amassed by a private individual.

He was the first to describe a rare giraffe, which was named *Giraffa camelopardis rothschildi*. Another 153 insects, 58 birds, 17 mammals, 3 fish, 3 spiders, 2 reptiles, 1 millipede, and 1 worm also carry his name. He famously drove a carriage harnessed to 6 zebras to Buckingham Palace to prove that zebras could be tamed.

In 2000, 23-year-old Raphael de Rothschild died of a heroin overdose in New York City.

David Mayer de Rothschild is a 32-year-old billionaire environmentalist and adventurer.

And Nathaniel Philip Rothschild, age 40, is said to have generated approximately $600 million from his stake in the hedge fund Atticus Capital and the launch of Vallar PLC, an investment company focused on mining.

The point is that the Rothschild family is made up of diverse individuals with varying abilities, just like yours. Yet they have been able to hold on to significant wealth for 200 years. They've done it by creating, nurturing, and sustaining a family culture that appreciates expertise in high finance. In the early days, this meant strategic marriages, forcing family members into the family business, and other, more extreme measures that would not be prudent today.

But they answered the question of what it means to be a Rothschild, and they continued to answer that question through the generations as the answer changed. They maintained a firm identity and successfully passed along the ability to generate new wealth in the family business.

The Rothschild family identity was carefully developed and nurtured from the beginning. Its model of expanding the family business by placing family members in strategic locations was followed by other Jewish financier families, like the Bischoffsheims, Pereires, the Seligmans, and the Lazards. . . .

While positive aspects of the family identity need to be nurtured, negative features need to be suppressed. Alcoholism or suicide might be in the family history or DNA, but, certainly, you'd want to push those out of the family brand. That doesn't mean that you sweep the issues under the rug. You have to deal with them. But you counter them with positive messages and a positive example.

The Kennedy family fortune was made partially from stock manipulation, insider trading, and bootlegging. But they managed to successfully brand the family into a political force that would ascend to the U.S. presidency and various other high-level positions within the government.

The Bush family also managed to parlay its family identity into a political dynasty.

In each of these cases, each generation is able to build on the successes of the previous generation. Again, we don't approve of either of these family examples. As Monsieur Mulliez explained, you want to avoid publicity. You should avoid talking to the press. And you should avoid the lure of becoming insiders. But at least these examples show how powerful family branding can be.

Keep in mind that all your family members have identities of their own. They will react negatively if you try to impose a brand, or an identity, that they don't like. You can't do these things by force. Instead, you have to lead by example and exert a positive, nurturing influence. You can help them see things from (your) family perspective. A family identity must be a vision of the future that family members share. And it has to be farsighted. It has to be fixed, like the North Star—something that will guide generations. But it must also be flexible enough to take on changes from the next generation.

In forming the family identity, think about what you want to be in 20, 50, or 100 years. You'll need your family members on board with everything. You'll need your vision of the future to match with theirs.

Career and Educational Development Programs

You should use your own family money to help keep the family from regressing to the mean. Family businesses and family investments challenge family members. They cause them to stretch, to grow into the responsibilities in front of them. You can help them grow by providing internships, jobs, investment analysis, and on-the-job training in business and finance, as well as more "store-bought" educational opportunities.

Heed the words of Baron Rothschild: "A hired hand is very different from your own blood!" The job of the family office—its ultimate aim, in fact—is to prepare and harness the potential of your family's human assets. Some of the ways of keeping family members engaged and learning include:

- Involvement in the family business.
- Involvement in family philanthropy.
- A role on the investment committee.
- A role in the management of family property.
- An administrative role in the family office.
- Starting a new business venture with family funds and support.

These things directly help support the family enterprise and the family money. Remember, family wealth needs to be replenished by each generation or it will disappear. That's why you should run the family office like a business. You need to make sure you seek a return on investment (ROI) on its assets.

This often happens indirectly. For example, when the family bank lends for a new business start-up, or for professional education, family members reach a level of success in their careers so they can support themselves. In this way, they cease to be "liabilities" to the family office.

Put another way, the purpose of the family office is to help current and future family members develop their talents and become productive. This, in turn, helps the family office endure. Because when family members discover meaningful work, they are much less likely to become "liabilities" on the family balance sheet.

Delaying Gratification

One simple characteristic that can help your children succeed is their ability to delay gratification.

You want to start emphasizing the benefits of delayed gratification to family members at a young age. Family members need to understand how delayed gratification was key to building the family wealth in the first place. And they need to understand why delayed gratification is also necessary to continue growing and preserving wealth for the future.

This is even more important because of something family wealth advisers call "generational mathematics." This is a fancy way of saying that families get bigger over time. And that family wealth gets eroded as families grow larger without becoming increasingly productive.

Also, when you take into account the setbacks, stock market crashes, business trouble, lawsuits, and taxes—never mind a black swan or two—you simply have to increase your wealth to give the same opportunities that you had to your children and grandchildren.

Mentoring and Internship Programs

From our business partner, Mark Ford, we learned that you always want to "pass it on." You want to transfer your knowledge in a position or a skill to someone else so that they can take over when the time comes. That frees you up to move higher up on the ladder and attend to more important business.

This is completely the opposite of what many people think. Most people think they need to hoard their accumulated knowledge so that they become more valuable. Maybe they think it protects their jobs.

Even in a family setting, sometimes the "old man" doesn't really want others to know anything about the business . . . or investing. A TV show called *Arrested Development* shows where this can lead. The show is a spoof on rich families who have businesses. The father is in jail for various crimes. The son wants to make it clear that he is now running the business. So he burns down his father's favorite mini-store. Then the father reveals that he had hidden $250,000 in cash in the store walls.

Don't wait too long to "pass it on"—it could be too late!

The bottom line is that it's never too early for a wealth creator to start grooming protégés. But beyond that, if you are the wealth creator of your family, you need to let go of the reins. *And the sooner, the better.* This ensures that your protégés gain real-world experience in managing the family money.

It takes 1,000 hours of focused effort to become competent in anything. That means you need 1,000 hours of actively managing family money before you can expect to be competent at it. But since investing is such a competitive activity, you'd be a lot better off if the person managing your family wealth were a real master who had worked at it for 5,000 hours or longer.

Does someone in the next generation of your family have that kind of experience? Does someone have the stamina and persistence to get it? You need to make sure they do.

And you want all family members to be passably competent in financial affairs. Let them each manage a small portion of the family wealth, say somewhere between 0.5 percent and 1 percent. There is no better way for them to learn the ropes. The earlier they make mistakes, the better. Mistakes are a great teacher, especially if there is real money involved.

Of course, creating the opportunity for family members to gain experience comes at a price. But that price will be much greater the longer you wait—and perhaps catastrophically high if you wait too long to take advantage of the wealth creator's guidance. Ideally, you want all family members to be passably competent in financial affairs. They can gain this competence by managing some portion, however small, of family assets.

Mentoring and internships can take many different forms. We like to send young people to work in foreign countries. We figure it gives them more options, a wider range of experience and particular skills that they would not otherwise have. Besides, you never know what the future holds. The more options that you have in terms of where you can live, work, and move your money, the better. And, of course, this gives your family office much more flexibility in terms of wealth preservation.

Giving family members the opportunity to explore new cultures helps develop your family's human capital. Understanding another culture raises your self-awareness and keeps your mind limber and open. And these foreign skills, such as language and cultural understanding, could prove to be very financially valuable in the coming years as wealth shifts from the developed to the emerging world.

People in the developing world understand and respect family business, more so than in the United States. In Latin America and Asia, family businesses are more ubiquitous than in North America. It can be reassuring for them to do business with a family member of the business owner, rather than an unrelated employee.

We create internship opportunities for our family members and friends as often as possible. These internships are not just in our family business, but also in the businesses of friends and colleagues. Sometimes these develop into careers, sometimes not. But the experience helps young people learn about themselves and what they want from their work.

Also, you never know where the next business superstar is going to come from. The college roommate of your younger author is now a valuable employee in our family business.

HOW TO BRING "OUTSIDERS" INTO THE FAMILY

The introduction of an "outsider" into the family dynamic can be tricky. And the statistics are not encouraging. Half of all marriages fail.

In our business experience, too, we find that it is difficult to import upper-level employees. Typically, people enter as very young adults. They absorb the culture of the business. They fit in. Outsiders often don't fit in.

But families must bring in outsiders. Sons and daughters will marry outsiders. You naturally want to protect your children and your family wealth. But you also know of the potential pitfalls involved in meddling in your children's love lives!

The family, by way of the Family Council, should make policies regarding spouses. That's because you don't want to make decisions like this on a case-by-case basis. That could create feelings of bias and even resentment. Instead, you just want prospective spouses to know what the rules are. Nothing personal about it. You want policies that put everyone on an even playing field. You want to be able to say something like: "It's nothing against so-and-so. Those are just the rules. We decided on them together long ago. Everyone follows them."

So what kind of policies are we talking about?

The first is not a formal policy. But it is important. Family members should understand that when they marry, they bring someone into the family. Whom they marry is an expression of the family identity. Will the person they marry "fit" into the family culture? Obviously, this can be a sensitive subject. But you might at the very least ask your son or daughter to consider this if it seems like they haven't done so already.

Is a "Prenup" Really Necessary?

In terms of more formal policy, you need something that addresses wealth protection in the context of the 50-50 potential for divorce. At least, there should be a policy that asks the family member getting married to consider the wealth protection options available. That does not necessarily mean a prenuptial agreement. This kind of thing seems a bit anti-romantic. But under certain circumstances, it is recommended. It depends on the financial situation of the person getting married and the legal structures the family is using to hold wealth.

We're not lawyers, but as we understand it, the beneficiary's assets in a perpetual trust, such as the one my family uses, would not be considered marital property. But income or profits derived from money distributed from the trust during the marriage would be considered marital property.

If there has been a distribution before a family member gets married, there's greater potential for that money—and especially the income derived from that money—to be considered marital property.

Should a Spouse Become Involved in Family Financial Affairs?

It depends on your family culture. Your younger author's wife has not been a part of our Family Council meetings. That's partly because we've had only a handful of meetings, and we're still getting the hang of how they will work.

Although we would like her to be involved, it's something we still need to figure out. If she is in our meetings, would that give an extra, unofficial vote to her husband? Would family members with spouses then have a greater voice in the meetings than unmarried family members? What if all six children married in quick succession? The addition of so many "outsiders" would change the makeup of the family's governing committee very quickly.

And in the event of a divorce, how is the ex-wife or husband removed from the Family Council and other family office activities? (Or should they be removed at all? If there are children involved, maybe an ex-wife or ex-husband has a right to stay involved.)

These are questions we'll need to answer. And the place to do that is a family constitution.

Writing a family constitution sounds like a daunting prospect. But it really is just a collection of guidelines to help the Family Council make consistent decisions. And consistency—especially in regard to spouses—is critical to maintaining family harmony.

We'll look at this in more detail in Chapter 8.

FIGHTING ADDICTIONS AND TROUBLESOME FAMILY MEMBERS

Substance addictions can be devastating to a family. And no one is immune to this problem. Even the most successful families can succumb to these threats. For instance, as we mentioned, after graduating top of his class from Brown University in 2000, 23-year-old Raphael de Rothschild, scion of one of the world's wealthiest families, died of a heroin overdose at a friend's apartment in Manhattan.

Families with a strong matriarch and strong institutions, such as an active Family Council, do not avoid these problems. But perhaps they can detect problems sooner; they are usually in closer and more frequent communication with one another. Whether they can do anything about the problem is another question.

Once a problem is detected, concerned family members should deal it with privately. We're no experts on this, either. But one route is to have a procedure already spelled out in the family constitution. Then, without making judgments on any particular family member, you can merely apply the rules as necessary. There are no guarantees that this will help the troublesome family member, but it will protect the rest of the family and its resources.

The Family Council can allocate funds for treatment and other health-related matters. Beyond that, the Family Council should stick to its wealth-oriented mission and avoid getting involved in personal, emotionally charged issues.

CHAPTER 3

WHAT ABOUT THE MONEY?

After the family, the other essential element of family money is the money itself. Where does it come from? How much do you need? How do you get it?

Good questions.

As with so many other things we discovered—or inferred—successful Old Money families do things very differently from other people.

First, who has "family money," and how did they get it?

The surest way to get a fortune is to be born with a silver spoon in your mouth. Better yet, a gold spoon. Money begets money.

But probably more important than the money are the other things we inherit from our parents. It's a competitive world. Those who inherit money have a head start. But those who inherit drive, ambition, energy, the right attitudes, intelligence, the right culture and so forth will probably pass them somewhere along life's highway.

If you're lucky, you've already got your family money in hand. Now your only challenge is how to hold on to it. That won't be easy. Partly because there are so many clever people trying to find ways to take it away from you, and partly because you might be eager to get rid of it yourself.

As to the first point, you have to understand that nature does not favor outliers. She tolerates them—but just barely. That's why they are outliers way out on the fringe of the bell curve—statistically important, but numerically insignificant.

That is, family money is a relatively rare thing. Just as nature mixes up and redistributes genes, she tends to mix up and redistribute wealth, too. Nature detests a monopoly and abhors a vacuum. Family wealth is like a monopoly; it is a concentration of assets in a family, monopolizing wealth that might otherwise be spread to the four winds. Nature doesn't like it. And she sends out agents of all sorts to try to eliminate it.

As mentioned often in this book, there are many of them, both inside and outside the family. Outside are tax collectors, lawyers, wealth managers, business advisers, investment analysts, luxury salesmen, and many others.

Inside are the vengeful spouses, neglected children, incompetent brothers-in-law, and spiteful siblings.

But the worst inside risk is the heir himself.

First, he might not be up to the challenge of managing wealth. Second, he may feel guilty about having it and be eager to get rid of it.

The desire for "fairness" seems to be innate in humans. The law of reciprocity decrees that when we give something, we should get something in return. So does the law of fairness tell us that if one person gets a good deal, the rest of us should get it, too.

But then, suppose you were born to a rich family, while many others were born to poor families. What are you to think of that? Where's the fairness in it? What can you do about it?

Most people are able to see through the thin veil of unfairness to the more profound truth behind it. We are all born with strengths and weaknesses. We take what we get. We make the best of it. That's fair.

Some are born tall, for example. Some are short. Studies show that tall people earn more money. Where's the fairness in that? Some are born good looking. Some aren't.

Studies show that good-looking people find it easier to get a job. One of the studies followed lawyers. It found that the more attractive the lawyer, the more rapidly his career developed. At the end of 15 years, he earned 13 percent more than his less attractive peers.[1] Where's the fairness in that?

Some people are born smart. Others are stupid. Again, studies show what you'd expect. Smart people, those who score highly on IQ tests, earn more money, are less likely to get divorced, live longer, and more rarely go to jail than stupid people.

One controversial book on the subject, *The Bell Curve*, by Richard Herrnstein and Charles Murray, argued that intelligence was more important than any other variable. The authors studied 12,000 young adults. They found that IQ predicted success much better than socioeconomic status. In other words, being born into a rich family or a poor family mattered less than if you were smart (as measured by IQ tests).[2]

Other researchers complained that Herrnstein and Murray had oversimplified socioeconomic status. They had included only parental income, occupation, and education. Adding in other social status indicators—family size, presence of two parents in the home, geographical residence, and so on—they found just the opposite: Socioeconomic status markers were more likely to be predictive than intelligence.

We don't know. And we don't care. Whatever you've got to work with is all you've got. Maybe your youthful socioeconomic status is a good forecast statistically, but so what? You make the most of what you've got. You don't care what the statistics tell you. What if they told you that your chances of success were less than those of someone down the block? Would you stop trying?

Probably the thing that makes one most successful in life is merely luck. As John D. Rockefeller put it, the way to success is to (1) get to work early, (2) stay late, and (3) strike oil. Give us a confident, energetic, ambitious young person, one whose natural pluck will put his luck to his advantage, and we will put our money on him, rather than on Old Money, any day.

But where do these qualities come from? And where's the fairness? Who knows? But some people are very troubled by the apparent unfairness of unearned money. And, in one sense, they are perhaps right. The system, at least in the United States, is rigged in their favor.

No, we don't mean by low tax rates; the rich still pay proportionately far more in taxes than the poor. The average top marginal federal tax rate imposed on the rich is 35 percent of income. Yet approximately half of all citizens have a net tax rate (net of money received from the government) of about zero. Where's the fairness in that?

But a lot of people feel guilty. They feel they have benefited unfairly, either because they personally did not earn their money or because the system benefited them at the expense of millions of others. While

we probably agree with their analysis, we disagree with their conclusion. Yes, the rich did benefit from the government's lame-brained
monetary and economic policies. Yes, the rich benefited from lower
tax rates. Yes, many of the rich benefited from special favors given out
by an increasingly corrupt government. The question before us is not
where the money came from but what to do with it now?

Moved by a sense of fairness, incompetence, or public service, many
rich people will shirk their responsibilities and shuck their wealth. But
successful Old Money knows better.

MOST CHARITY IS A WASTE OF TIME AND MONEY

We are racing ahead. We haven't told you how to make a fortune or
how to manage it yet. But we are telling you what to do once you have
one. Why? Because it shows you how difficult it is to do what you're
trying to do. The more money you have, the more reasons you find to
get rid of it. You think you're being smart by investing it. You think you
are being cool by spending it. You think you are being good by giving
it away.

Often, you might just as well throw it down a storm drain.

Most people with money have no reason to feel guilty or proud.
They were neither particularly smart nor particularly greedy. They
were just lucky. And they are not likely to do any good by giving their
money away or advocating higher tax rates on the rich—unless, of
course, they actually want to give it away or pay it in taxes. If they do,
it merely shows that they are not fit to have it. Better to move it along
to more able hands. What the hell? Spend it.

Ultimately, the government is responsible for tilting the playing
field. Why reward the culprits with higher tax revenues? As for giving
the money to charity, good luck with that. It's hard enough to manage, preserve, and pass along money to your own family. Try doing it
for someone else's family. Most likely, you'll do more harm than good.

Or maybe you think you'd like to find a cure for cancer? Pay for
a new gym at a local college? Provide scholarships for the children of
one-armed paperhangers? Good luck again. The world is full of people who want to get ahead. Everyone wants as much power, status, and
money as possible, with the least effort. Some work for the government.

Some for private business. And some for charities and public interest groups. All are good at one thing: transferring your money from you to them. Whether they actually cure cancer or accomplish any of the other worthy goals you hoped for is an entirely different matter.

Think of private, profit-making businesses. Even with the threat of bankruptcy and the need to trim costs and boost sales close at hand, even with the smell of profits in the managers' nostrils and the fear of Chapter 11 staring them in the face—private businesses are still prey to bureaucracy and position padding. Imagine what happens in an institution with no profit motive! Your money is capital. It is a call on resources. As far as we can tell, the best thing you can do for yourself and others is to invest it wisely, with the hope of a real profit. Profits are the only things that tell you with reasonable certainty that you are actually adding value.

Look at it this way: If you give money to charity, how do you know that it is worthwhile? How do you know that you don't do more harm than good? If your money is merely used up, with no positive outcome, you have done bad. That is, you have wasted precious resources that might have been used to make people's lives better. But how can you tell when people's lives are better?

You may think that people would all be better off if they lived in blue houses. So you buy blue paint and give it to people. Some paint their houses blue. Have you done good?

You may think that people would be better off if they had access to free bread. So you hand out bread on the street corner. Have you done good?

You may think that people should all drive energy-efficient cars. So you endow research into battery-powered vehicles. Have you done good?

Answer: You don't know. But if you have actually done good, it is by accident. Because you don't have any way of measuring it. And you surely don't know—by intuition or revelation—what would be good for other people.

MORE HARM THAN GOOD

We began to doubt the merit of charity work many years ago. A friend of ours had volunteered to go to Nicaragua during the Sandinista years. He felt guilty about the way the U.S. government had reacted to the communist takeover of the country. He wanted to help out by building houses.

So he went to Nicaragua at his own expense. There, he enlisted in a brigade of foreign volunteer workers. They toted blocks and laid bricks, without pay, helping to build shelter for the Nicaraguan population.

"You wouldn't think a country like that would have a shortage of labor," we suggested. "What's the going rate for a day laborer down there?"

"Oh, it's about $2 a day."

"Then, when you work a week down there, it's the equivalent of a contribution of $10."

"Yes, I guess it is."

"What do you earn in the United States?"

"About $10 an hour."

"Would they be better off if you worked in the United States for a week and sent them the $400 you earned?"

"Well, I guess so. . . ."

"Forty times better off."

"Yes, but they'd probably use the money to buy weapons—after all, the United States is supplying rebels who are trying to kill them."

Yes, dear reader, life was not set up in a way that accommodates the fantasies of world improvers. Instead, it is almost impossible for them to do any good—except by coincidence.

Don't believe us? Think someone who gives money to the Red Cross or Save the Whales or to fix the cleft palates of poor people *must* be doing good?

Not so. How does anything have value? Things don't have value in and of themselves. They are given value by willing buyers and sellers. If no one wants a Hula-Hoop, it has no value. None. It has value only when someone has a want or a need for it. Otherwise, it is worth zilch.

While there is obviously a demand for a Save the Whales group, signaling a value to the group itself, there is not necessarily any whale saving going on. Or even if there were, you wouldn't have any way of knowing what it was worth. Whale saving is not subject to market pricing.

Imagine a do-gooder who thinks he can make the world a better place by giving people Hula-Hoops for free. What has he done?

He has taken valuable resources and turned them into something for which people may have neither a use nor a desire. He has made the world poorer.

He has done bad.

You can know when something has value only when people want it. So why not give them something they want, like bread? Then, surely you will be doing good, right?

Wrong.

If you give away bread, what happens to the person who used to earn his living growing rice? Doesn't the competition of free bread doom him to failure? Is that a good thing?

And where would you get the bread? You have to buy it, right? And as people switch from expensive rice and other cereals to free bread, you have to buy more and more of it. So you drive up the price of wheat and bring other farmers to switch from whatever they are doing to providing you with wheat so you can provide free bread.

Does the world have more food as a result of your generous offer? Not necessarily; producers have merely shifted from producing what people wanted—and were willing to pay for—to what you wanted. And since it is free to consumers, they take it up with both enthusiasm and contempt. Unless controls are put on, they are soon feeding it to their pigs so that they can enjoy some free bacon on their free bread. Feeding bread to pigs almost certainly makes the world a poorer place. Pigs can thrive on cheaper food. So you apply various systems of control to make sure your free bread program is not abused. You hire agents and controllers. You give out ration cards. You insist that recipients register and prove that they really need the bread.

This, of course, costs money, too. You are now replacing the market system, which needs none of these things, with a system of centralized, bureaucratic management. Instead of honest buyers and sellers, now your paid functionaries decide who gets bread and who doesn't. These management systems divert further resources from actually providing food to paperwork and administration.

Soon, you will have lawyers and auditors on the case, too. And then you will eventually discover that every loaf of bread you distribute free costs you 10 times the previous cost of a loaf of bread. This means that you have destroyed resources equal to nine times the value of the loaf of bread itself in your effort to make the world a better place.

In fact, you have done bad.

The problem is simple enough. You can know if something has value only if it is allowed to trade in the free market, where willing buyers and sellers discover its value every day. Any attempt to give away something for free, or even subsidize it (to say nothing of controlling it in other ways) distorts the price. Now you don't know whether you are paying too much or too little. You don't know whether you are doing good or bad.

You think, for example, that the world is generating too much carbon dioxide. You subsidize a windmill. It generates electricity, but at twice the cost per kilowatt. Have you done good? What does it mean when you say "twice the cost"? Doesn't it mean that you actually use twice the resources? And doesn't that imply that you also use up twice as much energy? Someone had to make the steel to build your windmill. Someone had to put the parts on a truck to bring it to you. Someone had to drive out to install it and to service it. If the inputs cost twice as much as normal, you use twice as much energy to create it.

Prices, freely determined, are what tell you when something is worth doing and when it is not. They tell you how much both resources and energy cost.

Without freely set prices, you are wandering around in the dark. That is why so many charity efforts are hapless and vain. In fact, it wouldn't surprise us to discover that all the world improvement projects from the beginning of time to the present were a net drag on man's happiness.

It's a hard thing to believe. The world's smartest, richest, and most respected people are firmly behind charities. Bill Gates. Warren Buffett. Andrew Carnegie. The Rockefellers. How dare we contradict them?

Clearly, the burden of proof is on us. We gave you some of our reasoning already. Here is more:

Bill Gates and Warren Buffett are certainly geniuses. At least at making money. Wouldn't it be asking a little much to expect them to be geniuses at getting rid of it, too? They know what it takes to make money—good ideas, properly managed, properly funded. It's not easy. But if you do it right and get lucky, you add to the world's wealth. More people get more of what they want. That's what adding to the world's wealth means.

If you are good at adding to the world's wealth, you will accumulate a huge pile of capital as a result. This capital represents resources that could be put to use to add even more to the world's wealth.

So what are you doing when you give them away? Resources pass from the hands of people who add to the world's wealth to the hands of people who ... who what? Nobody really knows. Presumably, they are people who mean well. Presumably, they do a good job at what they do.

But if they were adding to the world's wealth, they wouldn't need a handout. So, by definition, they are not adding to the world's wealth. Are they adding to the world's well-being? Who knows? Their output is not priced and not subject to the rules of a market economy. They are operating like the government, whose output may or may not be useful or beneficial, but almost certainly lowers the world's wealth, rather than increases it.

VANITY

Says our friend Doug Casey:"The essence of a charity transaction is to transfer wealth from those who have shown they can create it to those who have not shown they can."[3]

But the fact that something is ineffective doesn't make it unpopular. People like giving away money. It makes them feel good. In order to fully understand how "good" it makes them feel, you have to understand what you're dealing with.

Giving money away is the spirit, not the practical doer, at work. It may not make sense from a purely economic point of view; that is, the net effect is probably to depress output. But it may increase human happiness. A man can be made happy by a number of things. Not all of them are the sort we are proud of. Not all of them increase the world's well-being.

Included in the evolved human species' genetic material is a desire to mate with the most attractive partner. We have developed a range of strategies and deceptions for that purpose. Women enhance their bosoms to show what good mothers they would be. Men like to show how rich and desirable they are. Some do this by driving cars they cannot really afford. Some endow hospitals with amounts that are pocket change to them. Some like to show how little money means to them—by tipping the cigar girl with a $100 bill or blowing a fortune on a worthless painting.

Vanity, vanity, vanity—money talks and bullshit walks. That's just the way we are.

Ted Turner must be as vain as Narcissus. He actually gave the United Nations—the UN!—a billion dollars.

Why on earth would he do such a thing? Wouldn't the world be better off if he used his money to build houses, hotels, and other things people might actually want? Why give it to a bunch of hacks who have never built anything?

But the *grand geste* got his face in the paper. He was happy.

You can see the vanity and competitiveness of it at work at a charity auction. There, the desire to spread your tail feathers is almost irresistible. There is often no relationship between the bids and the object on sale.

In fact, the greater the distance between one and the other, the more it flatters the vanity of the bidder. One fellow bids $1,000 for a luncheon with a faded sports star. Another bids $2,000. And then, the *grand geste:* "I'll make it $10,000...." He struts up to the stage to the enthusiastic applause.

The man is a hero. Is the money well spent? Is the charity worthwhile? Is the result greater wealth/more happiness—or less? Nobody knows. Nobody really cares, either.

That's another problem with charity: The giver is not more blessed; he is a bigger jerk. He cares only about his own status and about his own vanity, not about what harm his money actually does to people.

That's another big difference between other kinds of money and family money. You "give" money to others in the form of taxes. You have no choice. The money is transferred from you to someone else. Many people take pride in paying the taxes. They're happy to do it. They imagine that it does some good, but they must know that its consequences are mostly malign:

- Killing people in pointless wars.
- Locking people up in the war on drugs.
- Paying bureaucrats to sit on their fat derrieres and meddle in other peoples' affairs.

- Corrupting the poor with welfare.
- Corrupting the middle class with handouts.
- Corrupting even the rich with contracts, tariffs, and special favors.

That's the difference. Give the money to your own family, and you care whether it hurts them or helps them. That's why so many people don't bother to do it, of course. They don't want to harm their own children; they'd prefer to harm someone else's.

HOW DO YOU ACCUMULATE A "FAMILY FORTUNE"?

Most people earn their money from salaries or wages. But this kind of money is unlikely to bring you much in the way of capital. You can't earn that much. And most, if not all, of what you earn will be taken up with daily expenses and retirement financing.

Unless you are an exceptional wage earner, you're not likely to be able to use your earnings to build a real family fortune. There are a lot of people in the world. When you work for wages or a salary, you are selling your time. And your time is not going to be much more valuable than another person's time.

Of course, there are exceptions. If you are a currency trader for Goldman Sachs or a celebrated brain surgeon or a football star, your time might be valuable enough to fund a family fortune. Most people, however, won't be able to do it on wages alone.

That's true for those who have their own businesses, too. If they are selling services that they provide themselves, they face the same limits as a salaried worker. They are selling time. And their time is not that valuable.

They are also limited by time itself. You can sell only so many hours per day because there are only so many hours in a day.

Nor does family money usually come from investing. This is probably contrary to everything you've heard on the subject, so the burden of proof, again, is on us. We take it up as follows:

First, unless you are lucky or especially gifted, you are likely to get the same rate of return from your investments as just about everyone else. Even if you do exceptionally well from time to time, over the long run, your investment returns should regress to the mean.

It may surprise you to know that the stock market in the United States over the past century was not as rewarding as most people think it was. In 1900, the Dow index was at 51.60. In 2011, it ended the year at 12,100. That may seem like an incredible return. And it is. But it is not as incredible as it appears.

First, let's look at the Dow in Figure 3.1.

But now let's remember that a dollar in 1900 was worth a lot more than a dollar in 2011. In 1900, for example, you could buy a typical house for about $5,000. Today, the price is about $160,000.

We can also adjust the prices of Dow stocks by looking at gold. In 1900, gold sold for $18.96 per ounce. At the end of 2011, it sold for $1,710.

You can see for yourself that the Dow's ascent is not as impressive when adjusted for price increases. Still, had an investor put his money in the Dow and left it there for all those years, he would have done well, right?

Well, on one hand, he would have done better than this chart suggests because he would have also collected dividends. Include those

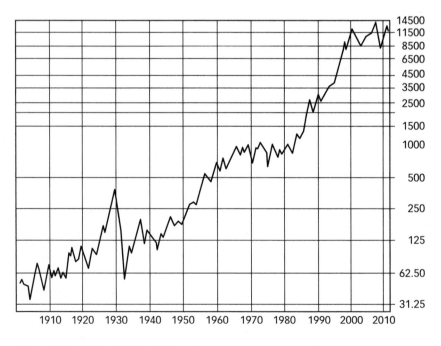

Figure 3.1 The Dow, 1900–2011

and the typical investor would have made much more money, especially if he reinvested the dividends in the stock market.

Of course, dividends are taxable. Tax rates have varied over the past 100 years and depend on your income and other details, so it's difficult to make a precise calculation. The total return over the past 100 years, net of taxes and inflation, may be only about 2 percent per year.

But before we go on, let's address a niggling little point: numbers themselves. You will notice that we say "about 2 percent" rather than 1.3 percent or 2.8 percent. You have to understand that precise numbers are a bit of a lie. They pretend knowledge that really isn't there. The fact is, nobody knows how much investors made over the past 100 years, with or without dividends. It is impossible to know such a thing.

There are probably many little reasons for this uncertainty, but there is one major reason: You never know exactly what is "real." We adjust numbers for inflation. But we never know exactly how much inflation was. In the preceding example, we adjusted stock prices to the price of gold. But not all consumer products rose in price along with the price of gold. Some exceeded gold's price. Others lagged.

And then, when you talk about "the typical stock buyer," you are also suggesting something that never actually exists. In practice, each stock buyer is different. Each buys different stocks. Each has a different experience.

And even if you presume that the stock buyer buys all stocks, there you are just raising more questions. When? The moment they went public? Or a day after? And then, what did he do when the companies went out of business? And did he reinvest all the dividends? Even if it were theoretically possible to do this sort of calculation, you can be sure that nobody ever invested in this way.

Almost all the numbers used in modern finance and economics are artificial, made up, and often fraudulent. You say the gross domestic product (GDP) rose 3 percent. What does that mean? Does it mean anything at all? When you dig into the numbers, what you find is a remarkable lack of precision. Assumptions. Adjustments. Estimates. Beneath the numbers is a swamp of slimy guesswork.

Yet the numbers are reported with decimal points, as if they were matters of scientific fact.

Here's just one example: Computer processing power increased greatly in the 1990s and 2000s. Moore's Law decreed that it would double every 18 months. Yet, because manufacturers became better and better and more competitive, prices remained fairly stable.

So one year, a computer might cost $1,000. Then, every one that was sold added $1,000 to total output. Two years later, the price might still be $1,000, but the computer could process twice as much information. What to do?

The quants who figure out such things decided that a computer that is twice as powerful should be twice as expensive, no matter what its real price. They added $2,000 to the GDP.

These "hedonic" adjustments made GDP numbers look better. But was there really any more "output"?

If bridges were built with such self-serving calculations, they would all fall down. Airplanes designed by economists would never get off the ground.

So, for those reasons, we distrust numbers generally and keep our distance from them. We use them as a chef uses his nose, just to get a whiff of what is going on in the kitchen.

A man with $100,000 in stocks was a rich man in 1900. Now, perhaps, he has $10 million in stocks. He has gotten richer. But so has almost everyone else. He was a rich man then. He is a rich man now. Is he any richer, compared with other people? Hard to say....

NOW BACK TO OUR STORY

Of the 30 stocks in the Dow in 1900, only one, General Electric, is still there. The others have been taken out of the index. Why? Because they weren't doing so well! The keepers of the index change the makeup of the Dow as new companies rise up and old ones fall away. This distorts the performance figures greatly.

Who would leave money in the original Dow stocks for 111 years? No one. Alas, human beings are not programmed for stock market investing. They tend to project forward their recent experiences and forget the experiences of those who went ahead of them.

What probably would have happened to the typical investor is that he would have panicked out of stocks in the crash of 1920 or the crash of 1929—that is to say, at the worst possible moment. Stocks hit epic highs when people believe that there is nowhere to go but up. They hit epic lows when they think that down is destiny.

It is only when the majority of investors come to believe such things that the stock market can fully express its extreme highs and lows. And since the typical investor must be counted among the majority of investors, it is reasonable to expect that he would do the wrong thing at the wrong time along with everyone else.

Even if he had the fortitude to sit through such alarming crashes and held on through the Great Depression . . . and through the calamity at Dunkirk . . . and through the bombing of Pearl Harbor, he certainly wasn't going to make it all the way to the end of the war. Most likely, he would have given up somewhere along the way. He would have sold his stocks and switched his money to the safety of bonds.

Market historians are smirking. It turned out that moving into bonds at the end of World War II was fatal. Bonds went down for the next 30 years! Here again, the typical investor was the victim of his own perverse instincts. As bonds fell, the logic of getting out of bonds became more and more persuasive. If the typical investor didn't get out by 1970, surely he cut bait by 1980!

This time, he wasn't going to fall for stocks or bonds. He bought gold!

You're smirking again, dear reader. You know what happened next. Gold collapsed over the next 20 years, while stocks and bonds rose!

Go figure.

Few fortunes are made by what most people think of as investing. Investing is what you do to preserve and enhance a fortune, not to make it. That is not to say you can't make a lot of money in the financial industry. There are many ways to make money in the financial industry, but few in ordinary retail-level investing.

The difference is simple. If you are in the financial industry, you are a seller; if you are a retail investor, you are a buyer. You make money, generally, as a seller, not as a buyer. To put it another way, you make money as a producer, not as a consumer. Few people make money by consuming Wall Street's products. Many make money by creating and selling those products.

Most retail investors are not content to buy the Dow stocks or to hold the stocks they have in hand. They try to avoid the bad companies and chase after the good ones. This only aggravates the "me-too," "buy-high-and-sell-low" pattern, which is so costly. The investor hears about a "hot" stock. He buys, along with everyone else. The stock rises, so he buys more. Then, the stock sells off as the insiders unload their positions.

Buying and selling also triggers another noxious phenomenon: taxes. The investor shares his gains with the government. As for his losses, they are more often kept to himself. Over time, the combination of taxes and investment losses is deadly.

But wait, there's more. The man who wishes to make his fortune by investing is doubly cursed. First, the market rarely obliges anyone. Second, it least favors him. Because he is in a hurry. He knows that he cannot wait to compound gains of 2 percent or 3 percent or even 5 percent. He won't live that long. He also knows that the companies he understands are not likely to provide much more than that.

The U.S. economy grew at an average rate of 3 percent over the past 100 years. There is no reason to expect the typical company to grow faster than the economy that supports it. In practice, some grow faster, some slower. The average is in the middle.

Since the typical investor is much more likely to be acquainted with the typical company, rather than the extraordinary one, he knows that if he wants extraordinary gains he must look beyond the companies that he knows. In fact, the further, the better. Because the more the terrain is unfamiliar, the more he can imagine what ever he wants.

That was much of the steam behind the high-tech bubble of the late 1990s. The companies often had no earnings and no clear way forward to get them. They claimed they had entered a new world, which made it sound very exciting. They even claimed that they did not really need capital, because they were leveraging information and knowledge via the Internet. And even if they did need a little money to get going, they wouldn't need it long, since these businesses would be so profitable. They would soon be minting money and paving the streets to their headquarters with gold.

And who could have known better? The stocks had plenty of P (price), but no E (earnings) to measure them against. Investors didn't know what they did or what they were worth. The fantasists could believe anything. The hallucinators thought they would all get rich. So the stocks went up and up and up . . . and then down. The Nasdaq, where these stocks were listed, blew up in January 2000 and has still not recovered (Figure 3.2).

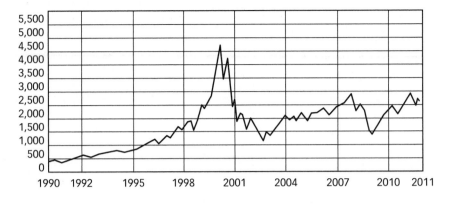

Figure 3.2 The Nasdaq, 1990–2011

Before we go any further, this is probably a good place to show how money grows. Everyone has heard of "compound growth" rates. How do they actually work? Here, we are greatly assisted by our chief financial whiz and the chief economist of our own family office, Robert Marstrand, who prepared the following explanation:

THE SIMPLE WAY TO DOUBLE YOUR MONEY

Exponential growth is a key concept to understand. Exponential growth is also exactly what we want with our investment portfolios. It is just another way of talking about the power of compounding.

If something grows at a fixed percentage each year, the *amount* it grows in each successive year will get bigger over time (even though the *rate* of growth remains the same). And small differences in the yearly growth rate result in big differences in long-term results.

Let's say an investment grows at 10% per year. Invest $100, and after one year you have $110. The investment has gone up $10. In Year Two, it goes up another 10%, which is now $11. So the profit has increased from $10 to $11. *This is because there are profits on the earlier profits.*

This is what we call the power of compounding. Which, as you should know by now, is the most effective way to grow your wealth over time or, as market guru Richard Russell famously put it, is the "royal road to riches."[4]

(Continued)

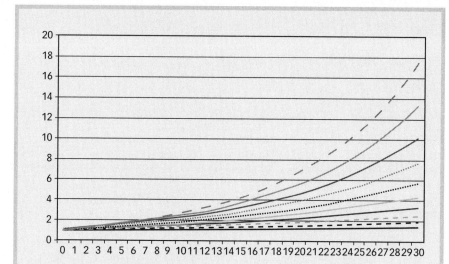

Figure 3.3 Exponential Growth

The Picture of Compounding

Figure 3.3 shows how exponential growth looks over 30 years (roughly a generation) using various growth rates from 1 percent per year (the lowest line) up to 10 percent per year (the highest line). Values are shown on the vertical axis and all start at 1. The years are shown along the horizontal axis.

The really important thing to grasp here is that the lines are curved and not straight. This is how the power of compounding looks over the long haul. You could call it the "picture of compounding."

A steady gain of 5% per year means the initial value of 1 goes up to 4.33 after 30 years. A steady gain of 10 percent per year means that initial value rises to 17.45 over the same time. The yearly rate has doubled. *But the end result after 30 years is over four times as much*. The longer the time period, the bigger the effect.

Of course, there is price volatility along the way with any investment portfolio. You won't get a perfectly smooth curve. But what matters for long-term investors is the end result. And the power of compounding still works its magic, even when there is price volatility along the way.

Most people don't understand compounding and exponential growth. This isn't because they are stupid or uneducated. It's just that it's not intuitive to most people. We're not wired to think in a nonlinear way. But it's increasingly essential to start to think this way if we are to truly understand the world we live in.

Annual growth rate (%)	Doubling time (years)
1	70.0
2	35.0
3	23.3
4	17.6
5	14.2
6	11.9
7	10.3
8	9.0
9	8.0
10	7.3
15	5.0
20	3.8
25	3.1

Figure 3.4   Annual Growth Rates and Their Doubling Times

Mine's a Double!

If you know the rate at which something is growing, you can work out how long it will take to double in size (assuming the growth rate stays the same). The rate of growth is the percentage that it goes up each year. The number of years taken to double in size is called the "doubling time."

Figure 3.4 summarizes the doubling times using a range of different annual growth rates.

At lower rates of growth, small differences in the rate make a big difference to the doubling times. If your investments beat price inflation and taxes by 1%, they will double in 70 years, measured in today's money. If the outperformance is just two percentage points higher—at 3 percent— they will double in just over 23 years (again in today's money).

Doubling Time = 70/Yearly Growth Rate

There is an excellent rule of thumb for calculating the doubling time of anything. You take the number 70 and divide it by the yearly growth rate to give the number of years for something to double.

If you aren't good with numbers, you can use a memory trick to help you. By creating mental images, we help your brain retrieve information more

(Continued)

easily. So you could imagine seven clocks all at 10 o'clock—combining the number 70 with the idea of time. Or you could think of your 10 fingers and the seven days of the week. Just try to think of something that works for you.

Conclusion: *To maximize long-term investment performance, you need to keep investment profits up and costs and taxes down. This allows the power of compounding to work in your favor.*

Reach for the Low-Hanging Fruit

Figure 3.5 shows the same data for the first 10 yearly growth rates in the above table—from 1 percent to 10 percent per year. The horizontal axis shows the yearly percentage rates of growth, and the vertical axis shows the doubling times in years.

Looking at it this way, something jumps right out. The relationship between growth rates and doubling times is not a straight line, but a curve. More growth always leads to a shorter doubling time. But there are bigger absolute differences between lower rates of growth than between higher ones.

(You can also see this relationship in Figure 3.3. Not every line gets up to a value of 8. But look at those that do. And compare the year at that point with the year when they crossed through the value of 4. The

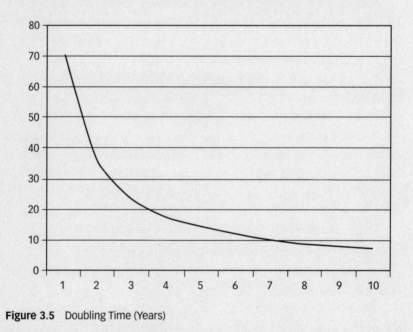

Figure 3.5   Doubling Time (Years)

difference is the doubling time. You'll see that it gets shorter and shorter as the growth rates increase.)

So in any investment portfolio, there is a huge advantage to increasing your net return (after tax and inflation) from low single digits to high single digits. Of course, short-term price moves in a single week, month, or year could be much better or worse. The crucial thing is that they average out at a higher level in the long run.

At the same time, at higher rates of growth, each additional increment is still good news. But the effect on the doubling time is less. Moving from 20 percent to 25 percent per year—an increase of a whole 5 percent per year—only reduces the doubling time from 3.8 to 3.1 years.

Conclusion: *If you have a strategy to give already high returns, taking on the extra risk to squeeze even more out of your investments is probably not worth it. The priority is to get those first improvements. These are the low-hanging fruit of enhancing your long-term investment returns, when viewed through the prism of doubling times.*

Double Your Money in Eight Years

Assuming a tax rate of 40 percent and inflation rates of 5 percent, you would need 8.33 percent gross return (before taxes and inflation, but after fees) just to break even. . .

Let's say you have 50 percent of your investments in 10-year Treasury bonds and the other 50 percent in the Standard & Poor's (S&P) 500. Your T-bond has a yield to maturity of 2 percent, at time of writing. Over 10 years, you will make exactly 2 percent per year gross with this investment—50 percent of the portfolio in this example.

But you need a gross return of 8.33 percent just to break even. So your S&P 500 stocks will have to make up the difference. This means the S&P 500 would have to return 14.66 percent over 10 years for the net result to be 8.33 percent per year gross.

Think about it. . . .

Inflation: A Stealth Tax on Your Wealth

Using our simple formula, let's think about price inflation. If the inflation rate is 3 percent, the doubling time is 23.3 years. This is close to the average official (CPI-U) inflation rate in the United States since 1987.

(Continued)

Prices would double in just over 23 years. Because they think in a linear way, most people wrongly assume that this doubling would take 33.3 years. For something to double, it has to go up 100 percent. So the thinking goes that if you add 3 percent per year, it would take 33.3 years to double. But because inflation is exponential—*because it compounds*—the doubling time is much shorter.

Put another way, a bundle of dollar bills in a safety deposit box would buy half as much in 23.3 years. The bills earn no interest. But consumer prices would double.

Real (nonofficial) price inflation is substantially above official rates. Government statisticians use various tricks to fiddle the numbers. The result? Inflation-linked pension payments and the like grow more slowly than actual price increases. Bond investors are conned into accepting lower coupon payments. And "real" (inflation-adjusted) GDP growth is systematically overstated.

Now, let's say inflation is 5 percent, instead of 3 percent. Divide 70 by 5 to get the doubling time, and we're down to 14 years. Just 14 years for a stack of cash to lose half of its purchasing power! This is why many people view inflation as a "stealth tax": It's just as dangerous to your wealth.

Some say that inflation is already running way above this level, most notably John Williams, author of the website shadowstats.com. He calculates a current rate of around 7 percent per year. This would mean prices would double in just 10 years if the rate stays the same.

So holding cash is a losing proposition in the long run. This is why we recommend you hold cash only as "short-term parking."

Compounding Is Not Always a Good Thing . . .

Of course, exponential growth can work against you too. Here are some more "doubling times" at *current* rates of growth:

1. **World Population:** The amount of people drawing air on planet Earth grows 1.1 percent per year. The doubling time is under 64

years. At this rate, this means the planet will add 7 billion in two generations.

2. **World Energy Use:** Energy use across all sources grew 2.2 percent per year since 1985, measured using millions of tons of oil equivalent. At that rate, it will double again in less than 32 years—or about one generation.

   This increase in demand is happening at the same time as reserves are depleting and new energy is becoming harder to extract. It's not the cost that matters most, but how much energy is required to produce new energy. If it takes a barrel of oil to make a barrel of oil, it's game over for oil production.

3. **Social Security Claims:** The number of retired Americans on Social Security rose 4.4 percent per year between 1999 and 2009. At that rate, the doubling time is just under 16 years. This refers to numbers of claimants, not dollar amounts. (The dollar amount grows faster due to inflation adjustments. It also doubles faster.)

   Since 2007, the rate of claimant growth has accelerated. By comparison, the U.S. population is growing at just under 1 percent per year. At current benefit and tax levels, even the U.S. Social Security Administration expects payments to be greater than new contributions from 2014 onward. This means the money will run out by 2037. I'd be willing to bet that the reality is worse.

4. **U.S. Federal Debt:** This grew at about 9.1 percent in 2011. At that rate, it will double in less than eight years. This illustrates the urgency of controlling the U.S. budget deficit. And the fatal math applies to most other countries in the developed world.

Of course, these growth rates could change. If food supplies don't grow fast enough, many people will starve. And population growth will fall. New higher energy prices could reduce the growth rate of energy usage—and even send it into reverse. And it's not impossible (although from our perspective, it is highly unlikely) that the United States, Europe, and Japan could all have growth spurts, balance their budgets and start reducing their debts to manageable levels.

Otherwise, bond markets are likely to be graveyards for investors' money.

The trick, for families interested in building and maintaining wealth, is to make sure compounding is working for you, not against you.

So let's go back to the stock market.

ARE STOCKS A GOOD IDEA?

The whole idea of stock market investing is a bit of a scam. The idea is to sell people bits of businesses they know nothing about at prices that the people who *do* know something judge too high. Otherwise, why would the insiders sell?

If you had a profitable business, why would you want to sell it to strangers? And why would strangers want to buy it?

You may say that you are going to retire. And you want to sell. You want the "liquidity event" wealth managers talk about. But why? If you sell, you will get money. What will you do with the money? You must put it somewhere. Assuming it is more than you can spend, you will either leave it in cash or put it into investments. There are only two major investment choices that are liquid (readily converted to cash): stocks or bonds.

If you buy stocks, you are merely taking money out of a business you know and putting it into a business you don't know. Good luck on that. If you buy bonds, you are trading your own equity for someone else's debt. Why would you do that, unless you believed that your equity wasn't really as solid as the alternative?

You say you need income to live in retirement? What kind of a business was it that it didn't produce enough income for you to retire on?

When you sell a business, you typically think in terms of price to earnings. People buy a stream of income. They pay according to how much income they think they will get. So if you have a business that is producing $100,000 in income, a buyer will compare your stream of income to others available to him.

In our experience, private buyers who know what they are doing will pay between four and eight times earnings. Typically, they know the businesses they are getting into. (Note that our experience is limited to the publishing business. Perhaps if you have a monopoly of some sort, or if you have a more reliable income stream, you'll be able to get more.)

But whatever you get, you have to do something with it. And whatever you do, the same calculations will work on the other side. You will then buy someone else's stream of cash, either in a stock or a bond. Or you will take a flyer on "growth" or a business opportunity that might really "take off" and reward you far beyond the expectations of the income stream itself.

It probably happens, from time to time, that business sellers find better opportunities elsewhere. But the logic of the situation suggests that if they do, the buyer has made a mistake. If he were a private buyer, perhaps he did understand the business. Perhaps he was able to add value to it. Perhaps he got a good deal at four times earnings.

But what about the public market investor, the fellow who thinks he should get into computer technology because "it's the wave of the future," or into agri-business "because there are a lot of hungry people in the world"? What about this poor schlep?

Public market investors usually pay higher multiples (higher prices) on investments they understand much less well. They get less for their money, and they don't know it. The price-to-earnings (P/E) ratio on the S&P 500, as of this writing, is 16—or more than twice what a private buyer would pay.

Sharp investors make money on the difference. They look for businesses that might be sold into the public markets. They buy them at the private market multiple and then sell them to the public at the public market multiple. This is the business of "private equity" and venture capitalists. You buy a business from a retiring entrepreneur at $10 million and "take it public" with an initial public offering (IPO), pricing the business at $20 million.

It's not as easy as it looks. In order to "list" a company in the public markets, you have to do a lot of work and pay a lot of expensive professionals. In addition to the venture capitalists themselves, you will need a small army of accountants and lawyers to prepare the company for a public offering. This adds huge costs that will have to be paid by the public market investor, which is part of the reason he gets such a bad deal.

Our personal experience tells us that the venture capitalists also sometimes ruin the businesses that they are taking public. They rarely understand how they work. And they don't really want to know. Their interest is very short term. Often, businesses work in ways that are quirky and hard to analyze. So when the suits come in, their eyes are so fixed on the prize—the IPO—that they neglect the business or actively destroy it.

We have seen our friends sell businesses to major venture capital firms and then buy them back later at a fraction of the price, after the venture capitalists had wrecked them.

After a business is public, the damage continues. It is one thing to run a private company. It is quite another to run a public company. The advantage of a private family company is that it can pursue a business or financial objective over a long period of time without worrying too much about what others think of it.

Family businesses are careful to protect their reputations. They watch out for anything that would undermine the value of their asset, even if the danger is far in the future. Farmers who own their own land do not wear out the soil. Families that own timber are not over-eager to cut it down and sell it.

Privately held enterprises operate without the glare of the financial media or public stockholders (strangers) looking over their shoulders. Of course, this may mean that they're not very serious about making money, either—but that's another story.

Public companies, however, run the race with a ball and chain clapped on their ankles. They cannot make a move without worrying about how the market will react. They live in fear of the Securities and Exchange Commission (SEC), too, and usually employ a phalanx of lawyers, public relations people, and accountants to try to stay on good terms with the regulators.

They often bring on celebrity board members or CEOs, pay them fortunes, and hope they get their names in the paper and boost their stock prices. In our (limited) experience and observation, these people often have no idea what business they are in. Their job is to glad hand, back slap, and give speeches. Their goal is to goose up quarterly results, get a big bonus, write a book, and move on. They know that what counts are the short-term, quarterly reports.

A private, family investor may be able to follow the long-term progress of his business and appreciate what is really going on. Public investors seem to care about only the last quarterly profit report. So the public CEO pursues good quarterly results, often to the detriment of all else.

Probably the most famous example of the successful celebrity CEO is Jack Welch, who ran GE for the decades of the 1980s and 1990s. The company seemed to prosper fabulously. Earnings rose. Sales rose. Profits rose. And the stock price rose from $7 to $40.

But nothing rose as much as Jack Welch's own fortune. He was getting $4 million per year when he retired in 2000. But then he got a retirement plan of $8 million per year, including a free apartment in the New York Trump Tower and use of GE's corporate jet, an office, a secretary, a limousine, and a driver. By 2006, his personal net worth was said to be $720 million.

But what about the company? When the credit bubble blew up in 2007, it became apparent that GE's success under Welch's reign was not all it appeared to be. He had transformed the business, taking it out of manufacturing and into finance. In fact, GE had become a quasi–hedge fund with huge exposure to bad debt. The share price fell, wiping out almost all of Welch's gains. Had the whole financial sector not been rescued by the federal government, GE might have gone bankrupt.

The stock market is not the source of riches that most people think it is. And while some people make a lot of money by investing in stocks, most investors do not even get the average offered by the market indexes, which, adjusted for inflation, are not that great anyway. And those who actually try hardest to make money fastest—by trading in and out, following hot stocks, looking for a pot of gold in unfamiliar territory—usually do worst of all.

But what about investing in bonds and compounding sure gains over a long period of time? This is known as the "royal road to riches." It is usually more reliable than stock market investing, even though in any particular year, rates of return may be lower. The trouble is, compounding gains from bonds works only in periods of monetary stability or, better yet, when bonds are rising in price. That is the world we've lived in for the last 30 years. It is probably not the world we will live in for the next 30 years. In any case, your authors judge it too risky now. (More in Chapter 5.)

Even if the currency and the bond markets were safe, however, you'd still have to reckon with a very long period before you could compound real after-tax gains from bonds into serious money.

SO HOW DO YOU GET REAL FAMILY MONEY?

"Behind every great fortune there is a crime," said Balzac. He was mostly right. The great fortunes of the pre–Industrial Revolution period, especially those in France, often resulted from some kind of ancient larceny. There was no other way. Capitalism in its modern form had yet to be invented. Land or special monopoly privileges granted by the king were the basis of most great wealth. The former was usually the result of a crime of some sort; the latter was a crime itself.

Land could be taken by force. In fact, that's how most of Europe's nobility got it. The Germanic tribes that overran France in the second to fifth centuries did not stop to check with the local office of deed registry. They took the land they wanted. Those who took it and held it were men of arms—strongmen—who then attached the names of the places they had stolen to their own names. Charles de Tancarville. Charles d'Argenton. Charles de Gaulle. In the nineteenth century, it was relatively common for people to add a "de" to their family names to make themselves a bit more distinguished.

Settled on their *terres*, the rough warlords of the early Middle Ages built castles to defend their lands and took on all the pretensions and *droits de seigneurs* of a permanent aristocracy. They were even excused from paying taxes.

If you wanted a family fortune back then, your best bet was to take it, as the ancestors of the Queen Elizabeth II of England or those of Prince Albert of Monaco did. The queen's remote ancestor, William the Conqueror, got his name by taking over England. Its lands were distributed to his soldiers, who became England's ruling class, its gentry, and its rich. They even gave England a new language, Latinized English, which is still used to write legal documents and school term papers.

Monaco was taken by force by an armed band of Genoese led by Francois Grimaldi in 1297. This was the beginning of the dynasty that still runs the place. It was greatly enriched after Charles Grimaldi sacked Southampton in 1338, bringing the booty back to Monaco.

Once the social and political order of Europe was more or less settled, with kings and queens firmly in charge, it was very hard for an upstart to make much headway. Roles were fixed, so they believed, by God. A man who was born a field hand was meant to stay put. An occasional gifted student might make his way to the court and thereby gain a favor. But for most ambitious people, there were few opportunities to accumulate wealth.

The discovery of the New World opened up opportunities. For the conquistadors, these opportunities were very similar to the opportunities afforded to the Germanic tribes that had invaded Western Europe 1,000 years earlier. It was an opportunity for theft. They could gain vast fortunes and vast domains by stealing from the local people.

In North America, there was less to steal and more to take. The native peoples had little portable wealth and loose claims to the land they lived on. Settlers could take as much as they wanted and then sell it on, at low prices, to new arrivals. An ambitious land speculator, such as George Washington, could make a family fortune for himself.

But the really big boost in wealth accumulation began with the Industrial Revolution. Then, it was possible to create a fortune without committing a sin or a crime. Capitalism is civilized, in the sense that it depends on willing exchanges of labor and property. There is no theft involved. And it encourages ownership of assets other than land. For the first time, people could own shares in businesses that they did not personally control. And by pooling their resources, people could undertake projects on a much larger scale, which brought even more wealth creation.

Capitalism is what made most modern family fortunes possible. And it continues to be the source of most family wealth. Gone are most of the fortunes from the land grabs of bygone centuries. Today's wealth is based on trade, commerce, production, financing and the other moving parts of a capitalist machine. Even land-based fortunes, of which there are many, are usually the result of rising demand and increased prices caused by the pressure of a growing capitalist economy.

Obviously, the ways in which you can make your family fortune in the modern capitalist era are as varied as the ways it can be lost. But there are some ways *not* to make it.

NOT SO FAST

You don't want to get rich too fast . . . or too easily . . . or by accident. If you get rich by luck alone, you'll probably lose your money as soon as your luck changes. It's much better to get rich from hard work, careful saving, and/or attentive investment in the real economy. Then you'll know how hard it is to come by and be much more careful to hold onto it.

As we say elsewhere in the book, you can have money by accident. You can have a family by accident. But you can't have family money by accident. That's why people who win the lottery, for example, are usually broke within 48 months. And why major sports stars and Hollywood celebrities, who earn millions during a few short years, often end their lives in complete poverty.

Take Travis Henry. He got a $25 million contract with the Denver Broncos in 2007. Now, he says he's already broke.[5]

Evelyn Adams won the New Jersey lottery twice, in 1985 and 1986. Talk about luck! She won $5.4 million in total. But don't go looking for Evelyn in a Beverly Hills or Palm Beach mansion. She lives in a trailer.

"Everybody wanted my money. Everybody had their hand out," she says.[6]

Or take the case of William "Bud" Post. He won $16.2 million in the Pennsylvania lottery in 1988. Think he's fixed for life?

"I wish it never happened. It was totally a nightmare," says Post.

Within a year he was $1 million in debt and had to declare bankruptcy. Now, he is said to live on food stamps.[7]

Suzanne Mullins won $4.2 million in the Virginia lottery in 1993. Now she's in debt—with "no assets."

Ken Proxmire won $1 million in the Michigan lottery. He moved to California and went into the car business with his brothers. Five years later, he filed for bankruptcy.[8]

Do you need to be rich to have family money?

By our definition, no. Family money is different money. It is not necessarily a lot of money.

Researchers asked rich people how much money they needed to be rich. A million dollars didn't get you very far in the eyes of these rich people. They said you needed $7.5 million, minimum.

Why so much? How much does it cost to live well?

Well, it depends. When the elder of your authors began his career, he worked for $100 per week. That became $100 per day after a few years. And then, it became $100 per hour. And so on. He doesn't recall being any less happy at $100 per week than he was at $100 per hour. And today, he says he would readily trade: make him 25 years old again, and he'll work for, well, $100 per day.

But as his income rose with his years, so did his expenses. At about $40,000 per year, he bought his first new automobile, a Datsun pickup truck. At $100,000, he had a Volvo and a Ford pickup. And a farm in the country. Every increase in earnings came with a price tag attached. Whenever he thought he was getting ahead, he found some new necessity—something he had to have.

That is why so many people with high incomes have no money. As soon as they get a raise, an entrepreneur offers them something they can't live without.

In our experience, you can live "as though" you were rich on, say, $350,000 per year. That's about what two good lawyers, or doctors, or small-business people might earn, together. They pool their earnings. They can enjoy "the good life." Vacations. A nice house. Nice cars. All the gadgets.

Demographers call them HENRYs ("high earners, not rich yet"). People think these people are rich because they live as though they were rich. But they are far from it. In many ways, they are in the worst possible situation. They earn a lot. But they pay high taxes and, usually, high living expenses. For all the money that goes through their hands, after years of hard work, many of them have little to show for it.

But wait. If you could get a steady rate of return of 3 percent on your money, it would require $11.5 million in capital to replace those earnings. And if you had $11.5 million in real capital, most people would agree, you would be among "the rich." But it's very hard to live off $350,000 as though you were rich and also accumulate enough money to really BE rich. Not unless you're earning a lot more.

And you can live a lot better with $11.5 million in capital than you can on $350,000 in salary income, for reasons we will explain.

If you had only $7.5 million, for example, at 3 percent yield, you could expect income of only $215,000. That may seem like a lot of money, but it is hardly the kind of money that would give you and your family a lavish lifestyle. After taxes, health insurance, tuition, autos, mortgage payments and other real necessities, there wouldn't be that much left. Wealthy? Yes. Rich? Not quite.

Having investable assets in the $250,000 to $5 million range simply makes you one of the "mass affluent," as the financial services industry now calls them. To be truly rich, you need quite a bit more than that. Silicon Valley has a useful, if gratuitously rude, phrase for the sort of money that will free you from ever having to take a job again: "F-U money."

F-U MONEY

The idea of F-U money came to us long before the money itself arrived. A friend of the family comes from a very rich family. But he had a falling out with his father. He was given $1 million, a paltry sum out of a $200 million fortune, and told "good luck."

But you need more than good luck to build real wealth. In fact, good luck is more often a curse than a blessing. It brings you wealth too easily and too early. In the late 1970s, $1 million was a much bigger fortune than it is today.

Our friend, who was still in his early 20s, was considered immensely rich by the rest of us.

A smart young man, he figured he could parlay a small fortune into a very big one. He set up an investment firm. He made some bets. Within a few months he had lost it all.

"You should have been happy with what you had," we suggested.

"A million doesn't do you any real good. You need real F-U money."

Our friend was a visionary. And a philosopher. And a great success. He quickly recovered, worked hard over several decades, and built a large fortune. Finally, he had F-U money.

But what is F-U money, exactly? And how much do you really need?

William Faulkner gives us a hint. When he was fired from being postmaster of Laurel, Mississippi, allegedly for drunkenness, he said he felt liberated: "I reckon I'll be at the beck and call of folks with money all my life, but thank God I won't ever again have to be at the beck and call of every son of a bitch with a 2 cent stamp."

F-U money is the money you need so that you are not at the beck and call of every son of a bitch with a 2-cent stamp. It is the amount of money you need to be free. It could be a lot or a little, depending on your ambitions. But it is the money you need so that you can do what you want.

That sounds almost egomaniacal. And there's always that risk. The man who can say "F-U" is tempted to do so. But being financially independent doesn't mean being antisocial. On the contrary, financial independence frees you to cooperate, create, and collaborate on an equal basis with others. It frees you from dependence on the government or on an employer. You have no reason to give false praise and no reason to pay sycophantic allegiance to any creed or salute any flag—unless you really believe in it. You don't have to be a "good citizen." You don't have to be a "good employee." You don't have to be a zombie.

The rich are often accused of being overly concerned with money. In our experience, it's the poor who spend the most time thinking about it. When we were poor, we had to think about how we could afford to get the radiator fixed in our old truck or how we might make ends meet if we lost our job. When we built our first house, we scrounged materials in junkyards because we didn't have the cash to buy them new. We studied the classifieds to find old cars. We saved coupons, and we knew exactly how much was in our wallet and how much gas we could buy when we stopped at a filling station.

Later in life, we became much less interested in money. We thought about it less. We knew we had plenty. We turned our attentions from our standard of living, measured in dollars, to the quality of our lives, which we couldn't measure at all.

That's the advantage of F-U money.

When you don't have F-U money, you tend to be interested in politics. You want the government to pay for your pills, your children's education, and your retirement. You figure it's written somewhere in the "social contract." Or even in the constitution. You will be a good citizen, vote, and pay your taxes. The government will look out for you. If you have no independent means of your own, the bargain is almost irresistible.

That's the trouble with money that comes from government subsidies, bailouts, regulations, and sweetheart contracts. It's not really F-U money. You depend on the feds. You can't say "F-U" to the feds. They can say it to you. They're the ones with the power. So you tend to keep a keen interest in politics, buying politicians if you're able, sucking up to them if you're not.

F-U money is liberating. It doesn't really matter how much it is, just as long as it is enough so you can make your own decisions free from the pressures of politics, desperation, or envy. F-U allows you think clearly. It permits you to do what you want, too. It makes it possible for you to go where you want, when you want. It gives you the wherewithal to survive as a free person in a largely unfree world.

HOW MUCH MONEY DO YOU NEED?

How much do you need to be really rich? $10 million? $100 million? One hundred million, at 4 percent interest, brings you $4 million per year. Or about $2.2 million after tax. But wait, there's inflation, too. If the real loss to inflation is 5 percent, you're losing ground. Even if it is 3 percent, you're still losing ground, after taxes.

So let's explore the numbers. Imagine you have $100 million and you earn 5 percent per year. After taxes and inflation, you might have $500,000 left. Maybe $1 million. (The numbers are never precise, never sure.) On $1 million per year you can live like a rich S.O.B. Less than that and you have to make do, watch expenses, and live on a budget (even if is it a large budget).

But who cares? We're not really concerned with living like rich people. And planning for a family fortune is nothing like planning for a specific objective such as retirement. If you are preparing your retirement funds, the rule of thumb is that you need to save about eight times your annual salary. That is supposed to leave you with an annual income of about 80 percent of your income when you were working.

The math is a little funny, because it involves a drawdown of capital. At 4 percent interest, eight times your salary will result in about only a third of your salary. But then, you're not trying to leave the money to your children, so you can spend capital as well as earnings, based on how long you think you and your money will hold out.

When you are planning for a family fortune, however, there is no question of spending capital. You cannot spend it; it no longer belongs to you. Even if it still belongs to you legally, if you think of it as spendable, personal money, it won't remain "family money" for very long.

That's why, in our previous example, we have to reduce the earnings by losses to inflation. If you earn 4 percent on your money, you can't spend 4 percent. You can spend only the portion of earnings that is above and beyond inflation. So if the inflation rate is 3 percent, you have to put back 3 percent each year just to stay even with it. That leaves you 1 percent to spend.

But wait. You're taxed on the whole 4 percent. So you have to pay the tax and then put back 3 percent to cover the inflation loss. As you can see, this is a losing proposition. That's why our calculation, earlier in this chapter, showed that you need a gross return of about 8.3 percent just to stay even! Which is why bonds are a losing proposition. And so are most stocks.

Hmmm . . . do you see what we see? You could have $100 million in the bank and get nothing from it. Nothing. If you were committed to preserving the family capital, you could spend only the amount in excess of 8.3 percent. And it is almost impossible to earn more than 8.3 percent. So even if you had $100 million in the bank today, and you followed the logic of our Old Money rules, you would not likely have an extra penny to spend. (We'll get to methods we use in Chapter 5.)

So as to the question of "how much you need," we are tempted to say that it really doesn't matter. At least, not when you think about how well you could live. If you follow this logic, you're not likely to get anything that you can spend from your family money. You'll have to live off what you earn, like all the other working stiffs.

This might cause you to wonder why you bother. Instead, we encourage you to think about it in a different way. Think about how much you can put into the pot and what you can do with it that does not involve spending it. As we will see, as little as $300,000 can be a worthwhile family asset. But the more the merrier. As your resources grow, so do the things you can do with them.

When we were driving through western Pennsylvania recently, we were struck by how cheap it would be to live there. Houses are very inexpensive, at least compared with what we're used to in the Baltimore-Washington metro area. You could have your own garden.

A few goats, chickens, and rabbits. An old car. A wood stove. A library card and an Amazon account.

What more do you need? Once you were set up, it's hard to see what you could spend money on. There are no shops worth frequenting, no restaurants worth dining at, no nightclubs, no theatres—not much of anything.

Would this be a barren and boring life? Not at all! Gardening, building, reading, visiting with friends, watching movies on the home computer. What more could you want? And with such low fixed costs, you could easily splurge from time to time with a weekend in Manhattan or Miami.

What would be a reasonable budget for a life like that? Maybe $1,000 per month. So let's take that as a point of departure. And let's ask, if you wanted enough family money to pay for a $1,000-per-month lifestyle, how much would you need? We're going to ignore taxes and inflation for this part of the discussion, just to keep it simple (besides, at today's rates the numbers quickly become squishy and probably impossible). The answer: At 4 percent interest, you could earn $12,000 per year on just $300,000 of capital. Would you want to live on $12,000 per year? It's up to you. But the point is that even with only $300,000 of family money, you could support a small family in a small community in a small way.

Most people would find that not worth doing. But what's wrong with having $300,000 on hand? In fact, it could be very useful to a family. With that kind of money you could finance an education—even medical school. You could support a family member who was out of work. You could build a house. You could start a business.

Remember, family money is different. If you spend it, it's not family money anymore. You don't have it anymore. It's gone.

Typically, families establish rules for how they will handle family money that are different from how they will handle personal money. And typically, they will spend only the interest on the money, not the principal. That way, the family money will last.

Looked at that way, a $300,000 capital fund becomes less useful, but still extremely helpful. It is enough to finance a house. The family could simply take the mortgage, rather than leave the money in T-bonds, and make sure the mortgage gets paid.

The family might also advance the money to a student as a loan. The student would repay it as he took up his career. Then, too, imagine that a family member is incapacitated or merely falls on hard times. The family money could be lent out to help him get over the hump, or the interest on the money could be given to him until he gets back on his feet.

The same thing applies to starting a business. The family could fund the business start-up, either as a loan or as a capital participation. Either way, it's much better to have a fund of family money available than to not have it.

Remember, too, that if your money is properly protected and managed, it grows. Three hundred thousand is not a lot of money. But if you added the $12,000 every year instead of spending it, eventually, it adds up.

Even a very modest "fortune" can be very useful if it is properly managed.

Let's say you have $1 million. Is that enough? Well, it depends.

If you could realize a net 3 percent real return (above and beyond inflation and taxes), that would be $30,000 per year. This is hardly a grand sum, but it's better than nothing, and it could begin to give you many of the benefits of having a family fortune.

For example, you may not want to live on $30,000 per year, but you could if you had to. That alone is a great thing, because it means that if you wanted to do so you could be free to pursue some interest that was not immediately financially rewarding. Or you could use the money to become more independent and secure in other ways—perhaps by simply insulating your house, paying off a mortgage early or saying "F-U" to the whole world.

Obviously, you could always simply improve your standard of living by spending the $30,000 or by letting it accumulate. In just three years of accumulation, you could add nearly $100,000 to your wealth. In 10 years, you'd have $400,000 more.

WHAT KIND OF MONEY IS FAMILY MONEY?

Apart from how you get it . . . and what you do with it, we'll also note that family money tends to hang out in different places than other kinds of wealth. As we'll see in Chapter 5, the investments you make are different. But also the nature of the wealth itself tends to be different.

Probably the most agreeable way to build a family fortune is just to own something you like owning that subsequently becomes very valuable. That happens from time to time.

You might, for example, have a painting hanging on your wall. Perhaps it was given to you by your grandmother, who bought it from a starving artist in Paris just after World War II. You like the painting. You like it even more when it turns out to be a forgotten painting by Picasso.

Sometimes art goes wild. An artist may struggle to survive, giving his paintings away for a bowl of soup or a glass of wine. Years later, for no reason that bears much analysis, the artist becomes a sensation. His works fetch millions.

Another friend decided that he wanted to stimulate and encourage artists in Latin America. He set up a prize—$10,000—for the most promising artist of the year. He handed out his prize—and then, he brought the winning artists to Paris, where he lived, and introduced them to the galleries in town.

He also bought the artists' works. By the time he died, he had a whole apartment stuffed with them. He had bought the works when the artists were unknown. He paid a couple hundred dollars each. He never sold a single one until late in life. Then, he put two of them up for auction. They sold for $185,000 each.

It happens. Things you want to do can be very profitable. It may also be true of a much more widely held asset: real estate. An advertisement ran in the *New York Times* in 1912. It offered a house on the coast of California, in a place that must have been little known to New Yorkers of the time: Malibu Beach. The house was for sale at $2,500.

That may have been a lot of money at the time. It was just about the same as 110 ounces of gold. We have not been able to identify that specific house, but it is likely that the house—updated, rebuilt, expanded, tarted up to 21st-century standards—might sell for more than $10 million, or 6,200 ounces of gold at today's price.

The rate of return per year is much more modest—only 8.73 percent. But what a way to make your money! The family had the pleasure of living and using the house for a century—and made $9 million to boot.

Note also that real estate proved an effective way to build family wealth for three reasons:

1. Growth of the United States, and especially California, pushed the price of choice properties up faster than GDP growth rate over a very long time.
2. There were no income or capital gains taxes to pay along the way. You pay property taxes, upkeep, maintenance, and so forth. But those are just the costs of maintaining a house.
3. There was no "liquidity event" to tempt the spenders in the family or to divide up the family asset. A "liquidity event" happens when a family business or family asset is sold. It brings cash into a family. This is usually a prelude to disaster. Cash is dispersed to family members, who then have something to argue about. It typically remains only briefly in the family's hands. It is soon in the pockets of yacht merchants, ex-wives, investment hustlers, wealth managers, lawyers, and other predators.

What makes wealth ideal for family fortunes makes it awkward and inconvenient for other purposes. If you are saving money for a house or a retirement, it needs to be liquid. You need to be able to get to it when you want it.

Family money is generally better when wealth managers, yacht salesmen, and family members can't get to it.

Few people can tolerate an investment that grows, even at 10 percent per year, for a very long time. They want the money now. They have spending plans. They may even need the money for very legitimate and worthwhile purposes. Education. Health care. Weddings. Funerals.

Costs rise to fill the budgets available to them. That is true in government agencies. It is true in business. It is true in families. Make money available. It is soon consumed by spending that has been "necessary and appropriate."

FINANCIAL ESCAPE VELOCITY

It is not enough to make a lot of money. You'll find that your spending keeps up with your income. There is some universal—or near-universal—law that decrees:

Expenses rise to meet the available income.

So no matter how much you earn, you'll have little left over at the end of the day. You won't be the first to observe this phenomenon. You won't be the last, either.

But what's the solution?

Wants and needs rise to meet the income available to them; that is a financial law as rigorously enforced as the law of diminishing returns or the law of supply and demand. That's why it's so hard to be rich and get rich at the same time.

The way to beat this phenomenon is either to exercise remarkable self-control or to outrun your wants and needs with "escape velocity" wealth. That is, wealth that rockets up so fast, you can't shop fast enough to keep up with it.

Typically, people reach "financial escape velocity" when their wealth surprises them. A family may own a farm or an apartment building. The asset is not very exciting, so they forget about it. And then, one day, they wake up to the fact that it is in the path of a major development, and they are being offered far more than they expected for it. That's the beauty of real estate. It does not go up any faster than anything else, but it is hard to spend. As it increases in value, its owner has no more income to dispose of. He is trapped. He gets rich in spite of himself. Nor does he pay current taxes on his rising wealth. This allows him to build wealth on a pretax basis, greatly enhancing the rate of return.

Another way to reach financial escape velocity is by using the miracle of compound interest. You make a small investment. You add to it. You keep at it.

Compounding works its magic. After a few years, you may notice that your wealth has raced ahead of your expenses. If you are lucky, you will be able to hide the fact from the rest of the family, allowing the compounding more time to reach escape velocity. Imagine, for example, that you have an account that has grown to $2 million, compounding at 10 percent per year (just to keep the math easy). You will earn $200,000 from the account this year. If you take it out and spend it, the compounding effect will stop. You'll have $200,000 to spend. But your wealth will cease to grow. And your family will have a chance to bring its spending habits up to the level of your income. Better to say nothing and let it run. After another five years, you'd have $3.2 million—giving you more than 50 percent more income.

Another place compounding works is in business. Often, businesses reflect the kind of compound growth you might otherwise get from an investment; only, it is less obvious. Accumulated effort compounds like dollars and cents. Work, capital investment, contacts, skills and a little luck are a great combination. Earnings can creep up on you. One year, your business earns $100,000. Ten years later, it earns $1 million. And if you've been putting your earnings back into the business, you would not have gotten accustomed to spending more and more. Your spending wouldn't have kept up.

If you had taken your earnings out, the business would have been unlikely to grow. Instead, your expenses would have grown, making it even harder to ever build up any real capital.

But let the business grow, and one day you could realize that you've reached the point where your earnings and capital can grow faster than your expenses; you've reached financial escape velocity.

One year, you earn $100,000. The next, you earn $300,000. If you act quickly, you can put that extra $200,000 into a special account, before spending catches up to it.

Another way to reach FEV is by owning assets that can't readily be turned into cash. Timber, real estate, a business itself—these can go up 10 times or more without giving you any easy way of adding to your expenses. You don't do an appraisal or even an up-to-date balance sheet very often. When you do, you're surprised by how much your assets have appreciated. You may feel as though you should increase your spending, but since the assets are not easily converted to cash, you'll be reluctant or even unable to do so.

After a few years of this, you'll find that you have reached FEV without realizing it (which is almost the only way to do so).

The other way to reach FEV is simply to make so much money that your ability to get rid of it is overwhelmed and may even break down.

Of course, there is a big psychological element to this. Ostentation is roughly the divide between old and new money. The *nouveaux riches* seem to want to spend their money to announce to the world that they've "made it." They want to show off, to prove something, to flaunt it.

Old Money is different. It is more likely to drive an old car and wear old, threadbare fashions. Old Money doesn't want to prove anything, except to other Old Money families. Old Money already feels superior. And it cultivates its superiority with its own codes, such as the reluctance to show off wealth.

Since you have to go through the new money stage before you can become Old Money, you have to get through the FEV. Otherwise, the new money disappears in gaudy, showy demonstrations.

LOCK IT UP!

Locking money up for long periods of time can help money go from new to old without getting wasted. Not only does this protect it from you and your family, it protects it from the government. The feds tax transactions. They tax liquidity events. They don't tax unrealized, compounding gains. This why most successful families favor very long-term investments in very illiquid assets. Typically, this is a business or real estate. Or some form of concession, such as timber or mineral rights.

Among our friends is a family that owns vast tracts of forest. They have been in the family for five generations. The present generation could sell the land. But it would so shock the family culture and family conscience that it is almost impossible to do so. It would take a very ambitious, very brash business school graduate to even suggest such a thing. And then, with luck, the rest of the family would overrule him.

Another family we know bought a gold mine. The gold is deep. Even at today's prices, it is scarcely worth bringing the gold up out of the ground. But what a great family asset! Since the gold is so deep, the family cannot expect much in the way of ready money by operating the mine. It just sits there, waiting for the next generation, the next round of inflation and repricing. It is an asset that is hard to spend, hard to dissipate, and even hard to appreciate. It is just there.

Between the Malibu beach house and the gold mine, there is a whole world of real estate: farms, ranches, apartment complexes, office buildings, shopping malls, and parking lots.

As a general rule that applies to businesses as well as real estate, the less desirable the property, the more profitable it is on an annual basis. Slum real estate and parking lots produce decent yields. Horse farms produce less income than soybean farms. Pawnshops are more profitable than art galleries.

You can easily see why this is. People want to own art galleries. They only own slum apartment buildings for the money. So the money has to be good in the slums. It doesn't have to be good in art galleries. As they say, an art gallery is a good way to make a small fortune out of a big one.

That is why the beachfront house in Malibu is so exceptional. It was something that people would want to own. That it made its owners wealth is all the more remarkable.

But sticking with our theme, we see that while old, rich families may own "prestige properties" and racehorses, it is likely that the new fortune was made elsewhere—perhaps in ghetto housing or chicken farms.

But every family has its weakness. Our own weakness is for old stones. We love broken-down houses, preferably mansions with walled gardens. We can't resist wanting to fix them up. This really has little to do with the subject of this book, at least not directly. But we might as well reveal our obvious defects; it might help hide the unobvious ones better.

We began restoring houses in Maryland. Our first project was a farmhouse in the southern part of the state. We did it in a cheap way and later sold the house for about what we had invested, not including our time.

Then we went on to Baltimore. There, we found that we could buy beautiful old houses—three-story brick mansions—for $25,000. We bought a few of them. We fixed them up. We later sold them when it became unsafe to continue living in the ghetto. We made a little on the later ones, but not much.

The city of Baltimore was at that time trying to attract businesses. It gave us two buildings near the downtown area with the condition that we would have to fix them up and put our young publishing business there. You'd think that you couldn't lose on buildings that you got for free. But you would be wrong. We invested about $80,000 renovating them and sold the two of them for $67,000.

Baltimore has been very instructive to us. We've learned that city government can destroy a city, no matter how many advantages it has.

Baltimore has one of the best ports on the East Coast. It is at the railhead of a vast network of train lines. It is only one hour by highway from the nation's capital, only an hour and a half from Philadelphia, and only three hours from New York. It is also in the middle of one of the fastest-growing, richest corridors in the United States, which just happens to be the world's richest and biggest economy.

It has some of the best schools in the nation, too: Johns Hopkins University is well known worldwide and attracts some of the brightest people in the world. There is high-tech research and development in almost every direction, and the nation's largest and most growing industry, the federal government, just minutes away.

It also has some of America's best architecture and whole square blocks of empty housing and a redeveloped harbor area that attracts millions of visitors every year.

Yet despite all these advantages, the city has been in decline for three-quarters of a century, with a rapid, almost terminal decline over the last two decades. The population has been cut in half. Even poor people have moved out. Followed by the rats. The public schools are largely dysfunctional. And real estate prices, adjusted for inflation, have been in a slump since 1927.

That is not to say that there still aren't nice areas in the city. There are also many good people doing good work. And there are many profitable enterprises, too. But if the city of Baltimore had been a stock, you should have sold in the run up of the 1920s—and stayed away ever since.

Nevertheless, we have made Baltimore our home, both for ourselves and our business. We work in mansions that no one else wanted that are inefficient for office use, but nevertheless bring a certain charm and graciousness to business life. We have fixed up more than a half-dozen of these buildings. We have never tried to sell one.

After having renovated properties in Maryland, we were ready to take on projects overseas. So far, we have worked on two semi-abandoned chateaux and a tumbledown ranch house in Argentina.

But we are under no illusions that these are good investments. They are a hobby. They are fun. They engage the family in projects that don't make money, but that do lock up family money.

But the general rule is this: The more the property is attractive, the less it is a good investment.

That general rule applies to business in this way: The more the business is prestigious, the less it is profitable. And the easier it is, too, the harder it is to make money in it—which we explore in Chapter 4.

CHAPTER 4

MAKING YOUR FORTUNE IN BUSINESS

Most family fortunes are created by successful businesses. Not by careers. Not by professions. Not by investing. Not by winning the lottery.

What follows is more of a romp through our own experience and thoughts about business than a serious rehearsal of successful techniques. There are plenty of "how-to" books on the subject already. You don't need another one. Besides, in our experience, there are no real "how-to" rules that will do much good. Instead, there are general ideas.

Just as multigenerational families invest differently, so are there some things about family businesses that make them different from regular businesses. And so are there some things that most people take for granted about business that are probably not so.

Successful businesses are a bit like family fortunes themselves. They are difficult to bring to life. Once you've brought them to life, they are even more difficult to keep alive. Especially over more than one generation.

Which brings us to a pretty good starting point: The ideal fortune is not money. It is a business. A family business. Fortunes die easily. They're like delicate birds you buy in the pet shop. Once you get them home, they are already half dead. You can give them the *coup de grâce* in a matter of months.

Money is easily spent. Easily neglected. Easily wasted. It is not solid enough to hold on to. In today's world, it is something that usually exists only in our imaginations—or in ghostly electronic form.

You could get a statement that tells you that you have $5 million in your account. But what does that mean? How do you know you have anything in your account? Have you ever seen it? What if your next statement told you that you had nothing? Would that be any less real? And what would you do about it if the bank insisted that it was not there? Would you go to the bank and look around in the corners to see if you could find it? Would you ask the tellers if they had seen it recently? How would you describe it to them?

And if it were suddenly gone, would you miss it? Chances are, you wouldn't notice that it had gone at all. For what did you ever do with it? You couldn't eat it. You couldn't wear it. You couldn't play with it. Scrooge McDuck kept his fortune in gold coins. In the comic books, he loved to dive into it and play with it. But you can't do that with an electronic fortune.

That's why it is so easy to say goodbye to it. You never got to know it in the first place.

A business is different. It is much more real, tangible, in your face, and demanding. It has doors that need to be opened in the morning and lights that need to be turned off at night. It has people, too: employees who need direction and salaries; customers who have questions, needs, complaints, and desires; and directors, managers, lawyers, bankers—all with their own points of view.

- Money is quiet. A business talks back to you.
- Money is anonymous. A business has a distinct personality.
- Money does what it's told. A business has a mind of its own.
- Money is fickle and runs around. A business is steadfast and loyal.
- Money is easy come, easy go. A business drags its feet in coming and digs in its heels when it is time to go home.
- Money is easy. A business is tough.
- Remember our general rule: The harder it is, *ceteris paribus*, the better it is. The longer it takes to make money, the longer it is likely to stick around.
- The harder it is to make, the less likely you are to lose it.

THE BEST WAY TO GET A FORTUNE

Getting a fortune by running a business is the best and most common way to get and maintain a fortune. Here's why:

- It is a more permanent form of wealth than just cash.
- It usually provides an onward stream of income that can be used to support a family and/or add to its wealth.
- It is dynamic and alive, not moribund. It requires attention.
- It causes the family members to work together toward a common goal.
- It helps family members understand the value of money and how it is earned.
- Over time, businesses give families a way to leverage their own skills and knowledge.

Let's examine each of these, briefly.

First, money from a business is more reliable than money from stocks or other investments. This is a dubious assumption. Small businesses have good times and bad times. Most are out of business within five years of their founding. So what do we mean by "more permanent"?

The trouble with cash is that it is hard to develop any real attachment to it. One dollar bill is the same as the next. People don't really care about them. What they care about is what they can be exchanged for. In other words, the only real value in cash is that it can be gotten rid of in favor of something else.

That is not true of business wealth. Businesses take many years to build. They are sold off only reluctantly and with considerable difficulty. Businesses are illiquid; they cannot be exchanged for other things readily. They are, at least in that sense, more permanent than cash.

Besides, in our reading of the family wealth stories, it appears that families with only liquid assets are less likely to have any assets at all 10 years on than those with family businesses. Families have no loyalty and little sense of responsibility toward money. They often feel very loyal toward businesses and work very hard to keep them alive.

Second, one of the reasons families like businesses is that they earn money from them. Money invested in other ways may pay little or no dividends (see below). Businesses, typically, can be managed so as to provide their vigilant owners with substantial streams of income.

This is partly because it is difficult to sell off a business in little pieces. If you have 200,000 shares of a stock, it is easy to sell a few shares every time you need a little ready cash. Each time you sell some shares, your stream of dividend income gets smaller.

Not so with a business. You can't sell it in pieces, normally. It's all or nothing. So as long as you have it, you get the full income stream.

Third, a business is not dead capital. It is alive in almost every sense of the word. It includes living people: customers, employees, managers, competitors, and suppliers. This requires owners to have real, human relationships, with the loyalties and responsibilities that go along with them.

It also requires dynamic, ongoing management. It needs control. It needs vision. It needs energy. And it is not just an abstraction. A business has a very real, physical sense, too. There are buildings. Machines. Trucks. There is a place.

Fourth, not only does this connect a family to the source of its wealth, it gives family members a way to participate. They can work together—even family members with very different skills. One may be a genius accountant. Another may be a good truck driver. Another may have great "people skills." In a business of a certain size, there is room—and need—for just about everyone.

Fifth, a family business helps the whole project of wealth preservation over several generations because it helps everyone understand how money is made and what it is worth. It helps avoid the "trustafarian" problem, in which young people are cut off from the source of their wealth and unable to understand it or contribute to it in a meaningful way.

Given these advantages, a family fortune based on a family business does not have to be as big as a fortune based on cash. You can easily see why that is.

The stock market currently has a dividend yield of about 2.5 percent. Ten-year U.S. notes have a yield of about the same amount. So if you are aiming for income of $100,000 per year, you need $4 million worth of stock. Or if you include replacing the money lost to inflation, you need maybe twice that much. At least.

But private businesses typically sell for multiples of only 4 to 10 times earnings. Or less. So a business that produces $100,000 worth of dividend income might be worth only $500,000 or $1 million.

However, a family business worth $4 million might produce $400,000 in dividend earnings (profits).

But that's just the beginning. Because the owners of the business control its spending, too. And its hiring. Often, two or more members of the family are employed by the business. They might easily earn $100,000 each, paid out of the expense side of the ledger, before profits are declared. They might also each have a company car. Even a company apartment. And a company credit card for business expenses and business entertaining.

The IRS has rules about these things. Readers are urged to scrupulously follow the rules. Dot every "I" and cross every "T." But in our experience, business owners often have considerable flexibility about how money is spent and frequently enjoy "perks" from before-tax income. Just providing an office is more than a trivial matter. If you had to do it for yourself—with assistants, copiers, computers, and so forth—it could easily cost you $100,000.

All together, a family might take out as much as $700,000 or so annually from a $4 million business, whereas a $4 million investment in the stock market would produce only $100,000 in dividend income.

HOW TO BUILD A FAMILY BUSINESS

The way to begin is simply to begin. But it's tempting to not begin at all. It's much easier to get a job. Let someone else do the thinking; you just do what you are told to do.

That's why people don't build fortunes working for the post office. In fact, they don't make fortunes by working for anyone. They build fortunes by operating a business—even if it is a business within a business, a form of intrapreneurship, where people operate small businesses in the context of a bigger one.

You begin by doing the hard thing: Try to figure out what you can do that people will pay for. People have unlimited wants and needs. You just have to figure out what you can do to help them. Then concentrate on doing it better than anyone else.

Where to start? Our old friend Doug Casey recommends going to Kinshasha or Mumbai:

When I used to land in some Third World country where I knew no one and had no connections, what would I do—sit in my hotel room and watch TV? No. I'd open up the Yellow Pages for that city—it'd be online today—and look at the different kinds of businesses listed and think of ways I could offer some value to those people in those businesses, such that they would be willing to give me money in exchange. I always started with the people who tend to be centers of power—lawyers, real estate agents, and the like. In most places, they either have the money or know the people who do. I'd call them up and arrange an interview.

Here it's an advantage to be in a different town, preferably in a different country. They don't know who you are—for all they know, you're an eccentric billionaire, looking for opportunities. You're interesting, simply because you're from elsewhere. With some of them, you'll establish a rapport, and next thing you know, you're being invited home for dinner, you meet some of their friends, you keep your eyes and ears open, one thing leads to another, and you can find some great opportunities.

This technique works best for people who have a wide array of knowledge and other connections. If you've done nothing significant with your life previously it's a waste of time—why should these people want to talk to you after the first five minutes, when they're sizing you up? Hitting the ground in a strange, foreign country is doing something significant—an excellent start. It both allows you to see opportunities that most people don't (stuck as they are in their medieval serf mentality), and to bring some new intellectual capital to the party—a reason for those with the money to deal you in.

You never know what the opportunity might be, but it will present itself. Ted Turner was absolutely correct when, in response to a question about how to make a fortune, he answered that you should go to where the action is and throw yourself in the middle of it. The law of large numbers will work, and some of the wealth will start coming your way.

If I were 18 or 21 again, what I would do is get *some* money—borrowed from grandmother, saved from mowing lawns, withdrawn from the college fund, raised selling possessions, whatever—and use that grubstake as seed money.

You have to start someplace. Most people could learn something from the average Chinese. As a culture, they've really been through the meat grinder over the last century, and know how important it is to save.

Anyway, I would take that grubstake and hit the road and go someplace new, as different as you can get from wherever you start. That way you're new, fresh, unique. If you're American and you stay in the U.S. where there are masses of people just like you, no one has any special reason to hire you; you are—at least at first blush—just one of millions with similar backgrounds. Better to go to Honduras or Bolivia or Laos or Nigeria, where you'll stand out from the crowd and have something to contribute that others do not.

You're interesting—and that opens up opportunities. And how interesting you are is a function of how many books you've read, how much thought you've put into things, how widely you've traveled, how many skills you've mastered, how many people you know. It's completely up to you. But you've got to get out of your comfortable and safe-seeming hometown—otherwise you're no better than a medieval peasant, chained to the dirt his ancestors toiled over and were buried in, for generations. Your chances of getting anywhere that way are slim and none.[1]

The important thing to remember is that you have to think like an outsider, not an insider. Insiders make money by succeeding in existing organizations. They can be very important, very competent, very hardworking, and very well paid. But it's very hard to build a fortune as an insider.

You have to challenge existing businesses. You have to be an outsider. You have to come up with something new or a new way of doing things or just a better way of doing things in an old industry.

Does that mean you have to try something really wild and weird? Not at all. Another old friend, Mark Ford, has studied the issue for many years. He's probably the world's leading expert on how new businesses are created, built, and developed into substantial enterprises. He points out that most successful entrepreneurs are not risk takers. They are interested in building businesses, not in gambling. They know that what they are trying to do—create a new business—is a risky undertaking. But they try to minimize the risk by following very sensible, conservative rules.

For one thing, Mark says they always stick to a fundamental rule:

ONE STEP AT A TIME

The idea is very simple. You begin very small. You try a number of things. If you're lucky, you'll find something that works before you run out of time, money and confidence. It may be a small thing. But it has to pay the bills. It has to generate enough money to keep the lights on and allow you to try other things.

In our business, we began with a single newsletter. In 1978, we figured there were lots of Americans who would be interested in opportunities overseas . . . not for tourism, but for deeper, longer experiences. We started a newsletter called *International Living.*

Until that time, the elder Bonner worked at a small public-interest group in Washington, the National Taxpayers Union. When he started, in 1973, he earned $100 per week. When he left, in 1978, he was earning (from memory) about $60,000 per year as executive director of the group. It was good money back then. But he had ambitions that went beyond what he could get from a job, and he was beginning to wonder about "public service," generally. He had worked to reduce taxes and government spending. Despite his best efforts, government spending was going up. It looked like he was fighting the tides of history.

Starting a newsletter was a gamble. But it wasn't exactly a step into the blue. He was familiar with direct-mail fundraising. Sending out direct-mail letters to get subscribers for his new newsletter was just "one step" away.

Still, it cost more to do his first marketing effort than he had in the bank. If it had not worked, he would have spent years paying off the debt. Fortunately, *International Living* was a success. It is still published today, from its headquarters in Ireland.

Thereafter, for the next 30-plus years, he took one step at a time, adding other publications, moving into the financial area, mastering the Internet, and building similar businesses in foreign countries.

The publishing industry suits us. In effect, we offer "outsider" ideas—on investment, health, and other subjects. There is no heavy lifting. It is not dangerous like truck driving or tedious like truck driving, or boring like truck driving, or dishonest like running the Fed.

We are writers at heart. It gives us a chance to write. We've been writing our financial blog, *The Daily Reckoning*, every day for over 12 years.

Of course, there were good times and bad times. Often, when we forgot the "one step at a time" rule, we lost money. Sometimes lots of money. We thought, for example, that we could turn a chateau in France into a conference center. Yes, in theory, it would work. But there were several giants steps required. We had to step across into a different culture and a different political and regulatory environment. We didn't know how to manage a conference center. We didn't know how to control the renovation. And then, we didn't know how to deal with the lawyers we brought into it to bring it under control.

Each error cost us heavily. It was a very expensive education. And since we had no desire to continue in that line of business, it was a tuition for no good reason.

Even in the publishing business, we lost money when we ventured out, taking more than one step at a time. Early on, for example, we thought we could make it in the magazine business. We published a magazine called *Frontiers of Science*.

The idea was not bad. But magazines are not newsletters. While newsletters are supposed to look amateurish, magazines are supposed to be slick and professional. And magazines require advertising; otherwise, the economics don't work. They're expensive to print and deliver, with editorial overheads that are much higher than in newsletters. But we didn't know anything about advertising sales. Or about newsstand sales. Or about magazine subscription sales. Or about magazine editorial, for that matter.

We published the magazine for a few years, losing money every year. Eventually, we gave up.

In another failed venture, we took up a satire newspaper. It was "publishing" in a broad sense. But it was several steps away from what we thought we knew. The idea was to lampoon everything that went on in Washington in a weekly newspaper, hand it out all around town, and support it with paid advertising. We imagined people reading it at the office and collapsing on the floor in spasms of laughter. We thought it was so funny radio and TV hosts would quote from it. We even thought that advertisers would call us to place their ads, for we had no advertising sales department.

It never occurred to us that advertisers wouldn't pay to be in a newspaper in which everything was a joke. (In retrospect, we should have tried getting them to pay to NOT be in our newspaper.) Nor did it cross our minds that Washingtonians were Washingtonians because they took the world of politics seriously. Making fun of them was good sport for us, but it was unwelcome to them.

The Public Spectacle, as it was called, failed within a few weeks. But it was early in our career and probably well worth the cost to learn an important lesson: Stick to the "one step at a time" rule.

Related to this rule is one given to us by a competitor:

"I take chances all the time," he said. "But I never take a chance so big it could sink the business."

Take small risks. Learn from them. Then, take some more small risks. Never put the business itself in jeopardy, because it is very hard to start a business, and it becomes more and more valuable as you learn more and more lessons.

If you are able to continue long enough, you will have accumulated enough capital and enough lessons that you will be only one step away from substantial success—substantial ventures with large payoffs.

Every start-up business is a "what," not a "why" undertaking. You know what works only by eliminating what doesn't. Of course, you try to draw general rather than specific lessons from each failure. But you are never too sure how much you can generalize.

Because you never know for sure why you failed. You have to guess at it and test it. Each test costs you time and money. Each one should bring you closer to what does work—and closer to your goal of accumulating real family wealth.

This is also why another rule is handy. We call it the rule of "accelerated failure." Since you don't know exactly what will work, and since there are usually quite a few things that won't between your initial efforts and where you want to end up, the trick is to get to the winning formula as quickly and as cheaply as possible. Time and money are limited. You don't want them to run out before you've come across a sustainable business model. And remember, as long as your business is "alive," you are still in the game—testing, trying, and failing.

"Accelerated failure" reminds us that we can't know what will work; we can discover it only by trial and error. It also highlights an important but underrated attribute of the successful entrepreneur: modesty. In investing, as in business, the know-it-all is often disappointed. The person who admits he doesn't have the answers, however, is more likely to discover them.

You can see why this is. Starting out, you can't know what will work. In fact, after 35 years in our career, we often feel that we know less and less. For every definite conclusion we can think of a dozen exceptions, caveats, and counterexamples.

The person who thinks he knows the answers without testing, though, is a risk to himself and his business. Because there are only a few formulae that will work. And an infinite number than won't. So the odds that he has fallen on a good one are small.

The popular idea of the entrepreneur is the man with a "vision" for the business he is creating. But the more cocksure he is, the longer he sticks with it—and the more he invests in it—the less likely it is to work. As the philosopher Mike Tyson put it, "Everybody has a plan, until they get punched in the face."

Life punches entrepreneurs in the face, sometimes more than once a day. There is hardly a real entrepreneur in the world who still has a straight nose. If he stands his ground and takes the punches—steadfastly enduring all that life can hit him with—he will soon be out cold on the mat.

The entrepreneur of myth is far from the real one. The real business builder knows he has to bob, weave, and duck. He has to roll with the punches, not take them in the head. And if he has a vision, he knows it is no substitute for real experience. When experience shows his vision won't work, he chucks it into the dustbin with the millions of other unworkable visions. Otherwise, he and his business will be chucked into the dustbin.

Contrary to popular myth, business builders try to avoid risks whenever they can. They soon learn that there are a lot of sucker punches in the world of business; they need to avoid them if they are to stay in business and succeed.

"Accelerated failure" is one way to control risks and find "what works" as fast as possible.

"One step at a time" is how to get where you want to go.

LEARN AT OTHERS' EXPENSE

Still another simple principle of successful business is to "learn from others' mistakes." We have heard so many stories about successful entrepreneurs who have pioneered new industries we forget that most new innovations fail. They are like mutations in the natural world. Most disappear. Only a very few survive and produce fertile offspring. Still fewer become major successes.

The trick is not only to learn from your own experience, but to take as much from the experience of others. You don't want to be a mutation. You want to be an improvement. And you do that by studying, watching, and listening to other people who have tried to succeed in your chosen industry.

Almost every industry has its sources. Magazines, blogs, web sites, trade shows—you can learn a lot about what works just by paying attention. You may not understand the "why," but who does? And you can check and find out what doesn't work, too. This is probably more valuable, since it can save you the time and expense of finding out on your own.

The inventions of the printing press and, much later, the Internet made it possible for almost anyone to learn from people they never met. Even from dead people. And cheaply, too. A book may cost only $25, but George Soros says you can make a billion dollars by reading the right book. He's right. People write down their experiences and their insights. Especially important are the memoirs of the old timers who've seen a number of innovations come and go. Read them carefully. They may be able to save you a fortune—and years of trial and error.

As successful people become older, they become more reflective. They wonder why they succeeded. They reminisce. They take guesses. And they are usually quite willing to talk to admiring newcomers. If you're starting out in an industry, find a successful older businessman. Ask for an interview. Just explain that you want to discuss the industry. Ask how he "made it," and what he sees as the important trends. You'll be surprised by how open and ready to talk he is.

In our own experience, a fellow we knew once came to us and said: "I like your business model. I'd like to do something like it. Would you tell me how it works?"

"Sure, we'd love to," we answered. We explained the whole thing, and he set up his own business, modeled on ours. When he had a question, he asked us.

He didn't invent anything. He just applied the lessons we had learned over many years (and at great expense). His new business took off almost immediately and is still going strong. Since he started about 10 years ago, he has made a few innovations of his own, which we are now applying to our business!

DON'T BE A PIONEER

Supposedly, the rugged entrepreneur sticks out his jaw and forces the world into the shape he wants it. He becomes the hero of his own success story.

In reality, he does nothing of the sort. He is like the successful beta investor. He does not create a trend. He does not buck the trend. He does not try to beat the trend. He just wants to find a trend that is running his way. He doesn't really try to make history; he just tries to make history work for him.

Here's another rule that might help: Don't be a pioneer. Be at the tipping point.

Malcolm Gladwell popularized a simple idea that some things seem to suddenly "catch on," while others don't. We look at it in a slightly different way. There are always new ideas, new inventions, and new innovations coming out. Most, like mutations, are dead ends. They never go anywhere.

The popular idea is that the successful entrepreneur comes up with a new idea. At the time, most people dismiss his idea as "too far out" or "ahead of its time." But with vision, hard work, and courage, he sticks with it, and despite all odds, he makes a success of it. It's the kind of story people like to hear. It has a hero. It has adversity. And it has a happy resolution.

Of course, this happens. But most wise entrepreneurs will not stake their successes on wacky ideas. They know that most ideas that are "too far out" stay too far out. Most ideas that are ahead of their time never get in the right time zone. And most entrepreneurs who are committed to the success of their ideas fail with the ideas themselves.

The smart entrepreneur looks for the idea—the business, the innovation, the industry—that has already proven itself, but which is not fully implemented. That is, he wants to launch his boat on a rising tide. Because he knows that success is not just a matter of his own genius and hard work. It is also a matter of luck—and the kind of luck you get when you have the wind at your back.

The smart entrepreneur wants an idea that has recently arrived at the "tipping point," where it has moved from the fringe to the mainstream. This is an idea that has proven itself, sometimes over many years in the wilderness of "out there" ideas. Once proven—and moving to wide acceptance—it is a great idea for an entrepreneur.

You can see this phenomenon clearly in the electronic revolution of the 1990s and 2000s. At least, *we* saw it clearly. In the early 1990s, we were exclusively a paper-based, post office–dependent publishing business, little different from those that existed 100 years earlier. We printed out eight-page newsletters on white paper. They were then folded by a mechanical folder, inserted in an envelope by a mechanical inserter, taken to the post office, and hand delivered all across the nation. It was a long, expensive process.

When the Internet came along, we knew that the industry was going to be rocked by change. But we didn't know how.

"You'll be out of business within three years," said one of our young associates. "Because now people can get all the investment information they want, for free, on the Internet."

The smart money was probably betting against us. Entrepreneurs were rushing to the Internet to put up web sites. The new medium was so attractive that it attracted not just entrepreneurs with vision but investors with money.

The combination was potent. In theory, the idea was to get there first and stake out a claim. It didn't matter that you didn't really know how you were going to make money. The race was on. And you could win it by getting more eyeballs to your web site than anyone else. And that you could do, it was widely believed, by spending a lot of money on graphics, content, celebrities, and other attractions.

Obviously, the doomsayers were wrong—at least about our business. Otherwise, we wouldn't be writing a book on family wealth. We'd be writing a book on family poverty, instead.

We are, after all, the "alternative" press. And the Internet allowed us to do what we do best: offer alternative ideas, information, and recommendations, without the huge expense of printing and postage. Our business boomed.

But there are several lessons about wealth building to be learned from this episode. First, the new medium was the place to be. There was no use ignoring it. The Internet reached the "tipping point" in the mid-1990s; after that, if you were an entrepreneur, it, and not the traditional paper-based medium, was the place to be.

Newspapers were hit hard. They lost their classified advertising revenue to Internet sites such as Craigslist. Then the ink-stained printers saw their revenues drop. The Postal Service, which had already lost much of its business to Federal Express and UPS, was hit with more bad news. In 2010, the Postal Service lost $8.5 billion. Then the bookstores were whacked by Amazon and other online booksellers. Borders, for example, went broke in July 2011.

While traditional paper-based media were in contraction, the Internet was soaring. An entrepreneur, starting out, has a much better chance of making a success in an expanding business. And probably no industry grew faster than Internet-based communications in the mid-2000s. You could make money by providing content. You could make money by selling hardware. You could make money by creating new "killer apps" or selling software. You could make money by offering Internet marketing services, creating Internet web sites, doing Internet graphics or Internet-based video games. Practically every industry offered an Internet opportunity. The entrepreneur just had to find it.

DON'T BE AN OPPORTUNIST

But there were two kinds of opportunities on offer. One was suitable for family wealth creation, the other less so. While many, perhaps most, entrepreneurs are opportunists, the person who is trying to build a durable family business is not. Not in the ordinary sense.

The opportunist is typically short-term oriented. And the Internet provided an incredibly rich ground for him to plant his fast-growing weeds, especially before the end of the 1990s.

The modus operandi of the short-term-oriented hustler is to come up with an idea that can be sold to investors—not necessarily an idea that will make a good business. Typically, he would lay out the idea to seed capital investors as though he were pitching a script to Hollywood. That is, he gave it the "elevator pitch," a selling proposition so short and sweet that it can be delivered during an elevator ride. The initial investors were also very short-term oriented. They weren't interested in building a real business or even in creating real wealth. What they wanted was an attractive idea that could be developed and then sold to other investors at a profit.

In the early days, it was all pie in the sky. Nobody had any real idea how much money might be made or how it could be made. It looked for a while as if the Internet might force all traditional businesses to close their doors. It also looked as if small investments in staking out valuable Internet turf might turn into real gold mines. So the hustlers moved in—thousands of them. Each had a vision. And many were able to raise money to see their vision come—more or less—to life.

For the lucky among them, the vision still looked attractive after they had fleshed it out a bit. They were able to take their companies public, raising billions of dollars, even though the companies had never made a cent and no one was very sure how or when they might ever become profitable.

A few entrepreneurs were able to cash out and walk away with millions. But after the washout in 2000, most ended up with nothing. Either way, they were not building family wealth, at least not the way we recommend. They were making fast money—a big score.

We don't recommend that approach for two reasons. The first reason is obvious: It usually doesn't work. It's hard to make fast money. In fact, the fastest way to make money is to make it slowly. You can try to make it fast forever and never get anywhere. But try to make it slowly . . . keep at it . . . and you'll probably end up with at least something—eventually.

The other reason is that when you build your business fortune slowly, it is much more likely to last. Because you're not just trying to take advantage of dimwitted investors. You're actually trying to build a successful business. And successful businesses are built, as we've seen, by trial and error over a long period of time. As time goes by, you develop not only the capital you need but also the skills, experience, and knowledge needed to preserve it. The quick-hit entrepreneur, however, has only money. And money goes fast, especially when it is in the hands of someone who doesn't know much about it. What became of the Internet fortunes built by twenty-somethings in the 1990s? We don't know. Our guess is that they disappeared in the 2000s.

The Internet gave wealth creators a huge boost; it still does. But the way to take advantage of it was by trial and error, slowly discovering how to use it to build a real business. Instead of investing a fortune of other people's money in a vision, the successful wealth builder invests little bits of family money to learn something. Then, only when he has proven out his concept does he put down big money.

This is not to say that this is the best way to build a big business or score a big financial success. We are only saying that is the best way for someone interested in building family wealth. Taking a flyer on an idea, such as setting up a Web-based business to make home deliveries of groceries or opening a chain of Internet cafes, may pay off. If it does, the entrepreneur gets rich and is celebrated as a hero in the financial press.

But the family wealth builder is not interested in becoming a media hero. He wants to be a family hero. And he will more likely succeed by not taking the risk of a big, expensive, flamboyant failure. He will play it safe. Test carefully. And never put the family fortune—even if it is tiny—at risk. He is not particularly interested in seeing *his* vision succeed. That would be vain and somewhat selfish. He wants something else: to succeed at building wealth for his family. He takes no giant leaps. He risks not his whole wad. He proceeds, one step at a time, accelerating his failures until he has found a model that works.

He is not an opportunist. He merely uses opportunities to give him a lift.

DON'T TRY TO DO IT ON YOUR OWN

The successful family wealth business builder is not much like the popular vision of an entrepreneur. For another thing, he is not at all a "lone wolf." He almost never succeeds on his own. A real business is a collaborative effort. It has to be. Businesses compete with other businesses. The one that relies on the talents, vision, ingenuity, and imagination of a single person is doomed to fail.

Our business is a collaboration of hundreds of people spread out all over the world. Its founder, the elder of your authors, explained its success at his 60th birthday party. His little discourse went something like this:

> You see before you a man of modest talents, but immodest achievements. For the modesty of his talents, he has only himself to blame. But for the immodesty of his achievements, he has all the people in this room to thank.
>
> And I want to take this opportunity to thank you all. You see, I have been extremely lucky. A lot of entrepreneurs are not so lucky. They are only marginally incompetent … good enough at a variety of tasks that they are hard to shove aside. They have opinions on marketing and management. Even worse, sometimes they have unshakeable convictions and absolute confidence in their own judgment. Those poor guys are practically doomed, in my opinion.
>
> I, on the other hand, owe everything to my own incompetence. When anyone new came into the office, I practically fell over myself to get out of his way. Some will generously say that I delegated authority. But that is not true. I shirked it. You and other partners, associates and employees just picked it up off the ground where I left it.

Mark Ford says that every successful business needs at least three key people: an idea person, a marketer, and a pusher. At the beginning, you have to make do, often doing two or all three roles yourself. But you cannot hope to go very far that way.

Mark believes new businesses progress through stages, each with its own challenges and each requiring something different from its owners. The first stage is one in which it must figure out if it can sell a product at all—and if so, how it can do so in a cost-effective way.

Typically, the business builder in this stage has few resources. He must be very careful not to waste time or money on things that don't matter. Often, a new businessperson will mistake the trappings of business for the essentials of it. He will rent an office. He will print up business cards. He will register with the Better Business Bureau and begin networking at industry events. He will even apply for licenses and permits.

All of that is usually a waste of precious time and resources. What he needs to do is figure out if he has something to sell and if he can sell it at a reasonable cost, leaving enough net income to pay his overhead.

Only after he has established that does he have any reason to go further. There's no point in getting a license to operate a drive-in movie theater for blind people, for example.

Of course, you have to do some bureaucratic chores and invest some money in infrastructure before you can test your idea properly. But you need to avoid expensive, time-consuming distractions.

Most start-ups fail. Many more never get much beyond the first stage, earning a living for the CEO but not much more.

The second stage is where the entrepreneur creates a real business. And that requires other talents. Most often, it requires real businesspeople who are capable of managing the key business processes: production, quality control, and sales.

The essential formula should already be in place. But the managers should refine it and make it profitable. Their goal is to build a real business producing real profits.

The third stage is where the business grows beyond the founder and its initial managers. Often, the founder—who tends to be a maverick, an eccentric, and often a royal pain in the derriere for his more mainstream managers—gets edged out.

This is a key challenge for family businesses. The goal of the family is not necessarily to manage the business itself, but it must understand it intimately and control it completely. Family members don't have to occupy all the top jobs in a family business, but the business must respond to the needs and goals of the family, and not necessarily its managers or outside stockholders.

This is a critical difference between family businesses and other businesses. The family business is the repository of family capital, the employer of family members, and the main source of revenue for the family itself. That's why it exists. And it's why the family must understand it and control it.

A normal business—especially one that is traded on public markets—answers to shareholders, but only indirectly and vaguely. Frequently, it operates for the benefit of its managers, not shareholders. Managers of large public companies answer to boards of directors whom they, typically, appoint. That is how someone such as Bill Weldon was able to earn $28 million in compensation as CEO of a pharmaceutical company last year.[2] He certainly wasn't worth that much. No one is.

True, the shareholders have a right to change board members or managers. But large groups of shareholders are like large groups of voters. They have little independent knowledge and little wherewithal to contradict the experts. So the managers tend to pay themselves far more money than they are worth. Plus, they give themselves huge perks and bonuses, far more than they deserve. Top ones create a cult of personality to convince the "lumpeninvestoriat" that they are responsible for the firm's achievements (which they have often jiggled and jived to flatter their own performance). It is a cynical truism that if people can get away with something, they will often try to do so. Managers of large public companies have been able to get away with a hideously large portion of the company's earnings—and often with its capital, too.

MORALE AND WHY IT SHOULDN'T MATTER

As mentioned earlier in this book, managers of public companies tend to be very short-term oriented, too. Their bonuses depend on quarterly or annual results. And their retirements are often larded up with the kind of cash and benefits that would make a pharaoh blush with shame. Their goal, typically, is to get as much as they can out of the company in the shortest time possible. This goal of the leaders is then transmitted throughout the whole business. All employees begin to take a short-term view. They come in and collect a signing bonus. They leave and collect a "golden parachute" severance bonus. Goals are set for quarterly earnings. Objectives rarely go out further than a few years. And soon the business is operating like a bank, where the profits are paid out in bonuses before they are even earned. Banks pay bonuses to employees for lending money. They don't even wait to see if the money comes back.

One of the justifications for overpaying managers is that shareholders feel they must keep them happy. That is a bad idea. Good shareholders don't care if managers are happy or not. What they should care about is whether the customers are happy. Good managers will care about that, too.

This is related to another insight. Not only must a business be started by "outsiders," it must continue to focus itself on the world outside of itself. Often, while shareholders believe they must keep management happy, managers believe they must keep the employees happy. This is a big mistake. It focuses the organization in the wrong direction, inward . . . toward itself.

Years ago, when our business was fairly new, a group of employees came to the elder Bonner with a problem.

"We've got trouble," they announced. "Morale is very low. What can we do?"

"Easy," he replied without thinking about it. "Ask for a show of hands on all employees whose morale is low. Fire those that raise their hands. We don't want employees with low morale."

By accident and instinct, he had hit upon a good idea. If he'd thought about it more, he would have added: "Oh yes, and fire any manager who ever mentions employee morale again."

Any business that begins to care about employee morale is lame. Because it becomes self-absorbed, like a teenager. It begins to care about itself, its problems, and its happiness. It will spend hours worrying about the wrong things. It will direct managers' attentions to problems that shouldn't exist. It will transform itself into an egocentric, self-serving institution. It will begin to act like a bureaucracy, in other words—which is the mortal enemy of all productive behavior. One study we saw said that a group of as few as 100 people could spend all its time trying to sort out its own interior "problems."

Instead of worrying about itself, a proper business should be focused outward, toward the people on the outside it is meant to service: customers, suppliers, partners, and associates. It should try to make customers happy with their transactions. Then, miraculously, employees will be happy, too. They will turn their eyes away from each other and toward their common objectives. Like soldiers quarrelling in their base, they turn to face the enemy. If employees are unhappy with this approach, fire them. Maybe they'll be happier somewhere else.

It is the role of shareholders, properly informed and motivated, to keep a business focused on what really matters. That is the grace and challenge of family-owned businesses. Good family businesses are managed either by the family itself—or by managers with very different goals and incentives than those in most public companies. Whether tied to the business by blood or by employment contracts, the goal is to increase the real value of the business over time. Quarterly earnings hardly matter. If it is a publicly traded company (some family enterprises are), movements in the stock price are largely irrelevant. Often, families have their own view of what the shares are worth. When prices fall below that level, they buy more shares. When prices rise above that level, they sell them. In no circumstance do family-owned businesses allow managers to undermine the value of their reputation or their patrimony.

Family shareholders are the kind of capitalists that capitalism needs. They are willing to make investments over years—even over generations—in order to build the value of their business. The business represents the family's financial and professional capital. They guard it, protect it, and nurture it. And they use time to do what no public company can afford to do: compound their knowledge, skills, and capital over generations. It is not the price of the shares that matters to them; it is the value of those shares. And it is not next week that they worry about, but the next generation.

WHAT KIND OF BUSINESS SHOULD YOU BE IN?

If you can ride a major boom in a new industry, like the Internet, at the tipping point, do it. If not, look for businesses that are not "prestige" enterprises. Instead, aim for something such as a chain of car washes, dry cleaners, or salvage firms.

The possibilities are too numerous, and our own knowledge is too limited, for us to give much specific guidance. But if you want to make a family fortune, pick a difficult industry, with high barriers to entry, low prestige, and little liquidity. Make it hard to get in—and hard to get out.

And make sure it is scalable. You can't make any real money selling your time, hour by hour. You want a business where you can leverage your time.

There is one other thing about family money that makes it different from other kinds of money—and one thing about the kind of business that supports family money that makes it different from other businesses. If you are a typical businessman or investor, you want a business that is as profitable as possible, as soon as possible. You also want one that is as marketable as possible. That is, you want one that is liquid, so you can realize whatever capital accumulation you manage to get. You will also want a business that you can run easily and one that does not require you to remain on the premises. You will generally have an "exit strategy" ready for the day you are ready to get out.

A family could benefit from the same kind of business, but with a few differences. It will not be concerned with getting out. In fact, as mentioned earlier, it will benefit from not being able to get out easily. Instead, it should want a business that traps future generations and leaves them without an easy exit. It should trap them close to the family's wealth, forcing them to remain near the source of their wealth and attentive to it. It is an added plus if the enterprise is remote from major metropolitan areas.

What is the ideal family business? Hard to say, but it might be a large, diversified family farm.

Here's why:

- It is a difficult business, perhaps with relatively low returns on capital.
- It requires active, on-site management.
- It is physical, tangible, observable—and something to which people can become sentimentally attached
- There is generally little liquidity, and a "liquidity event" is a very big deal.
- The main asset—land—compounds in value without capital gains or income taxes.

Of course, the best business for family wealth is the business you are already in, the business you know. That's the business that is most likely to make you the family money you are looking for.

General advice: Concentrate your forces when trying to get somewhere in life—diversify your assets when trying to protect them.

WORK HARD ... GET LUCKY

Life is competitive—especially business life. In general, everyone is trying to make money in the easiest possible way. One sure way to make more money than others is simply to work harder.

Resolve to work 12 hours per day. One well-focused, determined person will earn more money working 12 hours per day than two will make working 8 hours each. As we suggested earlier, that's why a two-income family, over time, may actually earn less than a one-income family. Do we know that for a fact? No, it's just an observation and a hunch. A person who works 8 hours per day should earn about as much as everyone else who works 8 hours per day. The way to earn more, *ceteris paribus*, is to work more. But you have to understand that it is not just the number of hours that counts. You cannot build a fortune on time alone. You have to do something in which your time compounds your earnings.

Starting out, the person who works 4 hours more per day should earn 50 percent more than his 8-hour-per-day colleague. One person's time is about as valuable as another. Neither has any real experience or skill that can be leveraged into great earnings.

So, starting out, a young couple, each working 8 hours per day, will earn more than the single worker who puts in 12 hours per day—25 percent more, in fact.

But earnings are a consequence of accumulated effort *over time*. So the guy who puts in 4 more hours per day accumulates much more experience and knowledge than either of the couple who each work eight hours. After five years, he's been on the job 5,000 hours longer than his colleague. That's the equivalent of 2.5 years more.

This gap between the 8-hour worker and the 12-hour worker continues to widen, year after year, so that after 10 years, the 12-hour worker is still working 50 percent more per day, but he also has 10,000 more hours on the job. A person with so much more experience should be much more valuable. His skills should have not merely added up but compounded. He is the rare person with substantially more experience and skill than his colleagues. At this point, he will probably not earn just 50 percent more than his coworkers, but more like 200 percent or 400 percent more.

Of course, this is not true for hourly work. But it is true in most businesses or professions where experience counts. The world is a competitive place. The winning players do not just win marginally—they win big. Because there are millions and millions of 8-hour workers, but relatively few 12-hour workers.

The statistics we found show that married men earn 11 percent more than their unmarried counterparts, and that the gap widens as they age.[3] This is consistent with our hypothesis. But it is far from the proof we would like to see. We believe that specialization, concentration, and accumulation pay off in a spectacular way—a lot more than 11 percent per year. In our ideal wealth-building family, the husband works like a dog—outside the home. The wife works, too, but inside the household, freeing the husband to concentrate on building wealth without undermining the integrity of the family itself.

Even working 12 hours per day and focusing almost exclusively on building a successful business, there are no guarantees. We recall from our own experience that it was a close run, with critical advances made by partners, associates and employees just in the nick of time.

COMPOUND EFFORT OVER TIME

You've heard of the "miracle of compound interest." Well, there's a similar miracle at work in the rest of life. . . .

One of the boys, 23, called recently. "I'm about ready to give up," he said.

The young man graduated from college two years ago. He could have easily entered the family business. Instead, he decided to try to make his career in one of the world's most difficult *métiers*, as a singer/musician/songwriter.

He moved to Brooklyn, which seems to attract young musicians like London attracts fund managers. He took courses at Juilliard. He wrote songs. He put them on the Internet. He sang at "open mic" nights in clubs and bars.

But after six months, it didn't seem to be going anywhere.

Meanwhile, his sister voiced similar disappointment and impatience.

She, too, has chosen a difficult career; she trained as an actress, moved to LA, and had—like her brother—approached her career in a disciplined, organized way.

But these are not careers in which discipline and organization come easily or pay off readily. There are no fixed hours. And no fixed route to professional advancement. Half the work you do, at least it seems to us, is just figuring out what work to do.

Our actress has had some success on TV and the movies. But she hasn't gotten the major roles she hopes for—yet.

"I've been in LA for two years already. I'm going to keep at it for another three years, according to my plan. But if it still isn't working, I'm going to have to find something else to do."

It's a rough life. She lives in a tiny studio apartment and works from dawn to dusk trying to get acting jobs. She supports herself, barely, by doing modeling work on the side.

Her brother, meanwhile, is literally a starving artist, working one day a week as a handyman to help pay the bills.

We don't know how others do it, but our children couldn't afford to be starving artists without family support. Rents are too high. Health care . . . transportation—if they were forced to pay 100 percent of their living costs, they'd have to give up on their artistic careers and find other lines of work.

The point we are making is that success doesn't always come immediately. And it's not easy to sustain a career that doesn't provide quick, positive feedback. But in our experience, it pays to stay the course.

Starting out in life, young people are practically interchangeable parts. They leave school not knowing much of anything. If they can read and write clearly, they have an advantage over most college graduates. But school doesn't prepare them very well for real life. School problems are bounded, controlled, and simplified. Usually, they are idealized, with the confusing parts taken out. In history, for example, they are taught broad themes and specific "facts." But the sequence of events in real life doesn't follow simple scripts. Instead, it is endlessly complex with "facts" that are always subject to doubt.

Historical characters are like cartoon figures, made into heroes or villains according to the storyline. In real life, they are like the people we know personally: They have their positive qualities and their negative ones; they perform well in some circumstances and poorly in others. They are neither good nor bad, but subject to influence.

That's why you cannot make a good history out of recent events; you know it too well!

In every discipline, the phenomenon is the same. In school, the complexities of real life are removed so that students can be tested on set groups of memorable, learnable, understandable bits of stripped-down, sanitized "knowledge."

That is why more education does not always lead to more success in the real world, and why we do not recommend too much "education" for children. It could be counterproductive. The better you get at handling the artificial world of academia, the worse you may do at solving the real world's infinitely nuanced challenges.

Problem solving in the academic world typically involves a part of the brain—but only a part of the brain. It is the "rational" part, the part that remembers facts, reads, writes, and connects the dots. That is the skill measured by the SAT tests, for example. They are tests of "scholastic aptitude." And they are pretty good at it. If you are able to do the kind of tricks the tests require, you'll be able to handle the kind of work they give you in school.

But life sends very different tests your way. Life's tests involve many, many more variables—so many that your "rational" mind is frequently overwhelmed. The human face, for example, is capable of hundreds, or thousands, of different expressions. Some people seem better able to read these messages than others. In the world of textbooks, other people scarcely matter. You read. You write. You check the boxes. But once you get into a workplace, you are confronted with faces—and an entirely new test. How well can you get along with others, motivate them, lead them?

In school, tests are anticipated. In real life, you never know when you will be tested. You never know what you will be tested on. And even when you are in the middle of an important test, you often don't know it.

In some careers—science, engineering, or accounting, for example—you are able to apply the body of knowledge you picked up in school. In many more, you're not. In most careers, you have to learn on the job a new body of knowledge, often additional, and sometimes completely new and different. And unless your job is to throw the switch on a toll bridge or to collect tolls on a toll road, your new knowledge is likely to involve a great many things that are uncertain, unknowable, and variable.

Even in "routine" careers, there is still plenty of room for career advancement and moneymaking. But it requires you to step beyond the routine. If you are a schoolteacher, for example, you might have to write a book on education or start a school of your own. If you are a carpenter, you could set up a carpentry business or use your skills to build something rare and interesting enough that it could be sold at high margin or mass produced.

Generally, the more formulaic the work, the less scope there is for making money at it. The more limited—that is to say, the more like school any job is—the less likely you are to turn it into a source of wealth, power, or outsized success.

But assuming you are doing something that is not routine, not formulaic and not limited, what is the secret to making a success of it? Ah, glad you asked. At least part of the secret is sticking to it. Here's why:

If your work is not simple and not formulaic, you need to use a fair amount of creative thinking, innovation, and entrepreneurship to get ahead. Sometimes your work can be reduced to simple, school-like thinking. More often, it is more complex, involving subtle judgments about people, guesses about how others will react, mastering new technology and leadership skills needed to get others to follow your plan, and so forth. It may involve raising money, "selling" your ideas, taking a chance on a new career or a new business, convincing clients to leave their habitual sources, or convincing employees to work harder—or better.

You may have to develop a new product. Or maybe you have an insight that tells you how to invest your firm's resources more productively.

Whatever it is, it is likely to require more than your "school brain" to make it happen. It is likely to involve wisdom, intuition, and "people skills." It is likely to require more of you: your brain, your personality, your heart. And maybe your soul, too.

It is likely to require trusted contacts, seasoned hunches, educated guesses.

WHERE DO THESE THINGS COME FROM?

There is no secret to success. Successful people just put in more hours than other people.

Our point is similar: Success is usually the product of compound effort over time. It takes time to develop contacts. It takes time to develop trust—both of your own team and outside clients, customers, and associates. It takes time and experience to develop the hunches and instincts that are useful in real life. It takes time, too, to understand other people and learn how to work with them. It also takes time to build a foundation of human and financial capital that allows you to take advantage of the insights and opportunities that experience bring you.

Time does not work in a linear, mathematical way. As with compound interest, time pays off geometrically. As contacts, experiences, wisdom, innovations, and intuition are added one to another, your opportunities multiply. A $100,000 deal that you might have made when you were 25 grows into a $1 million deal five years later. And instead of doing two deals a year, you might do 10 per year.

This is also why it is so important to put in lots of time. The leading figures in their industries put in thousands of hours—usually far more than their competitors. They may appear to be "gifted." Their achievements may seem effortless. But they are almost always the product of time.

Not only that, but the time spent at the end is much more powerful than the time at the beginning. You can see this by looking at charts of compound interest. Starting from a low base, the first series of compound interest produce little difference. But at the end, the results are spectacular.

Start with a penny. Double it every day. At the end of a week, you are still adding only 32 cents per day. By the end of the third week, however, you're adding more than $10,000 per day. So you see, the last increments of time are much more important than the first.

It doesn't exactly work that way in real life, of course. Hang around too long and you get tired, and the lessons you've learned might not be applicable to the new realities. Suppose, for example, that you had learned to make the perfect buggy whip, at age 55, in 1910! Or imagine that you were the leading expert on silent movies just before the "talkies" started. Or maybe you were cornering the classified advertising market just as Craigslist and eBay made their appearances.

But aside from that kind of a setback, time compounds your advantages. At age 20, you may know less than everyone in your business. But then you work 10 hours per day, while others work only 8. In 20 years, you may know more than just about anyone. Then who gets the new contracts? Who finds the new opportunities? Who has pricing power?

WHO MAKES MONEY?

Compound interest works because each addition is then put in service to earn another increment of gain. Compound effort works the same way. Every insight, innovation, and useful contact helps bring on another, bigger and better one.

Remember, success is competitive. While you are adding to your business capital, your competitors tend to wear out, move on, or retire. Sticking to it is not easy. People tend to get distracted. They often want easier, simpler, faster opportunities. They give up their accumulated capital and take up something new. That leaves you in a commanding position.

The longer and harder you work at something, generally, the more success you have. But there's an intriguing idea left dangling. What if you could work at something longer than a single life span? What if you could keep compounding for more than one generation? What if one generation could help the next succeed?

The idea is both self-evident and shocking. In America, you are supposed to be self-reliant, self-sufficient, and independent. You should believe that you are responsible for your own success. You are supposed to be able to do whatever you want to do—and go as far as your luck and pluck permit.

What if it weren't true? What if your success in life depended largely on your parents and grandparents?

We know that wealth is accumulated over many generations. We know that just by looking around. Our generation did not build many of the edifices we see, nor clear the fields where crops are planted, nor invent the automobile, the airplane, the television, or the toaster. We inherited those things and much more besides.

We know, too, that if you're born in New York rather than New Delhi, you're likely to be richer. And we know that if you're born to a rich family in midtown Manhattan, you're likely to be richer as an adult than if you're born to a poor family in Harlem. Yet how many people take responsibility for their children's wealth? How many figure out how to compound their success into the next generation and beyond?

There are many things that take longer than a single generation to accomplish. If you want mature oak trees lining your driveway, for example, you had better think in terms of generations or start very early. Olive trees can take an entire generation—35 years—before they produce a decent harvest. Then they live for centuries longer.

And what about a skill or a reputation? How long does it take to build a reputation as a great beer maker? A great winemaker? A great guitar maker? Or a great banker?

Not years. Generations.

The Martin family started making guitars in 1811. Now, everyone has heard of Martin guitars. The family is still making them.

The Beretta family is still making guns; the business was begun in 1526.

The Rothschilds have been in banking since the eighteenth century.

The Lemoine family started publishing books in Paris in 1772; they're still at it, too. And the Hoshi family in Japan has been running a hotel for 1,200 years!

Of course, these are rare examples. But there are a lot of businesses that involve delicate judgments, unusual habits, or the kind of specialized knowledge that is very hard to come by in a single generation or learned in school.

Parents mortgage their houses to send their kids to school. But the parent who advises his child to stay in school or attend graduate school may be doing him a big disservice.

The common belief is that people who get advanced degrees earn more than people who don't. Statistically, this is true. But it is misleading. It doesn't mean that any individual who gets a degree or advanced degree will earn more than if he didn't. All it means is that taking the whole population, average people who have more education tend to earn more than average people who have less education. Doctors earn more than carpenters. Engineers earn more than backhoe operators. But the average person earns an average salary. Obviously, if you want to earn an average salary, you are better off in a field where the average salary is high.

But what about earnings that are not average? What about the fellow who was going to be a doctor and instead decides to start a business of his own or goes to work for a pharmaceutical company? Would he be better off with more years of book learning or more years on the job?

To ask the question another way, would Bill Gates have had more success if he had stayed in Harvard and gone on to law school? We don't know. But it is unlikely.

STAY IN SCHOOL?

To turn to a more common example, what about the child who is destined to enter the family firm? Is he better off spending more time in school or going right to work? Almost every parent would say, "Let him stay in school as long as possible." If pushed to identify the merits of further education, the parent would say, "It can't hurt."

But maybe it *can* hurt.

People learn, no matter where they are and what they do. So the real question is, where are they likely to learn more, or which kind of learning will be more valuable?

Book learning has a value, especially in the sciences. But if the hypothesis of "Compound Effort Over Time" is correct, it may be more valuable to begin early accumulating the instincts, experience, and hunches that prove so valuable in real life. Plus, not only may time spent in school be less productive, it may undermine the process of accumulating real and useful knowledge.

Much of what is taught—depending on the discipline—is not knowledge at all. It is nothing more than intellectually fashionable claptrap that later proves to be completely false. Imagine the poor family that sends a child to an Ivy League school so that he may get a degree in economics or finance. Then it sends him to a business school so he may deepen his understanding of the subject. By the time the kid finishes school, the family has spent nearly $300,000 on his education.

Then, when his studies are finally completed, he comes back and applies the latest theories of finance to the family fortune. Had he arrived on the scene in 2005–2007, for example, he might have loaded up the family with a portfolio of mortgaged-backed derivatives, in order to earn higher yields from "safe" investments. He might have applied modern portfolio theory, too, and wiped out half the family fortune.

Or maybe he would have turned his education to the business itself. You can imagine him telling dad and the old-timers that there were new and better ways to do things and that they should be trying to "maximize shareholder value" by leveraging the firm.

The old-timers would shake their heads.

"No . . . debt doesn't seem like a good idea. . . ." they would say.

Or: "Hmmm . . . something doesn't seem right. . . ."

But asked to explain why they were reluctant to put the new learning to work, they would have a hard time arguing the point. They would have only hunches and habits, the accumulated wisdom of decades; it wouldn't stand up for long against the mathematical proofs offered by the young MBA!

Finally, the old guard would give up:

"Well, I guess you're right. We can increase our return on equity by borrowing money . . . I guess that makes sense."

And it did make sense—for a while. In 2006, the firm might have been more profitable than ever . . . and maybe even have bought a corporate jet and begun expanding into new markets.

"Well, I guess Sonny was right," the old man could say to himself. "It is a new era."

And so, the firm that had done business successfully ever since the War Between the States—like Lehman Brothers—loads up with debt. And then, when the next major cyclical downturn comes, it goes broke!

Julius Caesar never earned an MBA. Nor did Cornelius Vanderbilt. Or Henry Ford. Or Andrew Carnegie. Or practically any of the great successes of business and financial history. MBAs hadn't been invented!

Caesar learned his trade by following in his father's footsteps. His father showed him how to be a *praetor*, a senator and governor of an Asian province. Caesar learned how to talk to people. He learned how to think. He learned whom he could trust. His father made the introductions. His father set the pace. Then Caesar was able to step into his father's footsteps and keep on walking.

Caesar did not start from nowhere. He did not start with nothing. He started off where his father left him. He launched his career with the capital his father gave him: skills, reputation, experience, money, and contacts.

One of the many underrated legacies a parent can leave a child is a good reputation. Trust can take generations to build. We trust Mr. Martin to build guitars because his family has been making them for many, many years. We trust Mr. Ford knows how to make cars and Mr. Hershey knows how to make chocolate.

"The thing about doing business in China," said a man sitting next to us on an airplane, "is that it can take a very long time to build up trust. And without it, you're lost. They don't trust you. So they won't treat you very well. That's how they protect themselves, by cheating you first."

Trust reduces the cost of doing business. Less need for lawyers and contracts. No need for insurance, bonds, and hold-backs. That's one reason ethnic groups tend to prefer to do business internally. They understand one another. They know what to expect. They know whom they can trust . . . and how much.

Even in well-known, open careers such as filmmaking, banking and politics, trust, contacts, and "brand" awareness are extremely important. It's tough to break into acting or politics, for example, but it's a lot easier if your parents had already opened a breach in the wall. The number of people in the trade today whose parents and grandparents were also in it prove the point; there are far more of them than would be predicted by pure chance.

Of course, it's easy to see why. The children know how the business works; outsiders don't. They have the contacts; newcomers don't. People in the business trust them to know what to do and how to do it. So it's much easier to gain entry for someone such as Angelina Jolie (father: Jon Voigt), Michael Douglas (father: Kirk Douglas), Jeff Bridges (father: Lloyd Bridges), or dozens of well-known political figures.

Of course, that could be said of almost every career and every business, whether it is plumbing or haberdashery. One generation lays a foundation. The next can build on it.

That is another payoff of compound effort over time.

CHAPTER 5

MAKING YOUR FORTUNE IN INVESTMENTS

From every corner and every angle, the typical investor is urged to make a move.

"The train is leaving the station," say the brokers. "You have to act fast."

"This is an urgent opportunity," the promoters tell you. "You need to react now."

Twenty-four hours a day, seven days a week, come the financial updates. Each one screams out for action. Buy! Sell! Do something!

And everybody knows you have to be decisive if you're going to make any money by investing. "You snooze, you lose," they tell you. "You'll miss the opportunity," they warn. "I can't hold this open for you—are you in or out?"

Investment firms often have a "sucker list." It is a list of people with money but not much investment experience. So when they are told they need to "act fast," they believe it. You don't want to be on that list.

So the next time a broker tells you that you have to make a decision, tell him you'll get back to him—next year!

The typical investor believes he has to make his decisions quickly. And he thinks he could do much better if he only had more time to devote to his investments. He imagines the successful professional, glued to his computer screen, keeping an eye on the markets on a full-time basis, reacting to the news, taking his investments seriously.

Actually, nothing could be further from the truth. Serious Old Money investors barely follow the news and never react to it. They know that the really important trends take years to develop and then many years to play themselves out. You can take your time ... months ... years ... before making a decision. There is no need to feel rushed.

In fact, the more pressure you are under to make a decision, usually, the more likely you are to lose money. The investment pros want you to make a move. They don't know any better than you do whether investments will go up or down. But they know where they make money—on the churn. They earn commissions based on transactions, not on investment success.

Investment success happens by taking big positions in big trends and leaving them alone for a long time. The last bull market in U.S. stocks, for example, began in August 1982. You could have taken your time. Thought about it. And waited years before you were sure. The bull market ran for 25 years (depending on how you count it).

Likewise, the current bull market in gold began in 1998, with gold hitting a bottom of $268 per ounce. You could have bided your time for one ... two ... three years. Take it easy. Relax. There's no hurry. Big trends take time. And they pay off big, too, for people who are patient enough to let the market tell its story.

Now we're looking at opportunities we think will pay off over the next 30 years. We'll tell you more about them in the next chapter.

But 30 years is far too long for most people. That's the difference between serious Old Money and the rest of it. Old Money takes its time. And it uses the short-term, panicky nature of most investors in order to pick its opportunities.

For example, we've identified one very attractive opportunity. We could invest now and expect to earn three times the performance of the Dow, each year, over the next, say, 20 years. But what's the hurry? There's a better way. Most investors move in and out depending on the latest thing they've read or the most recent TV report. This sends prices rocketing up one month and falling down the next, even though the long-term, big-picture trend and the real value of the company remain unchanged.

Since we're in no hurry, we just wait for the short-termers to give us an irresistible entry price. Why buy at a reasonable price when you can wait for an absurd discount? We've seen good stocks sell for as little as two times earnings. Practically a giveaway. At that price, there is little downside risk left—and an upside that should multiply our wealth over the next two decades. That's an illustration of what we call "beta-plus." It gives you the benefits of being in the right market at the right time, plus you get the extra gain from buying the best investments at the best time.

THE KEY VARIABLE

But, first, let's put it in perspective. This chapter is about building—and keeping—a fortune by investing. Most people think you should invest one way to create a fortune and another way to protect it. That idea is wrong. Time, not the size of your portfolio, is the key variable. If you're interested in long-term, multigenerational wealth, you should use the same techniques whether you have little money or a lot.

Warren Buffett—along with countless others—has proven that you can build a fortune from investing. We don't recommend you try, for the reasons outlined in Chapter 3. But since the techniques for building and maintaining family wealth are essentially the same, you're going to have to know how investing works.

One problem with the typical investment fortune is that it is hard to hold on to. Because the next generation is not likely to have the rare investment skills (or luck) needed to build and maintain an investment fortune and because the conditions that created the fortune are likely to have changed. Buffett built his fortune by very cleverly investing in great companies at a great time. He studied the numbers. He studied the strategy. He studied the market. He met the management. When he was satisfied that all was in order, he made his bet.

We share Buffett's approach to stock picking. And we share his general philosophy. But only to a point. He's surely right about how to pick stocks. But picking stocks is not all there is to it.

The beauty of Buffett's approach is that it is simple. It is understandable. It makes sense. And it works. But what works for most investors won't work for us. And it is only one in a long list of things that won't work for long-term family wealth.

First, you can forget "get rich quick" schemes. They never work for anyone except the people who sell them. And even if they do occasionally make someone rich, you're better off thinking they never work.

Second, investing in something you don't understand will probably not work, either. There's no reason this is necessarily so. Anything priced in an efficient market should be properly priced, with about as many people who believe it is too cheap as believe it is too expensive. But markets are not necessarily efficient. And if there's any inefficiency in it at all, the ignorant investor will be the victim of it.

Do not invest in anything in which the fees and charges are significant—which is likely to be the case with things you don't understand. Derivative-based structured investment vehicles, for example, are things almost no one understands. And they are stuffed with fees—and fees on fees—because these are essentially confections of fee-saturated positions.

The further you get from the underlying investment, the more fees you pay. And the less desirable the investment becomes. Let's say, for example, that you have a woodworking shop. That is an asset. You can buy it or sell it. You can treat it as an investment.

But you can also "take it public." Now the fees begin. You have to pay lawyers, accountants, venture capital firms—a long list of professionals just to get your shares ready to sell to people you don't know. Then, the stockbrokers get a commission. And there are ongoing fees to meet reporting requirements and keep up with other necessities of maintaining listed company.

And then, you can take the shares and sell an option against them—more fees. And then, you take the option and you put it in a derivatives contract—along with any number of other positions. And then, you take the derivative and you structure it into a product that serves a particular purpose—or at least has a nice story to tell—you put on more fees, and you sell it to a person with more money than brains.

Fees and related investment costs are a nuisance to the ordinary investor. Over time, they are fatal to family fortune.

Here are some other things *not* to do:

- Do not invest in anything you see advertised.
- Do not put your money into anything you see on TV, unless it is presented in a negative light.

- Do not invest in anything that everyone considers safe or conservative.
- Do not make more than one major investment decision every five years.

That covers almost everything. But after eliminating all those possible investments, is there anything left?

What's left is the biggest, most profitable, and safest kind of investing. It works only for serious, very long-term-oriented investors who are willing to listen for the market to tell its story—and patient enough to let it come to the end. We want to invest in a long-term trend that is so basic, so unstoppable that you don't have to be especially lucky or particularly smart. We want to find the markets in which you don't have to be a genius to make money.

That's the difference between the usual investment approach and our approach. We're not looking for companies that will outperform the market in the next six months or next year. We're not looking for the next Microsoft, though we'd be happy to find it! We're looking for the fortune-making trends that will multiply our wealth by 10 times or more over a long period of time. We don't want to beat the market. We just don't want to get beaten by it.

BORN YESTERDAY

Probably the first thing you should understand is that the financial industry is largely parasitic. Of course, the pros are in it for the money. Nothing wrong with that. So are bricklayers and streetwalkers. But the bricklayers and streetwalkers, presumably, give you value for money and go on their way. Wall Street does not.

A parasite attaches himself to his host and drains him of his life's blood. He does not charge for services rendered and move on. Instead, he continues to levy his fees, commissions, spreads, and insidious charges. His interests are at odds with yours. The stockbroker, for example, wants to encourage you to buy and sell, when that is precisely what you shouldn't do. The fund manager, the dealmaker, and the structured products engineer all make their money by encouraging you to do things that are most often harmful to you. They want you to be a consumer, not a producer. They want you to spend your money on Wall Street products.

Wall Street sells dreams, hopes, and pie in the sky. And it's not cheap. Its labor force tends to dress well. Investment professionals often go to the best schools. They are smart. They are presentable. They wear deodorant to cover the smell of fear. They wear makeup to mask the moral strain of flogging hopeless investments to people who, when it comes to investments, were born yesterday. They are not bad people. They are not dumb people. Neither saints nor sinners, they are just like the rest of us. But their industry encourages a huge fraud: that they are there to help you make money. They are not. They are there to help themselves make money. How? By taking it from you.

The financial industry is very large and very profitable. The service it pretends to provide is helping to match worthwhile investment projects with the capital they need. The service it actually provides is separating fools from their money. And a lot of it.

In the early 2000s, the top 25 hedge fund managers earned more money than all of the CEOs of the entire S&P 500 put together.[1] In other words, these hedge fund managers made 20 times as much, on average, as the people who ran America's top businesses. Few executives earned more than $100 million in public companies; Wall Street had nine times as many people in that category. Hedge funds, generally, are a bad place for your money. As Warren Buffett explained, they are not an investment category; they are a compensation system.

But so are a lot of things on Wall Street. Every public offering—and every public company—involves large teams of people in "finance." There are the lawyers, market makers, underwriters, researchers, analysts, clerks, secretaries, administrators, brokers, dealers, speculators, and venture capitalists. Armies of them. They travel by limousine, helicopter, and private jet. They have offices in the gleaming towers of Lower Manhattan. They eat at the finest restaurants and typically have large, luxurious homes on Long Island or in Connecticut. They take summer vacations in Europe. In winter, they go skiing in Vail or Sun Valley. And they need to be paid. All of that money has to come from clients.

How can they coax so much money out of clients' pockets? They induce investors to levels of risk taking, transacting, spinning, leveraging, churning, and trading that are hallmarks of the financial industry. Of course, in any single transaction, you can look at the results. Some produce positive returns; some don't. But it is almost impossible for the amateur investor to know which transaction is a good one and which isn't. In most cases, Wall Street itself doesn't know. And hardly cares. It earns its money on transactions, not results.

Here's a simple rule: The more they want to sell you a financial product, the less you should want to buy it. In Paris, the best apartments never even show up in the realtors' windows. Instead, every one has a dozen admirers waiting for the owner to die. Buyers are usually friends or family with a special "in."

So it is in investing. The best deals are rarely presented to the public. They go to friends and family—the people who are "in the room" when the deal is done.

That's where you get the best assets at the lowest prices. The deals that end up in front of the public, however, are those that neither friends nor family wanted. When the insiders don't want an investment, watch out. But that's just what most investments are. They're the ones the really knowledgeable investors rejected. They are then sold to the public.

BORN THE DAY BEFORE YESTERDAY

We have a friend who came to us recently with an investment suggestion. Farmland in Brazil! Apparently, he said, you can make 20 percent on your money simply by buying productive land and renting it back to the local farmers.

But wait. How is that possible, we wanted to know? Why don't the local farmers buy it themselves? If they can make that kind of return, they should be able to get all the financing they need.

Good farmland, like good Paris apartments, is coveted by neighbors. When a productive farm comes on the market, it is usually snatched up immediately. But every once in a while, we are offered the opportunity to buy a farm. The first question, of course, should be "what's wrong with it?" Unless you're one of the neighbors, or unless you really know what you are doing, you have to assume that the neighbors are describing you as the "out-of-towner moron" who might buy it.

Occasionally, you see major efforts to market farmland to people in other countries. Expensive brochures are printed up. Sophisticated financial projections are made. Investors are permitted to see themselves making high returns on what seems like a can't-lose proposition. After all, the world needs more food! Sometimes investors are even told that their earnings are "guaranteed." What's more, they don't have to do anything. The organizer guarantees to lease back the land and operate the farm for you.

Wow, you say. What a great deal! Then, the next thought should be a question:

"How come such a great deal is being offered to me?"

The answer comes back polished and bright, from frequent handling: because the owner doesn't have enough capital. You've got him at your mercy. He needs foreign investors!

Most likely, the deal is a bad one. Capital is footloose. It wanders the world, always looking for a safe, productive home. It doesn't miss much. And local investors, like insiders everywhere, rarely pass on a good opportunity to strangers.

DESILUSIONADO

But you never know. And there are special circumstances in which the insiders don't take up a good investment. We are all moody. And sometimes we get in such a funk we don't see things for what they are actually worth. At least, that was our thinking when we bought our ranch in Argentina. It is in a desolate corner of the country. It had been for sale for years. No one wanted it. All the neighbors had rejected it. Heck, we discovered later that even the knowledgeable foreigners had turned it down. There were several active buyers in the valley; none wanted this place. Too remote. Too dry. Too hard to manage. Too unproductive.

"Aha!" we told ourselves. "They don't see the value. OK, it's not a great ranch from a productive standpoint. The cows are too skinny. The climate is too harsh. It's too far from the markets. But, boy, what views! Someday, people will pay big money for those views."

We imagined ourselves having discovered what others had missed. This might not be the greatest ranch in the world, but what a great place to come to visit. If we ever wanted to sell, we were sure we could poke some other gringo in the eye for at least as much as we paid.

It was then we learned the meaning of the word *ilusionado* in Spanish. Or more precisely, *desilusionado*. We had been *ilusionado* when we bought. Later, we were *desilusionado*.

It turned out that everyone was right. The ranch is too far, too high, too dry, and almost impossible to manage.

Our ranch is so dry that one day, cattlemen came up from the pampas and asked: "What do your cattle eat?"

We told them that we're creating a new breed of low-fat cow we call "sand-fed beef."

They laughed and shook their heads.

And then we wondered if we'd lose the farm altogether. A group of locals—descended, they said, from the original tribes who owned the place—tried to take it over! They claimed it had been stolen from their ancestors 500 years before. They wanted it back!

One challenge after another. But we've held on.

It's still in our hands. Still losing money. And still a pleasure to visit.

What was the point of that little anecdote?

Just that we all become *ilusionado* from time to time. We want to believe the sales pitches. We want to believe we see an angle others have missed.

We're usually wrong.

The best investment is one that no one tries to sell you. And that no salesman represents. Generally, you want to be the neighbor who buys the good bottomland, the person who knows more about it than any other buyer and who realizes what the value really is. That's why you want to be in business—and the best thing to buy is the thing that expands and improves your business, the thing you understand better than anyone.

But there are times when the neighbors really don't see the value in an investment. Sometimes they have been discouraged by losses. Sometimes they have lost faith. And sometimes they are wrong. Sometimes the whole market fails to see the real value in an investment. Sometimes people are just too *desilusionado*.

Remember, market psychology is often bipolar. Sometimes it is manic. Sometimes it is depressive.

Another simple rule: When it is depressive, buy. When it is manic, sell. You want to buy what no one tries to sell you from buyers who are completely discouraged. You want to buy things that mark you as a bit of a nut. Friends look at you with pity. Relatives doubt your sanity. And when you're really buying a good investment, you wonder yourself.

STAY AWAY FROM "CONSERVATIVE" INVESTMENTS

Successful Old Money does not invest the way most people expect it to. To put it another way, if you put Old Money into "conservative" investments, pretty soon it will be Dead Money.

Yet smart, professional wealth managers will tell you to do just that. Why? Because wealth managers are typically crowd followers. And parasites. And if you're trying to hold onto money over more than one generation, you can't afford either.

You can follow the crowd and make money for a year, two years, maybe even 20 years. But the crowd goes over a cliff about once in a generation. If you're trying to hold on to money for more than a generation, crowd following won't do it.

An investor who lived through the entire twentieth century probably would have gone broke at least three times. Maybe more. Let's begin by assuming he dodged the crash of 1920–1921 and the depression that followed. It was over quickly and stocks soared. He learned to stick with stocks. But then came the crash of 1929. It almost certainly wiped him out. Experience had shown him that stocks always went up, that they were a "safe, conservative" place to leave your money. That was the lesson of the 1920s boom. And hadn't they come back fast from the 1920–1921 bust?

But this time, they didn't come back fast. This time, something had changed. Now the government was actively managing the economy. After 1929, stocks waggled around for the next 10 to 15 years. Our typical investor learned another lesson: Bonds are more reliable than stocks. He switched his investments to U.S. bonds. Everybody said it was a good move, especially the pros. While stocks had been going down, bonds had been going up. They were unquestionably the "safe, conservative investment" of the postwar period. By 1949, they were higher than ever. But why shouldn't they be? The U.S. government was good for the money. It, and the U.S. economy behind it, were the strongest financial institutions on the planet. All you had to do was to buy bonds and let time make you rich.

Thus did the fellow in search of the "safe, conservative" ship run aground again. The next 30 years proved a disaster to the bond market. By the early 1980s, bond prices had collapsed and long-term U.S. Treasuries yielded more than 15 percent; the Fed's key rate was at 19 percent. Consumer price inflation hit 13 percent.

It was then that the wealth advisers began to refer to U.S. Treasuries as "certificates of guaranteed confiscation." Stay away from them, they all said. And stocks had not done much better; in fact, *Business Week* magazine said that the days of stocks were over. "The Death of Equities," proclaimed an August 1979 cover. What was left? The professionals looked elsewhere for a "safe, conservative" investment. And what did they find? Gold.

Both gold and commodities had been driven up by the trends of the 1970s. They were widely regarded as a secure refuge from inflation. We recall a popular investment adviser in the late 1970s telling a crowd of thousands that gold was headed to $5,000 per ounce! It was the only safe place for your money, he said. Everything else would be wiped out by inflation, he maintained.

But again, the safe, conservative investment turned out to be catastrophic. In 1979, Paul Volcker took the job of head of the U.S. Federal Reserve system. He vowed to stop inflation. At first, investors didn't believe him. They continued to sell bonds and buy gold. But "Tall Paul" meant business. By the summer of 1983, inflation was going down and bonds were going up. Those "certificates of guaranteed confiscation" actually outperformed all other major assets categories over the next 27 years. As interest rates came down, bonds went up. As for gold, from over $800 at the beginning of the 1980s, gold lost more than $500 over the next 18 years. Adjusted for inflation, it lost about 80 percent. Far from being a refuge, gold turned out to be a speculation—and a bad one.

Meanwhile, researchers were able to *prove* that stocks were not any riskier than bonds and that you got paid a "risk premium" for owning stocks without actually taking on any additional risk.

This idea was common knowledge in the 1990s, leading investors to their next ditch. While gold went down, investors piled into stocks as never before. By 1999, the stock market had reached an all-time high, and investors believed that they could not lose money by buying stocks. *Stocks for the Long Run* was the title of a popular book. *Dow 36,000* was another.

So what happened? Well, in 2000, the tech sector crashed, and over the next 10 years, the stock market had its worst decade since the 1930s—with negative real returns for the 10-year period.

By the end of the twentieth century, "safe, conservative" investments had blown up three times. Stocks went bust in 1929. Bonds went bad after World War II. And gold went bust after 1983. And then, at the end of the century, stocks went bust again—with no gain to stock market investors over the last 11 years.

So what do wealth advisors tell the rich to do now? What are the "safe, conservative" investments favored by the pros?

U.S. Treasury bonds! And who knows? While the Great Correction drags along, bonds may remain a good investment. For six months. For a year. Maybe even five years. But if your goal is to build and protect family wealth over longer than a single generation, bonds will be a disaster. Sometime in the years ahead, they will blow up. (More in Chapter 6.) If you're trying to build or protect a family fortune, stay away.

You see, Old Money is not like other money. It shouldn't try to be. Most people don't have any money. People who have money are different by definition. If you want to have money, you have to do things differently. It's that simple. Especially if you want to have it for longer than a single generation. Don't follow the crowd. Don't take the advice of people who make money by getting you to follow the crowd.

DON'T CHASE ALPHA

Most people think the secret to making money by investing is to find the stock that will go up. They all want to be an alpha investor, the big man on campus who put his money into Google when it opened for business or the guy who bought Starbucks went it went public in 1992. That's the whole game, they believe—seeking alpha.

"Alpha" is what they call the above-market gains you can get by selecting the right stocks. But the trouble with alpha is that it is unreliable. Of course, if picking stocks that go up were easy, everyone would do it. And if there were some formula that made it possible, everyone would follow it. Instead, the typical experience is mixed. You choose one stock that goes up. Then you choose two that don't. And then you get a real nightmare stock and you're wiped out. Over the long run—by definition and observation—most alpha-seeking investors cannot beat the market averages. And as we've seen, the market averages are not that high—not in real terms.

But what choice do you have? You're a typical investor. You've got 10 years to build up a small pile of savings for a retirement fund. You do your homework. You take your chances. You hope to get lucky.

If you did that for a short time, you might come out OK. If you happen to be in a bull market, the rising tide will raise your boat. Sometimes you'll beat the market. Sometimes the market will beat you. Sometimes you'd get a big run-up in a bull market. Sometimes a bear market takes you back down again. Provided you didn't make any major mistakes, you'll get what everyone else gets, more or less, over the long term. But you don't have the long term. You can't get average, long-term performance. You get only a piece of it, and you hope it will be the good piece.

A serious family, with a serious long-term wealth strategy, on the other hand, can't do that, for a number of reasons. First, the obvious: It knows that chasing alpha will give it only average returns over time. It knows that average, long-term returns are very small. As discussed in Chapter 3, it wants to do better than that.

Not only that, it knows it *must* do better than that. Otherwise, the money will disappear. Why? Because after taxes and a genuine adjustment for inflation, the real return of the stock market, over time, is trivial. And there are always errors, setbacks, taxes, and nasty surprises that cost you money. Mistakes and accidents are inevitable; the Old Money family needs to aim for a higher rate of capital growth to offset unavoidable calamities.

How to do it? The secret is to use the one big advantage of very long-term investors: time itself.

Instead of chasing alpha, successful multigenerational investors go after "beta."

In the long run, it's beta that makes fortunes, not alpha. Every study proves it.

Put simply, asset allocation is how serious investors think about investing. This approach is backed up by historical data. Two separate studies—one by Brinson, Hood, and Gilbert in 1986, and another by Ibbotson and Kaplan in 2000—showed that professional fund managers' asset allocation decisions are responsible for nearly 100 percent of returns.

In the first study, which was published in the *Financial Analysts Journal*, the authors looked at the asset allocation of 91 large pension funds between 1974 and 1983. To find out how much asset allocation mattered, they replaced the funds' cash, bond, and stock allocations with corresponding indexes.

The results were startling. The quarterly index returns—without a single stock or bond pick—did better than the funds' actual returns. And the correlation between the index returns and the returns that came from stock picking was 96.7 percent.[2]

The second study appeared in the same peer-reviewed journal. The study authors looked at the 10-year returns of 94 balanced mutual funds (that involved active stock picking) versus the corresponding index returns. Again, the actual returns failed to do better than the index (asset allocation only) returns. And according to this second study, asset allocation explained virtually 100 percent of the funds' returns.[3]

Now, these studies didn't look at any particular style of fund—just ones that were "actively managed." For our purposes here, these studies show that, contrary to what most stock market gurus would have you believe, a big part of investing success comes down to being in the right place at the right time. Being in the right place at the right time is much more likely to pay off than being smart enough to find just the right stock to buy.

A beta strategy is completely different from an alpha strategy. Instead of trying to beat the market, you make the market your friend. It's not your enemy. You don't try to beat it; you just want to join it. And go along with it.

150 TIMES YOUR MONEY IN 40 YEARS

Here's an idealized example of how it works: You could have multiplied your money 150 times or more just by making three simple investment decisions in the last 40 years. And two of the decisions were exactly the same! Note that these are not alpha-chasing decisions. These are beta decisions, choosing which market you want to be in and waiting until the best possible time to get in.

Let's go back and look at that period from 1970 to the present again. This time, we will look at in terms of the opportunities it presented, rather than the risks and blowups investors suffered. You remember that Richard Nixon cut the dollar's link to gold in 1971? It didn't take much imagination to see what would happen next. Inflation rates would probably increase, and they would inevitably drive up the price of gold.

So imagine that you started in the early 1970s with $10,000. There was no hurry; you had years of opportunity to buy gold at a low price. Just to keep the math simple, we'll say you paid about $50 per ounce.

By the end of the 1970s, your gold was shooting over $500 per ounce. You made 10 times your money. You were not sure what to do. You could not know what would happen next. But you read the paper. Paul Volcker, head of the Federal Reserve, vowed to crush inflation. He seemed serious. And by the early 1980s, it was beginning to look as if he might win his battle against rising consumer prices.

Again, you didn't have to have a PhD in economics to realize that falling inflation rates wouldn't be good for gold. However, they'd be very good for stocks or bonds. So you made your second decision. You sold the gold and put the money into the stock market. Gold rose over $800, but let's say you locked in your sale at $500—a "10 bagger," as they say. Again, you had plenty of time to make your move. The price of gold stayed over $500 from the end of 1979 until well into 1981.

The stock market took its sweet time, too. But that's the way beta investing goes. One decision. Lots of waiting. The Dow lollygagged around for five years after 1980 before it hit 1,500. So, let's say you waited five years and bought at 1,500. Then you waited again. Gradually, the Dow rose. And rose. And rose.

By the end of the 1990s, the Dow rose over 10,000. By January 2000, it was over 11,000. Then there were so many warning bells ringing you would have had to be deaf not to hear them. The Dow was up 1,000 percent. People were starting dot-com businesses with nothing. No business plans. No sales. No profits. They were making millions selling them to investors. Something had to give.

What should you have done? You should have made your third investment decision in 30 years. You should have sold stocks and bought gold again. Stocks were overbought. Gold was oversold. Adjusting for inflation, gold was down 80 percent to 90 percent from its 1980 high. Stocks were up about five times, inflation adjusted, from their 1980s low.

Had you done that, you would have multiplied your money at least another five times. Your original $10,000 would have become $300,000 by 2000. Then, in gold since, you would have multiplied your money another five times—for $1,500,000.

We want to emphasize that this is very slow investing. You don't have to make any fast decisions. All those in this example could have been made over many months or many years. You don't really have to do much guesswork, in other words. You can wait and let the markets tell you what is really going on.

And even if you miss a signal now and then, it is not necessarily fatal. Say you missed the clanging bells in 2000s. You just held your stocks. In fact, after a brief drop, they continued to go up. The Dow eventually rose to over 15,000, giving you a total of about $500,000 at the top. Not too shabby, right?

That's what beta investing can do for you. That's what the smart money, the Old Money, the family money does.

In any event, that's what we try to do in our family office.

So far, we have touched on several things the rich do differently. We have claimed that they do not buy "safe, conservative" investments. In fact, they buy what the wealth managers consider the least safe and least conservative investments. And they try to do so at the moment the pros consider them at the very height of their riskiness.

We also noted that they do not chase alpha. Instead, they try to ride along with beta.

And if they follow the professional wealth managers' advice, it is usually only in the inverse. When Wall Street is actively pushing an investment, it is usually something you want to sell, not buy.

As also mentioned, they worry more about asset allocation than asset selection (another way of focusing on beta, rather than alpha).

Many find it curious, too, that serious Old Money families are more concerned about minimizing fees and costs than ordinary investors with a lot less money. Old Money does not worry about day-to-day, quarter-to-quarter, or even annual results. It does not use sophisticated investment tools or complicated techniques. It especially eschews financial products targeted at high-net-worth individuals, for these financial products are typically those with the most built-in, compounded fees.

THE BETA PERSONALITY

But let's dig deeper into the alpha-beta question. It's essential to understanding the mentality of the long-term, Old Money investor. Alpha is all about winning. The alpha male is the leader, the hero, the winner. It's hard to resist wanting to be the alpha investor. The personality is everywhere. He's the big man on campus. He's got the big wheels and the big biceps when he is young. When he's older, he's got the big bank account.

In business, he wants to win—and win big. And fast. He dreams of starting a company or a hedge fund, making a big score, and retiring before he is 40. How? By outperforming his peers, by winning.

In investments, he likes systems, secrets, hot tips, new technology—anything that will help him make money fast. He's a winner in whatever he does. And he keeps score!

But long-term family investing is a different matter. We don't care about winning. We don't care about finding the stock that doubles, triples, or goes to the moon. We don't want to win. Instead, we want to succeed. Right here on Planet Earth.

Success means not getting distracted by short-term opportunities. It means avoiding getting involved in extraneous investments, businesses, gambles, projects—even when it looks as if you could win at them. It means seeing targets of opportunities and ignoring them. It means having a strategy that can take you where you want to go, and sticking with it, even when it seems that it might be much more fun—and more rewarding—to do something else. Our aim is not to get more profit than the next fellow. It's not about being right while others are wrong. And it's not even about having more money in our account at the end of the month or the end of the year.

It's success we're after, not victory. And success for the family beta investor means taking the time to listen to the market's story. Giving it time to tell its story. Letting it explain itself before you take a major position.

ALPHA MATTERS, TOO

There are only three main variables:

- Your choice of beta—your asset allocations.
- The number of years you are invested.
- Your rate of return per year.

We have discussed beta. Time is not worth discussing; it is immutable. So how can you boost your rate of return? We've seen fund managers consistently beat their indexes—outperforming their beta—over a period of 20 years by as much as 100 percent per year. Assuming he was in the right place, the right market, the right beta, this extra performance would give him a spectacular advantage. This is what we call "beta plus."

After displaying so much apparent contempt for it, we're a little embarrassed to be offering alpha-hunting advice. But for our money, we prefer a very old-fashioned, deep-value approach.

One of our partners has $375 million in his family office investment pool. He's beaten the market by an average of 5.32 percent per year by using a strict value approach to investing. His approach is very simple. He buys companies, not stocks.

Companies are real businesses with real assets and real cash flows. Stocks are claims on a piece of those assets and cash flows. They are *not* just blips on a computer screen. Those assets and cash flows have a value. So the stock also has a value. *And that value is almost always different to the traded stock price on a given day.* Underlying *value* doesn't change much or often. But the traded stock *price* changes every day, and often by a large amount. The secret to successful value investing is to buy stocks when the *price* is significantly below the *value*.

In this sense, short-term stock price volatility is your friend, not your enemy. When traded prices are well above value, you sell and move into better opportunities or cash. When prices are well below value, you buy the stock. No matter what happens to stock prices in the short run, if you buy below fair value, you should make healthy profits in the long run.

The key advantage that a family has is time. While others need to invest for a payoff of 5 or 10 years down the line, we can wait, even for generations, if need be. So we can take advantage of the "miracle" of compounding in a way others can't. We can wait for compounding to work its magic.

The secret to compounding is that, over time, even small incremental gains can produce huge results, with the biggest gains at the end.

Of course, the other side of the coin is that little expenses add up, too. Time is our friend. And also our enemy. Whatever you gain from higher returns, you lose if you allow your costs—such as management fees—to rise. That's why we need to be fanatical cost controllers, as well as fanatical increment-chasing investors.

You are not likely to beat the market in the short run. We accept that as a given. Most investors shouldn't even try. They'll only be carried into fads and overpriced Wall Street favorites.

And most investors don't have the time to benefit from long-term trends. But we do. And since we can compound our results over a long time, even if the improvement is only marginal, it is still well worthwhile.

CAPITAL GAINS, NOT INCOME

Even if you are investing for only 20 years, you should beware of the standard advice. It would have you putting your money into even more bonds and other income investments 10 years before that. So that's roughly an entire generation stuck in supposedly "safe" investments. Your grandchildren will have been born and started their own families over that kind of time span.

That's a long time to be parking your money in low-return investments. If you're planning to pass your money on to the next generation, they'll be getting a lot less as a result.

Let's assume for a moment that your investment strategy ends up making 15 percent per year on average over time, before taxes, but after costs. This is not a target or a prediction; it's just an example (provided to us by our chief strategist, Robert Marstrand). Profits are split 50-50 between income (dividends) and capital gains. Income is taxed at 40 percent, and capital gains are taxed at 20 percent. So the blended tax rate is 30 percent.

In this case, taxed returns would be 10.5 percent per year. Over 30 years, with compounding (profits on the profits), our money would multiply 20 times, or up 1,899 percent. If the profits grew without tax—for example, in a pension account or if you are a tax exile—the money would multiply over 66 times, or up 6,521 percent. (The difference between these two results is a reminder of how important it is to plan your taxes. A little money saved now can be worth a lot more in the future, thanks to the compounding of investment returns.)

Now let's assume that the money is moved to a standard retirement portfolio that is 80 percent bonds and 20 percent blue-chip stocks. The bonds return 5 percent per year before tax, all as coupon income taxed at 40 percent. So the net bond return is 3 percent. The high-yielding stocks pay an average 4 percent in dividends and also make 4 percent in capital gains, to give 8 percent total. Dividends are taxed as income at 40 percent and capital gains are taxed at 20 percent, to give net stock returns of 5.6 percent per year.

So the 80/20 bond/blue-chip portfolio returns 3.52 percent after tax. If the investments are untaxed, then the return would be 5.6 percent. (I realize dividends are taxed at a lower rate than earned income in the United States. But this may not always be the case. And this is only an illustration. The conclusions that I come to are unchanged.)

A return of 3.52 percent after tax over 30 years works out at 2.82 times the original investment—or a 182 percent gain. Untaxed returns at 5.6 percent per year would be 5.13 times your money—a 413 percent gain.

So 30-year taxed profits under the family office strategy were an estimated 1,899 percent. But under the "low-risk" strategy, they were an estimated 182 percent. Cutting the annual after-tax profit from 10.5 percent to 3.52 percent is a reduction of two-thirds. But over 30 years, it's a reduction of over 90 percent—all because of the loss of compounding.

After inflation, the "low-risk" strategy will most likely lose money, especially if inflation increases, as we believe it will. This is because the value of the bond portfolio will take a hammering. There is nothing "low risk" about that.

The immediate problems in the income portfolio are twofold. The returns are lower, and the tax rate is higher. So you get a double hit to long-term returns. Your profits are lower, and your profits on the profits are *much* lower.

Still, you may still need to live off your investments. But to do this you don't need to have low-return income investments. You just need profits. Each year, you could make sure you have a minimum of, say, 5 percent of all your money in cash. If you are very wealthy or spend little, the figure might be less.

That cash would cover your expenses for the coming year. When that is all used up, you sell just a little of your investment portfolio to generate some more cash. That way, most of your money stays at work generating higher returns.

Income is usually taxed at higher rates than capital gains. So you may think this is just a tax effect. But even if the tax rates were identical, capital gains would still beat income over time. Yet, again, this is about the power of compounding.

Here is another example to illustrate the point. Say you have two investments that give the exact same pretax return but in different ways. The first investment—let's call it the "Payout"—gives you a 10 percent dividend every year and no capital gains. The second investment—let's call it the "Reinvest"—gives you no dividend, but 10 percent capital gains every year. The pretax return to you is the same in both cases. But the way you get it is different.

Now to keep things simple, let's assume dividends and capital gains attract the same tax of 40 percent. And let's say you put $100 into the Payout and another $100 in the Reinvest and hold on to them for 30 years. You're a long-term value investor, both look cheap, and you want to buy and hold for the long run.

After one year, you get $10 in dividends from the Payout. You pay $4 in tax, giving you $6 net income, which you use to buy more Payout stock. You keep this up for 30 years, and at the end, you sell all your Payout stock. There have been no capital gains. You get back $574, with no more tax to pay. Your profit is $474.

The Reinvest doesn't pay dividends, but the stock price goes up 10 percent per year. So after one year, your $100 investment is worth $110. You stick with it for 30 years, adding 10 percent per year. At the end of those 30 years it's worth $1,745. Then you sell it. But you have to pay tax at 40 percent on the rise in value. Your profit was $1,645. So your tax bill will be $658. This leaves you with $1,087 and a profit of $987.

What has happened here? Your profit from the Reinvest is more than double your profit from the Payout. How can two investments that both return 10 percent per year give such different results after 30 years?

The reason is that profits from the Reinvest have initially grown tax free and been taxed only once at the end of the 30 years. Profits from the Payout have been taxed every year because you received income. In other words, the *profits on the profits* were bigger for the Reinvest. This is all to do with the power of compounding. By pushing back the day when you had to pay taxes, you have increased your total gains.

This gives yet another reason not to go into the "low-risk" income portfolio as you get older: Your gross profits will be lower. Your taxed profits will be lower, too. And your taxes will be paid earlier—another big hit to long-term returns. Over the 20 or 30 years that you might be in this strategy, it makes a major difference.

LET MR. MARKET TELL HIS STORY

One of the convenient fibs of the last half-century was that there was no story. Market movements were said to have been completely random and completely unpredictable. There was no point in trying to step back and understand the direction of the market or to see the big picture. There was no picture to see. As Peter Lynch put it, if you spent 13 minutes per year thinking about the big picture, you wasted 10 minutes.

Lynch got lucky. He was a stock picker when stocks were enjoying one of the greatest booms in history. His view might have changed if he had been picking stocks when they were going down.

But Lynch and stock picking were popular. So people stopped looking for the story. They weren't interested. It was as if they were on a train, playing cards. They were all having such a good time that nobody bothered to look at what was up the tracks. Why spoil the party? If you had joined the party in 1980, you could have enjoyed yourself for 20 years without trouble. Two decades' worth of investors could have made money without looking out the window. The bull market in stocks continued, year after year. You could have been a winner from the time you began investing at 35 to the time you reached 55. And by 1999, you were surely convinced that the train was solid, safe, and bound for glory.

That was when it paid to look out the window—especially if you were in tech stocks and getting ready for retirement!

The efficient market hypothesis, as it is known, was a convenient thing to believe; it allowed the financial industry—fund managers, wealth advisers, private client counselors—to "model" investment strategies based on past data. If, for example, you believe the price of oil bumps around without any underlying rhyme or reason, you can just substitute volatility for risk. You can look at what the price of oil has done in the past. Then, you assume (*big* assumption) that the price will continue to bump around more or less as it always has.

The academics had convenient digital records going back, say, only 20 years. So they used what they had. If they saw that the price of oil, for example, had varied from $9 to $35, they figured they had a range of possible "risk," with the extremes on each end. Then they could do all manner of mathematics to determine the likelihood of various movements in between.

Peak oil? The debasement of the dollar? Rise of the emerging markets? End of the world? What difference did they make? Price movements were supposed to be random. Like lottery numbers. There was no point in looking for deep patterns.

Jeffrey Snider describes why confusing volatility with real risk is a big mistake:

> Conventional thinking says that if a standard deviation is high, describing a "volatile" market or stock, then the chance of losing money is also high. . . . Conversely, low measures of volatility are thought to signify less risk. . . .
>
> We can compare two very different market periods to see if the common measures of risk/volatility are sufficient. Using the S&P 500 as a market proxy, in Time Period 1, the one-year standard deviation of weekly returns is 54 index points and the VIX index (a measure of implied volatility derived from stock options) is 16.67.
>
> Time Period 2 shows a much more volatile market: the one-year standard deviation of weekly returns is 234 index points and the VIX is far higher at 49.68.
>
> By the traditional measures of risk, Time Period 1 is far less risky than Time Period 2. The problem is that Time Period 1 is Oct. 8, 2007, and Time Period 2 is March 9, 2009.
>
> Traditional risk measures are backward looking and therefore assume that the future will look like the past. In the most common

statistical expressions, the problem is far worse; it is assumed that the near future will look like the recent past. In both the time periods above, the near future looked nothing like the recent past.[4]

Treating risk as though it were just a mathematical expression of the recent past permitted the modern wealth adviser to tell his client that he could get predictable returns by mixing and matching various investments according to their historical volatility and gains. If Japanese industrial stocks always went down when the price of oil went up, for example, you were supposed to be able to eliminate "risk" by matching them up. Put together the right combination of equities, bonds, foreign stocks and so forth and the investor could expect a steady rate of return, guaranteed by standard deviations and statistical probabilities that sounded rather impressive. In other words, the young business school grad made it sound like the money was in the bag.

Of course, the money wasn't in the bag at all. The pros were just guessing. Not only that, it was the worst kind of guesswork, because it pretended to be scientific.

The 20 years from 1980 to 2000 were exceptional. They were some of the best years in market history. These were the years after Paul Volcker tamed inflation and saved the U.S.-dollar-based monetary system. Stocks rose. Bonds rose. The Soviet Union collapsed. The Chinese turned to capitalism. Oil prices were low. The price of credit fell. Naturally, the markets reflected all this "good news." (Even so, an article in *Barron's* titled "The Money Paradox" tells us that in the 20 years ending in 2008, the average stock fund investor earned only 1.9 percent per year![5])

In particular, the falling price of credit meant that even bad investments could be refinanced at lower interest rates. The financial "accident rate" went way down, since errors were hidden—temporarily—under cheaper financing. Gradually, people came to expect no accidents at all—and certainly not in government debt.

DON'T TAKE A BIG LOSS

There's another very important reason to let the market tell its story. Family money must last through more than a single bull market. We want money that will last for generations. And remember, it's not enough to stay in the same place. You can't stay in the same place. Because the world moves. Try to remain in the same place and you will be left behind. You need to enlarge your assets to keep up with it—and to offset the inevitable setbacks. You can't afford to climb up the mountain and then climb down again. You've got to get somewhere.

And you can't afford to gamble, either. If you have a million dollars and you judge the chance of a big run-up in the cotton market as 50/50, you can put your whole wad on cotton—either you'll have a lot more money or you'll have nothing.

A speculator or a gambler might be perfectly happy to take that bet. We can't. We know that building a family fortune (even a very small one) is a long, hard process. We can't afford to lose it. Our goal is to succeed, not to win. And we succeed by respecting the first rule: Don't Take a Big Loss.

You don't take a big loss because you can't recover from it. As a custodian of Old Money or a builder of it, you have to make sure you do not bet the farm on anything. You also have to make sure you keep your eyes and ears open, letting the markets tell their story. The riverboat gamblers may have their eyes down on the table, waiting for the next ace to come up. But you have to put your head out the window and see where the boat is going.

The problem with "conservative" investments is that they usually aren't. The markets work their perverse magic to turn everything on its head. That which is most risky, as judged by the majority of investors, is actually the most safe. That which is supposed to be the most safe actually carries the most risk. Risk is not measured properly by volatility. It can be understood at all only by understanding the big picture—by listening to Mr. Market tell his story.

Where is the right place to be? When?

We use the word "beta" in the broadest possible way. Imagine, for example, that you are on the *Titanic* and that you just won big at the card tables when you feel the ship shudder. Or imagine that you are in Russia in 1910. At the time, the Russian economy was booming. After the U.S. and Germany, Russia was the place to be. By some measures, it even looked as though Russia could surpass all of its rivals.

So what should you do? Look for the best Russian bond, the fastest-growing Russian company, the best deal on the Russian stock exchange? Order another bottle of champagne from the waiter on the *Titanic*?

Or imagine that you lived in Germany in 1937. Finally, the country seemed to be pulling itself together. The Depression, the hyperinflation, the nationwide strikes, and Bolshevik lawlessness were in the past.

Germany's centrally planned, expertly managed economy, with that clever Mr. Hitler at the top, was the wave of the future; everyone said so.

What should you do? Buy property in Berlin? Build a factory in Dresden?

Oh, but that's ancient history. Let's come forward to Argentina in 2000. No more inflation; now the Argentine peso is tied to the dollar! The country is booming, except for the pesky problem of too much debt. What to do? Seek alpha? Try to find the best-performing Argentine stock?

And here we are in the United States in 2012. And you have a similar question to ask yourself. Should you be seeking alpha? Or something else completely? Should you be in bonds or stocks? Should you be in cash or gold? Should you be in the United States? You can answer those questions only by listening to the market tell its story.

There was no point in hanging around St. Petersburg in 1917, trying to find the very best investment opportunity. It was time to raise your head. Look around. Listen. And get the hell out. In just a few months, the Russian Revolution would bring the Bolsheviks to power. Forget about your money; you'd be lucky to get out with your life!

Similarly, Germany in the late 1930s was dynamic and interesting. It had many of the world's finest scholars, philosophers, scientists, musicians, and writers. Whether you were looking for beer or strudel, it was hard to beat. But it was not the best place to be hunting for the best long-term investment—especially if you were Jewish or belonged to one of many other "undesirable" groups. In 1939, World War II began. Before it was over, practically every major German city had been pulverized by bombs, and about a third of the country was seized by the Soviets. East Germany wasn't reunited with West Germany until 40 years later.

Imagine that you were in China in the late 1940s. The Maoists chased the nationalists under Chiang Kai-shek from the mainland to Taiwan. A significant number of Chinese went with him. Some few left the Far East altogether and moved to North America. What happened to them all? Those who remained in China suffered four decades of misery, including famines, poverty, Great Leaps, Cultural Revolutions, gray jackets, one-child policies, and quasi-enslavement. Those who moved to the United States and Canada enjoyed the highest standards of living in the world, with complete freedom of movement.

Which would you prefer?

The point is, sometimes it pays to stop chasing alpha—the next deal, the next stock, the next triumph—and step back and look at the big picture. It can affect not only your life but the lives of your children and grandchildren. Beta is a big question, much bigger than just the question about whether to switch from stocks to bonds. It is an essential question. Yet it is the question very few investors bother to ask.

THE RESOURCE ADVANTAGE

Here's a quandary for you:

Americans have enjoyed the land of milk and honey for more than 300 years. But in the past 10 years, the upward slant of progress has leveled out. This could be just a simple setback in an otherwise unblemished history of material success. It could be a fluke. It could be a blip. Or it could be more than that. It could mean that the advantages bestowed on previous generations of Americans have been tapped out. From here on out, Americans may have to fight for every bit of wealth—on equal terms with the rest of the world. Or even at a competitive disadvantage.

Let's look at why that might be.

First, Americans had a huge resource advantage. Arriving in the new world, they found forests that had never been touched by the saw, rich earth that had never been turned by the plow, native peoples who had never been murdered or exploited. Each time the land wore out or got crowded, they picked up stakes and moved West.

Abraham Lincoln described why his family left Kentucky for Illinois: Kentucky had gotten crowded and, he explained, "you could hardly go 10 miles in any direction without seeing the smoke from a neighbor's campfire."

This three-century push to the West gave American settlers an expansive sense of optimism. The further they went, the greater the wonders they discovered. From sea to shining sea, there were mountains and forests—land, land, land—and then, when they finally got to the shining sea on the West Coast, they found a remarkable country where almost everything would grow. They found valleys they could plant and waves they could surf.

That was the story of the United States from the seventeenth century to the end of the nineteenth and into the twentieth century, too. Onward and upward—better and better, year after year.

Now, the country is still thinly populated, compared with other parts of the world. But with 300 million people, it is no longer virgin territory. Neither are its land nor its water as limitless as they once appeared. Even its human resources are slowing and aging. Immigration into the United States is at a 20-year low. The population is growing at the slowest rate since before the Baby Boomers were born.

Wood and coal powered the first phase of U.S. growth and expansion. Wood was the fuel of choice in the seventeenth and eighteenth centuries. America had it. More trees than you could cut. More wood than you could burn. The Old World did not. The forests of Europe had been reduced by centuries of cutting. The country side was relatively crowded. It needed farmland, not woodland.

Then came coal and oil. Discovered commercially in Pennsylvania, oil packed much more energy into an even more dense and convenient form. Refine it a bit and you could put it in a tank and it would run directly into the burner—no shoveling, sawing, or toting necessary.

Oil made America what it was. Pumped from fields in Texas, refined at plants in New Jersey, America's high-octane fuels ruled the world.

We recall driving to from Maryland to New Mexico in the early 1970s. For some reason, there was a price war being waged along Route 66. One station advertised gasoline at 28 cents per gallon. Another went down to 24 cents. And they washed your windshield, too.

Today, the typical working man in America pays about 17 times as much for gasoline. Adjusted for changes in the Consumer Price Index, he pays about five or six times as much. In real terms, Americans pay more of their incomes for gasoline than they did in the early 1970s—much more.

AMERICA DEPENDS ON CHEAP OIL

Cheap oil may have sealed the success of the United States. It certainly determined the look and the makeup of modern America. Suburbs are dependent on automobiles and trucks—which run on oil. The vast build-out in Las Vegas, Phoenix, Miami, and other heat-plagued areas was possible only because oil-fired generators allowed for electrical power to cool buildings. The distant suburbs made sense only as long as you could get into town without spending too much on energy.

The United States was the world's leading oil exporter, up to 1974. But now Americans buy energy at the world price, just like everybody else. And the price is rising. U.S. consumers compete with consumers all over the globe, including those in emerging markets. Fifty years ago, the Chinese, the Russians, the Indonesians, Latin Americans, and Africans barely used any oil at all. But now they're in the market— billions of them—bidding for oil. The price of petroleum has risen from just $25 per barrel as recently as eight years ago, to about $100 per barrel today. And while the price may go down, it is unlikely to go down and stay down at the levels that gave the United States a competitive advantage.

Oil prices can move dramatically. But oil supplies are sluggish. It takes a long time to produce an extra barrel of oil and bring it to market. It also takes a lot of capital. And faith.

What you also see is that oil prices are much higher than industry experts expected. In oil, as in everything else, nobody knows anything. As you will see in Figure 5.1, there are vast supplies of oil that are profitable at $100 per barrel. But $100 per barrel is far more than the experts forecast.

So they didn't make investments for a $100-per-barrel world—they made investments for a $30-per-barrel world. Consequently, the supply of oil has gone up only modestly. Even with such high prices, output from the major oil companies has gone down. The big firms have been unable to increase production from their mature fields and have no new production ready to come online.

You've heard of "peak oil"? It is the hypothesis that there's only so much oil available and that at a certain point we will begin pumping less and less of it out of the earth. Whether that is true or not, we don't know. But it is definitely getting harder and harder—*and more expensive*—to expand oil production.

From the Sprott Asset Management report, "Oil or Not, Here They Come" by Kevin Bambrough:

> The EIA study revealed that the largest 1% of oilfields (798 total fields) account for over 50% of global production. Remarkably, in this group,

there are 20 super giant fields that account for roughly 25% of global production. All of these super giant fields were discovered decades ago.

What has been discovered and brought into production in the past few decades are smaller fields, which normally have higher decline rates. As these new smaller fields replace production from larger fields, and older larger fields age, we can expect the global observed decline rate to increase from the current estimated rate of 6.7% (or 4.7 million barrels per day annually).[6]

See Figure 5.1. It shows that there is considerable oil available. But it comes with a higher price tag. And it demands many years of investment to bring it online. Obviously, no one will make the investment unless they are pretty sure the price will be high enough—when they are finally bringing their product to market—to justify the investment. Mr. Bambrough concludes that $75-per-barrel oil is needed simply to maintain current levels of production.

But current levels of production aren't good enough. While the developed world's use of energy is on the decline, the emerging world can't get enough of it. The reason is self-evident. The emerging world has billions of people who don't already own all of the energy-guzzling paraphernalia of modern life. And they are acquiring the means to afford it (see Figure 5.2).

Figure 5.2 tells the China story. There's also Russia, Indonesia, Brazil, India, Turkey, and many other high-growth emerging nations. We don't necessarily believe that any of them will become the America of the twenty-first century. But we take it for granted that they will be the big oil users of the future. At present, the per-capita use of oil in

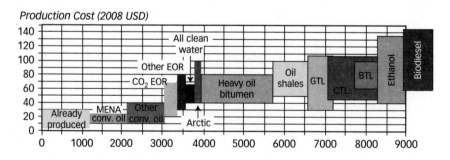

Figure 5.1 Available Oil in Billion Barrels

Source: Sprott Asset Management

the United States is 10 times what it is in China. But the trend is clear: Oil use in the emerging world is rising rapidly, as you'd expect.

Of course, the other thing that is rising rapidly in the emerging world is personal income. This is a crucial point. In America, the typical working man reached his peak earnings per hour in 1974. You can argue that he gets more in social services today, such as free cheese and free pills. But that seems like small comfort to him when he drives up to the gas pump. Looking at Figure 5.3, you'll see the adjusted wage cost of gasoline over the past 10 years has gone up. The Chinese buyer finds gasoline—as a percentage of his wages—has gone down because his earnings have increased so substantially. Chinese wages are up 281 percent over the last decade.

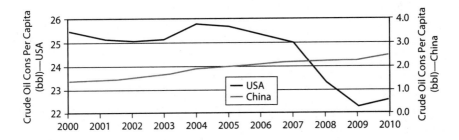

Figure 5.2 China vs. USA

Source: Sprott Asset Management

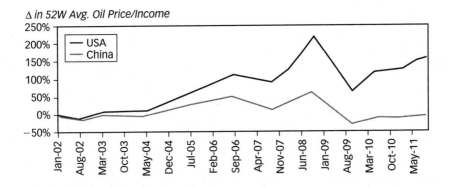

Figure 5.3 Divided by Change in Disposable Income, China vs. United States

Source: Sprott Asset Management

Even with Chinese wages up so sharply, they are still far below U.S. levels. The average worker earns roughly one-tenth as much in China as in the United States. So there is plenty of room for more wage growth in China. That means there is also plenty of room for more purchases of gasoline. And although we can perfectly well imagine a major blowup in China, we can't imagine a major change in these underlying trends.

This is one of the "beta" trends we follow. People in the emerging world are bound to earn more money. They're bound to use more oil. The oil price is bound to go up in real terms.

Should you bet on higher oil prices? Maybe.

Our point here is that as people in the emerging markets earn more and produce more, they are bound to use more oil. To do so, they must compete with Americans.

That's two strikes against America. It is no longer a source of cheap oil. And Americans' earnings are not keeping up with the growth in energy prices. And here comes strike three:

NO LONGER A FREE SOCIETY

Here's another reason America may not be such a good beta bet over the next 20 to 50 years. A big advantage that Americans enjoyed in the past was that they were relatively ungoverned. At the time of the American Revolution, the total tax take from the government is estimated at only 3 percent. When, in the Declaration of Independence, Thomas Jefferson writes about the English crown having "sent forth a swarm of agents to harass the people and eat out their substance," he was using a bit of hyperbole. There weren't many government employees. An American, especially one on the frontier, could live his whole life without meeting one.

Compared with the Old World, America had a big advantage. Her people were able to work, to invent, to produce, and to innovate largely free from the dead hand of centralized financial control, regulation, and price fixing. Work and investment produce wealth. Government, generally, redistributes, consumes, and destroys it. This is not to say you can have a society that is all production and no government. But you certainly can't have one that is all government!

"It's either control or money," says a friend of ours. He means that a controlled economy doesn't produce much money. But a free market economy that does produce wealth is "all out of control," which is even more unbearable to many people.

We described in a previous chapter why charitable projects do not increase the world's wealth in any measurable way. Value is determined, imperfectly, by price movements. Without freely moving prices—a market economy—you never know whether you are actually adding value. Most charitable activities are wealth-destroying vanity projects. Like government itself. But at least they're not financed with stolen money!

Mr. Market always tells you what things are worth—right now. Tomorrow, he changes his mind. Investors and business people are always guessing about which direction he will take next. And sometimes he makes major mistakes—such as the value he put on the tech stocks in January 2000 or the value he put on America's housing stock in 2005. So you might be tempted to say that Mr. Market is no better at determining real value than you are. If that is so, your charity project might be just as valuable as anything Mr. Market favors—and government spending might be just as productive.

But Mr. Market doesn't claim to know what things are really worth. He claims only to be discovering what they are worth—day by day, hour by hour. He is frequently wrong. But at least his mistakes are always corrected. That's what market "corrections" are all about.

The mistakes of philanthropists and politicians are corrected, too, in the fullness of time. But not easily. And not cheaply. Never "marked to market," they are corrected only by war, bankruptcy, poverty, hyperinflation, and/or revolution.

We believe the United States will be unable to adjust its current trajectory in a meaningful way. It is headed for one or more of these calamities. But wait, you say, the United States is a democracy. It is a capitalist system. Surely it will adapt, reform, and make the changes necessary before the big boat hits and iceberg. Right? Wrong.

In fact, democracy may, in some circumstances, be the least adaptable of all political systems. A king or a tyrant may be able to make a fundamental change in an economic system, in spite of what special interests, lobbyists, and even the people themselves want. But in a democracy, where special interests are well entrenched and well funded—and where more than half the voters receive money from the existing system and depend on it for their daily bread—a substantial change of direction may be impossible.

This is a beta issue. A big beta issue. The trends have favored America for the past 300 years. And the trends of the past 30 years have favored U.S. Treasury debts. Both trends may be coming to an end.

SPURTS OF GROWTH

Here's a thought: Each time humans make a breakthrough, their rate of growth speeds up. They then take advantage of it. They fill up the economic niche that opens up for them as fully as their new technology allows. And then what? Growth then goes back to "normal." But what's normal? Apparently, normal is very low or negligible rates of growth; that's what we had before the Industrial Revolution began. For approximately 199,700 years, the growth rate of the human species was negligible. Vanishingly small. Zilch. For thousands of years at a stretch, there was no change in populations or living standards.

Which, of course, only gives rise to a whole group of questions.

First, is it true? Is human history a long spell of stagnation or low levels of growth, punctuated by sudden bursts of above-trend growth?

If it is true, is it also true that the developed economies have reached the limit of the "cheap energy" dividend, which began with the large-scale exploitation of coal in the eighteenth century, followed by the wide use of oil in the nineteenth and twentieth centuries?

And if that is true, what next? Are there no new sources of cheap energy?

What about nuclear? Well, a possibility, but recently, nuclear power was dealt a huge setback. It's not cheap, not when you add in all the safety features and the cost of the occasional emergency. Many nations are now reexamining their energy policies to decide whether nuclear has any role to play at all.

What about conservation, energy-saving measures, going green?

Well, yes, you can stretch your energy. You can probably even increase your quality of life by using it more efficiently. But you don't get above-trend economic growth gains by reducing the inputs of energy. You appear to get rapid growth only from big breakthroughs that make new energy available—and put it to work for you.

Doesn't technology lead to big increases in standards of living? To growth? To higher gross domestic product (GDP)?

Apparently not. The biggest new technology to come along in recent years is the Internet and the accompanying communications revolution. Nowhere was this more promising or more fully elaborated than in the United States of America. The United States had the most innovators. The most new high-tech startups. The most applications and computers. The most capital invested in the new industry. The most educated, technically literate, well-financed people in the world. They also had the slickest capital markets, ready to grease as much money as possible toward a promising new company.

So what happened? Computer power doubled every 18 months from the mid-1990s to deep into the 2000s. Entrepreneurs concocted all manner of apps to take advantage of it. Billions of dollars were invested. Fortunes were made. And what did this florescence of new technology achieve? In terms of economic growth? Nothing. The real GDP of the United States grew insignificantly during the entire first decade of the twenty-first century. No—or very few—new jobs were added. No apparent wealth was created. The average person earned no more money. Nor did he possess greater wealth. Millions of people were happily distracting themselves with video games and tweets, but no gains were recorded for the economy—or its people.

Why?

We're suggesting that the kind of growth the United States saw in the nineteenth and twentieth centuries was anomalous. New technology—including something as important as oil—obeys the laws of economics. And one of those laws tells us that new technology, whatever it is, eventually arrives at declining rates of return. It is subject to the rule of declining marginal utility, in other words. The first inputs produce huge gains in output. Later inputs produce only incremental gains. Then, if the cost of the additional inputs rise, they may produce no net gain at all. A new technology or innovation or discovery or even a new method of organizing existing resources brings results—but not unlimited results. In the case of the human story, each new source of energy has been exploited, and then economic growth rates have fallen. Perhaps to zero.

Let's say you look back at when the bow and arrow was invented. It probably enabled primitive hunters to get more game with less caloric cost. Rather than run the rabbit down, they waited, pulled back the bowstring, and then they could walk over to collect the immobile animal. Thus, they could support more people. So the human population grew. Perhaps in a spurt of above-trend gains until a new, broader niche was fully occupied. But once the bow and arrow was widespread, the population probably stopped growing. We had squeezed all the juice we could out of that innovation.

The investment returns of the past 200 years actually may reflect this anomaly. That is, they may be the product of abnormal growth rates brought about by the introduction of fossil fuels. If so, investors may never again realize anything like the rates of return they enjoyed in recent history. It may also be that the prejudices investors developed—such as the bias toward the stock market over saving money in gold—may be the product of unusual circumstances, rather than the reflection of universal, eternal investment truths.

Does this mean, if true, that you should forget about investing altogether? Should you bury your talent in the ground, like the "wicked, lazy servant" of biblical fame?

Well, no. This analysis applies to the advanced, energy-burning economies of the developed world. There are many places where the "energy revolution" has not yet been fully exploited. There are huge parts of the world where modern economies do not yet exist. Again, more in the next chapter.

What this analysis suggests is that not only America but most of the developed countries are no longer a good place for your money. You might be able to get alpha. Here and there. But you probably won't get much out of beta. And it's beta that counts.

A FINAL THOUGHT . . .

Finally, here's another thing to keep in mind:

Anything that can't be explained in simple language in 15 minutes is not something you should invest in. The Jewish scholar Hillel was once asked to explain the Torah to a man standing on one leg (meaning someone who wasn't going to stand there for long). He said:

"That which you would not want done to yourself, do not do it to anyone else. All the rest is detail. . . ."

The same could be said for investment opportunities. If a project can't be explained to a man standing on one leg, it isn't a good investment. All the rest is detail.

Likewise (true in business, as well as investment), if the deal itself requires a lot of paperwork, it probably isn't worth doing. The deal—investment or business—has to be simple. There can be a lot of detailed paperwork behind it, but the basic deal must be simple enough that you can remember it.

CHAPTER 6

OUR BETA BETS

This chapter explores our "beta" bets. Remember, you can make money by guessing right about a stock. But you can make a fortune by guessing right about a major trend. Then, you take your time, giving the market time to tell its story. When you're sure you have the story right, you invest heavily for a long time.

Taking the world and the future together, we might choose among millions of beta possibilities. Will the Chinese begin to wear more hats? Perhaps we should invest in a haberdashery in Shanghai? Will an aging population begin to take more pleasure cruises? Maybe investing in the holiday cruise industry is a can't-lose proposition. Or how about India? Is it not inevitable that the world's largest democracy will flourish—or at least grow marginally richer over the next half a century?

So many possibilities. So little time.

The danger with these sorts of macro guesses is that they depend on rather sketchy and imperfect information. Nietzsche called attention to it. There are two kinds of knowledge, he pointed out. There is the knowledge you get from the bottom up—*erfahrung*. And there is the knowledge you get from the top down—*wissen*. *Wissen* is what "everybody knows," the kinds of things you find in the newspapers, for example. *Erfahrung* is the result of direct experience and personal inquiry. It's what you discover on your own. What you know to be true from personal observation.

Of the two forms of knowledge, *erfahrung* is usually much more profitable. All very well to know that ice cream consumption is going up. But more valuable to know that Joe's Ice Cream Shoppe on the corner of Broad and Dupont streets doubled its sales last year.

Most beta bets are based on *wissen*. And a lot of what people know to be true turns out to be not true at all. That is why you have to choose your beta bets very carefully and monitor them regularly. And it's why it's very important to remind yourself at all times that whatever you think, you may be wrong.

That said, let's turn to our big beta views. We have two of them. First, we think the "emerging economies" will continue to outperform the developed world. In short, we think there is a very long-term trade to be made. Short the developed world. Go long the emerging world.

BET ON THE LOSERS

Before we explain more fully, let's note two things:

First, this is a trade that only very long-term-oriented investors can make. Over the next year, or the next five, or even the next 10 years, the relative performance of developed and emerging market assets is unpredictable. Anything can happen. So if you're investing for an outcome five years out, you should probably ignore this suggestion all together.

Second, there is nothing particularly original about this view. In fact, the thing that bothers us most about it is that it is so compelling, so obvious, and so widely accepted. The investment gods do not give up their secrets so easily. There must be a trap. We have to find out what it is.

Of course, the trap could be somewhat obvious, too. In the near term, the world seems to be in a Japan-like deleveraging phase. This has the curious consequence of shifting capital from the fast-growing emerging economies to the United States—a slower, more debt-drenched, fully developed economy.

The Japanese syndrome has already lasted 22 years in Japan and 4 years in the United States (depending on how you look at it). If it intensifies—and expands—it is quite likely that the flow of investment capital from the emerging markets to the United States will increase, while the flow of goods and services from the emerging markets to the United States, Europe, and Japan will decrease.

This will have the perverse result of causing the developed world (or at least the United States) to outperform the emerging world for another few years. By then, even long-term investors will have thrown in the towel, selling out their remaining holdings in India, Russia, and Brazil in order to buy U.S. Treasury bonds. Again, perversely, that will be the signal for the end of the Japan syndrome, when the bond market finally crashes.

But with those words of caution, let's look at why—eventually—this beta play should pay off.

We begin by asking once again why we bother to begin at all. According to the efficient market hypothesis, you can't really improve your results. Prices are set by markets, which are always smarter than individual investors. Most investors would probably help protect their money by assuming it were true, just as they protect their marriages from infidelity by assuming they will be caught. Both assumptions are probably incorrect, but both are useful. But what if a careful analysis of the big picture permitted you to shift the odds just a little bit in your favor?

In random walk theory, one investment selection is as good as another. But in practice, investors act like befuddled crowds. They tend to bid up certain favorite investments far beyond what the random walk would suggest. This makes those investments—the very ones that most people want to buy—the very worst ones, because they are selling above what a purely random system might provide. Yet if that is true—if there are some investments so favored by investors that they perform worse than random motion would predict—the opposite must be true, too. There must be some unfavored investments that are so neglected and underpriced that they will perform better than random motion suggests.

This insight has been confirmed by countless studies. "Rich," popular stocks tend to go down. Pariah stocks tend to go up. The academic explanation: Markets aren't always "efficient."

Fortunately for us, popular investments—that is, those that are likely to underperform the market—also happen to be oriented to the short term. Not only do people want to make a lot of money, they want to do it quickly.

So if you are focusing on a long-term trend—one that will pay off many years into the future—it is not likely that you will choose popular, overpriced investments. Those will be the favorites of people who want their profits sooner rather than later. Since the payoff from favoring emerging markets could be far in the future, we are probably safe in guessing that it is not, generally, an overbought position.

WHY EMERGING MARKETS WILL OUTPERFORM DEVELOPED ONES

The idea is simple. The developed world is growing slowly, if at all. The "emerging world"—which includes all sorts of countries in all sorts of different phases of economic development—is growing more quickly.

Over the last four years, for example, there has been no real growth to speak of in the developed world. But China boomed.

This process, most likely, will continue. It doesn't mean that China has to continue growing at such a sizzling pace or that the developed countries will necessarily stay in a slump. It means only that the developed world will continue to underperform the undeveloped world for the foreseeable future.

Why might this be a reliable, long-term trend? Regression to the mean. One region is developed. The other is not. It seems more likely that the undeveloped region will play catch-up than that the developed region will sprint further ahead. Catch-up is easier.

If the developed world is to grow faster, the old dogs in its economies will have to learn some new tricks. But the young dogs in the undeveloped world don't have to. They just have to look at the mutts in the developed world and do what they do. Which is just what we've seen happening over the past 30 years.

The developed countries have heavy industry. So the developing countries put up steel mills and auto plants. The developed world has shopping malls. So they built them in Beijing and Mumbai, too. Developed economies have highways, ports, container shipping, banks, McDonald's, and all the rest of a modern economy's infrastructure and output capacity. The developing countries put them in place, too. The developed world appreciates the role of private property and a court system to sort out problems and markets to set prices and guide production. They now have those things in the developing world, too.

But the trend of faster growth in the developing countries isn't just about imitation. There is something more profound going on.

It is an expression of the principle of "regression to the mean." For approximately 199,700 years of human existence, a man's labor in India was about as rewarding as a man's labor in Africa or Europe. It's only in the past 300 years or less that wages in Europe and its Europeanized colonies raced ahead. Is there some inherent reason why one human should be more productive than another? Not that we know of. And, if not, we can expect the abnormality to be corrected, with the wages of humans in India and Indianapolis both regressing to a mean.

But how did they get so far apart? What, exactly, was going on—and why might it have come to an end now?

"PROGRESS"

Much of the growth and prosperity of the developed world—if not all of it—can be traced to innovations and discoveries brought "on line" in the eighteenth and nineteenth centuries and fully expressed in the twentieth. These were two: America and the use of fossil fuel.

When Columbus crossed the Atlantic in 1492, he was only marginally richer, more productive, and more technologically advanced than other seafarers from centuries earlier. The Chinese roamed large areas of ocean. So did the Phoenicians. And the Vikings. But America is much closer to Europe than to China, and the Europeans who followed Columbus were ready, willing, and able to take advantage of his discovery.

Europeans found almost unbelievable quantities of new resources. The Iberians—from Spain and Portugal—focused on what is today Latin America. The French and English directed their energies to North America. At first, the Iberians seemed to get the best of the bargain. They found money—gold and silver—which gave their economies an immediate rush. But the effect was short lived and harmful. What they got was the equivalent of today's sugar rush from printing-press money: an increase in the supply of money with no increase in the ability to produce things. The result was inflation—and the impoverishment of the entire Iberian Peninsula.

To the north, the haul was similarly huge, but it was in a different form. The English and French discovered no gold or silver to speak of but things that they could use to create real wealth: timber for fuel, rivers that made communication easy, abundant minerals, and vast expanses of virgin farmland. It took time. It took work, saving, and investment, but the treasures of the north were transformed into much greater and much more enduring wealth. This was especially true after oil became widely used as the fuel of choice. America had a lot of it.

Oil-fired machines soon increased output so greatly that the average person in America, Europe, and, later, in Japan became much richer than his contemporaries in the undeveloped world. (If there were a racial, cultural, or geographic hypothesis explaining Europeans' comparative success, Japan disproved it. Even after being defeated in World War II, it grew richer more rapidly than any nation ever had.)

Today, we take "growth" for granted. We think it is normal. And we presume that after a period of recession or stagnation, growth will resume. But what if the entire period from the invention of the steam engine to the invention of the Internet were not the normal thing but the abnormal thing? What if the "Lost Decade" we have just gone through is actually more ordinary? What if very low rates of growth were the "mean" to which we have just now reverted?

The typical person in 1750 lived better than the typical person in, say, 100,000 B.C., but not that much better. The person in 100,000 B.C. lived in a cave or maybe a wigwam. The typical person in 1750 lived in a hovel. There were some great houses, too, of course. By the eighteenth century, humans had been building with arches and columns . . . and domes . . . dressed stone with elaborate decoration for thousands of years. But they were like the palaces of the Orient, not a part of everyday life. Most people had no access to those monuments. Most people lived in houses made of whatever they could put together—usually wood or mud—just as had been done for many thousands of years.

Progress between 200,000 B.C., when mankind is now thought to have emerged, to 1765, when Watt produced his first engine, was extremely slow. In any given year, it was nearly negligible—imperceptible. Over thousands of years, there was little progress of any sort, which was reflected in static human populations with static levels of well-being.

Then, after 1765, progress took off like a rocket. Over the next 200 years, the lives of people in the developed countries and the human population, generally, changed completely.

It took 199,700 years for the human population to go from zero to 125 million. But over the next 250 years, it added about 6 billion people. Every 5 years, approximately, it added the equivalent of the entire world's population in 1750. "Progress" made it possible. People had much more to eat. Better sanitation. Better transportation, which eliminated famines by making it possible to ship large quantities of food into areas where crops had failed. The last major famine due to failed crops in western Europe occurred in the eighteenth century. After that, the famines, in the developed world at least, have been intentional—caused largely by government policies.

Progress permitted huge increases in population. And it brought rising real wages and rising standards of living.

By the late twentieth century, people in the developed world took progress and gross domestic product (GDP) growth for granted. Governments went into debt, depending on future growth to pull them out. So did corporations, insurance companies, pension firms, and ordinary households. Everyone counted on growth. Spending and tax policies were based on encouraging growth. Whenever growth stalled, governments rushed to try to get it going again.

The enormous growth in government itself was made possible by the internal combustion engine. The more it boosted output, the richer the host economy got, the more parasitic government it could afford.

Today, there is hardly a mortgage, stock, bond, municipal plan, government budget, student loan, retirement program, housing development, business plan, political campaign, health care program, or insurance company that doesn't rely on growth. Everybody expects normal growth to resume after we have put this sluggish period behind us.

But what if growth isn't normal? What if the growth of the last two centuries was a once-in-a-centimillenium event, made possible by the discovery of new continents and cheap energy?

Man fills the niche nature allows him. He probably lived on the African savannah for many thousands of years with no progress or growth of any kind. Then, the discovery of fire allowed him to extend his range. We imagine that there followed a "growth spurt" that brought him into the colder regions of Europe and Asia. He then discovered the bow and arrow, further increasing his available food supply and extending the range that nature permitted him. So, too, did the domestication of animals and the development of sedentary agriculture allow him to put more food on the table with less exertion, thereby permitting another growth spurt.

But once the new, wider niche was filled out, his progress and population growth leveled out and once again became stagnant. So we have to wonder: Is the developed world at the end of its growth spurt?

In Europe, the United States, and Japan, the use of fossil fuels has leveled off. The number of miles driven in the United States—which rose steadily from the day Henry Ford built the first affordable "Tin Lizzie"—has begun to decline. So has economic growth. So has the use of energy. In fact, the beginning of the decline, or perhaps the "topping out" process, appears to have begun in the 1970s.

Why the 1970s? We can only guess. Most of the tools and machines we take for granted today were invented in the 1920s, 1930s, and 1940s. After World War II, they were put into service in all the developed countries.

Growth was fast—and real—in the 30 "glorious" years following the end of the war. By the 1980s, most of the big gains had already been captured.

Thereafter, the rate of return on an incremental unit of energy went down. We could still buy new machines, but they produced only marginal improvements in output. After 1970 . . .

- Gross energy use per person peaked out (in the developed world).
- The rate of return on an incremental unit of debt went down.
- Rebounds from recessions grew progressively weaker; they were driven by making credit cheaper.
- Real hourly wages peaked in the United States.

In a nutshell, after the 1970s, people stopped using more and more energy. They also stopped getting richer. Then, both the United States and Europe turned to debt. The United States cut the link to gold, making it easier to borrow. American households borrowed to continue increasing standards of living. European governments borrowed to expand social services. The United Kingdom borrowed for both reasons. And now, the borrowing has gone exponential, while growth has almost disappeared.

THE CHINESE CENTURY?

Many people see parallels between the rapid growth of the U.S. economy at the start of the twentieth century and the rapid growth of the Chinese economy now. They are tempted to see this as the "Chinese Century" and imagine that China will be a powerhouse, like the United States, for the next 100 years.

Yes—maybe—but . . .

The U.S. economy was a powerhouse then because it was so *unlike* what it is today. It was a free-market economy back then. Willing buyers and sellers made capital allocation decisions. Sometimes they were right. Sometimes they were wrong. But the markets corrected mistakes, continually redirecting capital from weak hands to strong ones and from failed projects to successful ones.

Capitalism—not central planning—is how people get rich. China is a "capitalistic" economy, but with major guidance from the public sector. We don't know exactly how important those bureaucratic inputs are. We don't know if any Westerner fully grasps how it works. Even the Chinese we talk to are perplexed. But there is no question that central, regional, and local planners, by no means pure capitalists, direct vast amounts of investment capital.

As a result, there are perhaps trillions of dollars of misallocations of capital that are not readily or easily corrected. Shopping malls with no customers. Apartments with no buyers. Whole towns with no inhabitants. Many of these were built with debt. And much of that debt is bad debt.

It is impossible to predict how this will be resolved. Perhaps a blowup will be followed by a quick bounce-back, with corrections that allow for more sensible decision making. Perhaps real growth is so strong that it overwhelms and smothers the mistakes. Who knows?

But that's why we need to invest as though we expected to be surprised. We surely will be.

Where the surprise will come from, we don't know. But it looks as though people in the emerging world are bound to use more oil and earn more money. And emerging markets will be better places, generally, for capital investments than the developed world.

Another way to look at it: The emerging markets are just less zombified than the developed world. Tax rates are lower. Regulations are less stifling. Special interest groups are as likely to be losing their grip on power as gaining more. Zombie institutions are swept away more quickly, making room for new ones to arise. Businesses start up more rapidly, with less expense; they operate more cheaply and adapt to new opportunities more readily. Most important, emerging markets can still boost output by putting in service the machines and machine-age infrastructure that is taken for granted in the developed world. Emerging economies can still use more oil—a lot of it—and get positive rates of return from their energy investments.

WHAT ABOUT THE INTERNET?

But we know what you are thinking. The developed countries may be in a slump, but it is only temporary. We have the scientists, innovators, and breakthrough inventions. After all, we invented the Internet.

Be that as it may, so far, this twenty-first century has been a flop. A washout. At least for Americans, from an economic point of view. There are no more full-time jobs in the U.S. today than when the century began. In terms of per-capita wealth, Americans are now worse off than they were when the century began. The value of U.S. houses, for example, is about back where it was when the century began. Household earnings, adjusted for inflation, are lower. And America's industries, businesses, and enterprises—as reflected in stock market prices—are worth less, in real terms, than they were in 2000.

And now . . . the background.

You will recall that when the century began, most people thought it was the most promising period in history—especially in the history of the United States of America.

The Soviet Union had ceased to exist. China had joined the capitalists. And George W. Bush told the graduating class of the U.S. Military

Academy at West Point that America was the world's "single surviving model" for a successful system.[1] It was so successful, in fact, that Francis Fukuyama thought it might signal an "end of history." What more work had history to do? Perfection had already been attained. The United States was dynamic and flexible. Its democratic political system could adapt to whatever changes and challenges it confronted. Its capitalistic economic system could push ahead on every front. And its scientists and innovators were discovering new things at a breathtaking rate. History could pack up and go home.

You remember Moore's Law? It told us that computing power would double every 18 months. And with computers came not just a new world but a better world. Innovators could innovate faster. They had all the world's knowledge at their fingertips. There would be no more reason for error—darkness and sin would be banished from Planet Earth. We would all be smarter, richer, and healthier forever and ever. Amen!

What could go wrong? Well, so far, everything.

For starters, in 2001, a tiny group of fanatics brought down two New York skyscrapers and caused the Pentagon to panic—a very self-serving panic, we should add: Defense contractors have made billions in profits out of the Pentagon's hysteria. Since then, the United States has spent $8 trillion fighting "terrorism," easily the worst military investment in world history. For every single "terrorist" killed, the United States spent billions, to say nothing of the soldiers and civilians who died.

Then the digital revolution was a flop, too. An enormous flop. Millions of people may be using the World Wide Web, looking at photos of congressional crotches or planning the next "flash riot," for example. Hundreds of people may have become billionaires by selling electronic devices and Internet stocks to the masses. But how much has the Internet contributed to the wealth of nations? Apparently, not a damned thing.

At least as measured by GDP results.

Nowhere was the Internet revolution more focused than in the United States. Nowhere did people have higher hopes for it. And nowhere were the results more disappointing. The typical teenager now spends one-third of his life—not just half his waking hours, but one-third of a day—eight hours—on some sort of electronic device.

Does it make him smarter? Richer? More civilized? More coherent? Not that we've been able to detect!

Not every technological advance results in an increase in standards of living. Take Twitter, for example. Or nuclear weapons. Or dozens of other innovations and inventions. The Internet, like TV before it, is a great entertainment device. It is also very useful and extremely successful commercially. But has it boosted GDP growth or improved living standards? Probably not. From a GDP growth point of view, the Internet appears to be a dud.

Great advances in living standards and related increases in the value of equities have been driven by big increases in energy use. The Internet did nothing to change that. It was not a "game changer." The game is the same as it has been since the steam engine was first developed. And now, the "emerging markets" are using oil, too—lots of it. And they're registering growth rates above 5 percent.

Meanwhile, growth rates in the developed world have declined. In real terms, as mentioned above, U.S. growth in the twenty-first century seems to have fallen back to medieval levels. Why? Who knows? The concept we are presenting here—that developed economies have reached the point of diminishing returns on additional energy inputs—is a maverick idea, at best. Perhaps it is true. Perhaps it isn't.

A more conventional explanation is that the developed economies are merely in a period of debt consolidation. After 60 years of credit expansion, it is time to reduce debt. That alone could be responsible for the failure of growth and material progress. But why was there so much debt?

First, after the first oil shock in the early 1970s, the economy failed to produce much real growth per capita. Only by going into debt—effectively, spending money they didn't have—could households increase their standards of living. But we have to remember that the debt itself—and the subsequent deleveraging—are consequences of the same extraordinary energy-driven boom we have been describing. High growth rates over a long period of time convinced almost everyone that standards of living would always go up over time. This allowed both private and public borrowers to believe that they could move some of the inevitable growth forward, so they could enjoy it sooner. In other words, the belief in growth was somewhat self-fulfilling and thoroughly captivating. If growth were a sure thing, debtors could reach ahead to monetize future earnings in the present. States could run large deficits, confident that they would grow their way out of debt in the future. Households could anticipate higher wages and smooth out their lifetime living standards.

THE LOST CENTURY

In the summer of 2010, several articles in the financial press warned that America might face a Lost Decade, similar to the 1990s in Japan. They needn't have worried. The United States had already lost a decade.

But if our analysis of the effect of energy on GDP growth is correct, that is just beginning. Developed economies could lose a whole century. Losing a decade is bad enough, but losing a whole century is beginning to sound like carelessness. Or recklessness. Or inattention. Or robbery.

We will resist the urge to judge the motives or competence of our government authorities. After all, we need to be sharp observers; we can't afford too many illusions of our own. But if our "energy" hypothesis were correct, how many years of growth would be lost? One hundred? Who knows?

Why take a chance? Put your money in the emerging markets instead.

Relative to the developed world, the emerging markets look like winners. And remember, even if the difference is marginal—and even if the trend takes a decade or longer to express itself—that is OK with us.

BIG TREND NO. 2

Gold is a bet against the financial authorities and their institutions. It was a bad bet 30 years ago. But it looks like a good bet now. Here's why:

In 1971, Richard Milhous Nixon changed the world's money system. Detlev Schlichter, writing in the *Wall Street Journal*, marked the anniversary:

> Forty years ago today, U.S. President Richard Nixon closed the gold window and ushered in, for the first time in human history, a global system of unconstrained paper money under full control of the state.[2]

Of course, we know exactly where we were and exactly what we were doing on that fateful day. We were watching television. . . .

Richard Nixon, President of All the Americans, had something terribly important to say to his people. But he was worried. He summoned his advisers together and posed the key question to them:

"Should we interrupt *Bonanza?*"

Bonanza was a very popular TV show, featuring a prosperous rancher, his three sons, and their Chinese cook. Since *Bonanza* was much more popular than Richard Nixon, the president hesitated to interrupt it—even though he was going to change the entire world's monetary system—and, in fact, institute a bold new system of purely paper money.

In trials, run over the preceding 2,000 years or so, this new system of money had always failed. But Richard Nixon seemed unaware. In fact, he seemed unaware that he was changing anything important at all. Instead, he directed his attentions to another experiment in central economic planning—another one that also failed every previous test—wage and price controls. Taking a page out of Emperor Diocletian's book on "How to Screw up an Economy," Nixon announced that henceforth the authorities in Washington would decide how much a man should pay for a loaf of bread or how much his employer should pay him for his labors.

Naturally, this effort was a failure too—and was quickly forgotten. But Nixon's other initiative stuck. The world has suffered from it ever since. We are four decades into this latest experiment with paper money—the most successful effort so far, no doubt about it. People still use dollars with few complaints. As far as we know, nobody doesn't want them. As far as we know, nobody will not want them tomorrow, either.

But wait, while dollars are universally accepted as a medium of exchange, as a store of value—money's other purpose—green paper has been a disaster. It began losing value immediately after the Federal Reserve was set up to protect it. And then, when President

Nixon cut the dollar's last connection to gold, it lost value even faster. Today, a dollar will buy only about a penny or two as much as a dollar from 1913.

Until August 15, 1971, wealth was tallied in units of a real and natural thing: gold. It measured out the world's other real things: its resources and its output. Its main advantage was that it couldn't be diddled.

For proof: *Nuestra Señora de Atocha*, a Spanish galleon, sank in a storm off the Florida coast in 1622. When it was found in the 1970s, its treasure of gold doubloons was just as valuable as it was when the ship left Havana 350 years before.

But post-1971, we have a new, avant garde money system. Wealth is counted up in pieces of paper or as electronic "information." Each unit has no real value of its own. It represents only a claim against real goods and services. And each year, it purchases fewer of them.

What is most remarkable about this freakish new money system is that it is always on the road to hell, but never seems to get there. Since 1971, paper currencies have lost value at a breakneck speed. You'd think their necks would be broken by now. In 1972, we bought a gallon of gasoline for 24 cents. Now it is 16 times that much. Gold has gone up 50 times—for a 98 percent loss to the dollar holder. If this pattern continues for another 40 years, a gold doubloon will buy about what it does today. A dollar will buy nothing.

And then, in August 2011, along came Standard & Poor's (S&P) with more bad news: Not only is the dollar disappearing, but if you lend money to the U.S. government, you might not get it back. The stock market took the news badly. But bond investors bought with even more lusty recklessness than before. It was as if they really didn't want the money back anyway. Yields on U.S. 10-year notes fell from around 3 percent to scarcely more than 2 percent, giving investors a negative real yield.

But the fall in yields (the rise in bond prices) should not come as a surprise. Japan's government debt lost its triple-A status in 2002. Yields did not rise. Instead, they stayed between 1 percent and 2 percent. Then, when equities plummeted after the S&P announcement, Japanese 10-year notes—IOUs of the most deeply indebted nation on Earth—reached an all-time high, with yields just below 1 percent.

But it's not the nominal rate that counts; it's the real rate. For 20 years, stocks and property in Japan got hammered. Bond buyers are the only ones who made any money. A debt deflation causes prices to fall. When prices are falling, even a zero interest rate gives investors a positive rate of return. And it isn't even taxable.

WHO WILL HAVE THE LAST LAUGH?

When Richard Nixon cut the dollar's link to gold, there were many people who forecast doom and gloom. No nation had ever run a successful paper money system. How likely was it that the United States would succeed where all had failed before it? How much had the human character improved over the years? Would central bankers now be above temptation and mistake? Free from both error and sin?

It is hard to ask the question without laughing. But for a long time the laugh was on the doubters. Yes, the cynics had the first laugh. Inflation rates rose as the United States did as the cynics forecast. Government spending rose. So did prices. The price of gold rose, too, as people anticipated the crack-up of the system.

But the system didn't crack. Inflation rose to 13 percent annually. And no further. Volcker stopped it. And then it was the believers who laughed.

But the question is: Who will have the last laugh? And here it is worth looking at what happened between 1971 and today.

When Richard Nixon implemented his new monetary system four decades ago, he set in motion a huge expansion in the world's supply of cash and credit. Gold was limited. Paper money was left to run wild. Ben Bernanke famously announced how it worked in a 2002 speech, entitled "Deflation: Making Sure It Doesn't Happen Here." He explained:

> The U.S. government has a technology, called a printing press (or, today, its electronic equivalent), that allows it to produce as many U.S. dollars as it wishes at essentially no cost. By increasing the number of U.S. dollars in circulation, or even by credibly threatening to do so, the U.S. government can also reduce the value of a dollar in terms of goods and services, which is equivalent to raising the prices in dollars of those goods and services. We conclude that, under a paper money system, a determined government can always generate higher spending and hence positive inflation.[3]

Bernanke made it sound like a piece of cake. He should have appended a footnote. Inflating is easy when the credit cycle is expanding. When an economy transforms itself from grasshopper to ant, it gets harder. People switch from borrowing, spending, and investing to exterminating debt and hoarding cash. That's when stimulus measures—fiscal or monetary—cease to work. It's when the formula of the previous half-century becomes worthless. That's when the cynics begin warming up for their final laugh. But we're getting ahead of ourselves.

The boom had begun during the Reagan administration—in fact, it turned around on almost the very day that Ronald Reagan was inaugurated. We attended his inaugural ball, sure that the trends of the past 20 years would last a few more years. Consumer prices had been rising steadily—and were now going up at 12 percent per year. And gold had gone from $41 per ounce at the beginning of the 1970s, to more than $800 by the time the 1979 election results were in. How were we to know that that trend had run its course?

The country had seen what stagflation would do to it. It had had enough. Even economists recognized the need for a change. Easy money policies were out of the question; the bond "vigilantes" already had their eyes on M3, the broadest measure of the money supply. And consumers were ready to ditch the dollar. Volcker knew he couldn't hope to go along and get along. He had to jack up rates—over 20 percent—to save the dollar; damn the recession!

Recession came, with the economy going into the worst recession since the 1930s. But it worked, and the price of the dollar—measured in gold—rose for the next 20 years. Woe to the "gold bugs" who stuck with it. . . .

But wait, suppose the gold bugs actually did stick with it? Suppose they looked up on August 16, 1971, and read the handwriting on the wall. The day before, Richard Nixon had "closed the gold window" at the Treasury. Henceforth, you could rap on the glass all you wanted. Even if you were Charles de Gaulle, you still wouldn't be able to trade your paper dollars for the gold you were promised.

This was a major default. And it clearly augured more bad things to come. Now that the dollar was no longer anchored to gold, the entire world money system—which was anchored to the dollar—was adrift. And you didn't have to tell us gold bugs what that meant. It meant that the dollar would soon be worthless.

So let's imagine that they did exchange their dollars for gold. Just to make the math easy, let's imagine that they waited a few days after Nixon's announcement and got an ounce of gold for every $50 they traded.

We all know what happened next. They looked like geniuses in the 1970s—and then like morons for the next two decades. Gold rose to over $800 by the end of the 1970s. But then, the aforementioned Mr. Volcker put the kibosh on inflation. In doing so, he also pulled the rug out from under the gold bugs. The dollar was good. No need for gold, especially not overpriced gold. The price of gold fell for nearly 20 years, beginning at the onset of the 1980s and ending at the end of the 1990s. By then, the typical gold bug was broke and depressed. You could find him muttering to himself while picking up cigarette butts and looking through dumpsters for a half-eaten sandwich.

But the markets had a story to tell. And it wasn't over. Prior to the "Nixon Shock" of 1971, nations settled their trade imbalances in gold. This had the effect of keeping trade imbalances from getting too out of whack. If a country spent too much on imports, its paper money ended up in foreign hands. When this paper was presented to the central bank, a transfer of gold from the importer to the exporter settled the account. Nations with trade deficits were thus encouraged to raise interest rates to cool imports and protect their gold.

After 1971, imbalances were allowed to run unchecked. In effect, Americans could buy things without ever really paying for them. It was as if you sent a check in payment for a new washing machine and the check was never cashed. You might be tempted to buy more! Dollars shipped abroad were never presented to the U.S. Treasury for exchange. Why bother? The U.S. dollar was the world's reserve currency.

Americans bought more and more from overseas. In the four decades before 1971, there was not a single U.S. current account deficit. Since, the U.S. has run a deficit every four out of five years. Soon, the volume of goods coming into the country was far beyond the volume going out. Ships appeared at Long Beach Harbor laden to the gunwales with merchandise. They left riding high on the water—empty.

This resulting explosion of new dollars caused a worldwide boom. Much of the boom in the emerging markets in the 1990s and 2000s can be traced to this source. Not only were foreign factories running hot trying to keep up with demand from America but exporters were forced to print money of their own to keep up with the flood of dollars. They needed to redeem dollars from their own merchants and prevent their local currencies from rising too much. The higher the yuan or the yen rose, the less competitive were Chinese or Japanese products, respectively, to America's rapacious consumers.

What a system! The U.S. consumer spent money he didn't really have to buy goods (mostly from China and Japan) for which there was no genuine market. The local central bank took in the dollars—in exchange for local currencies—and lent them back to the U.S. Treasury! It was as if the money had never left home. As you can see in Figure 6.1, since 1975, imports have exceeded exports every year.

But debt was building up.

A crude way of understanding this is to say that today there are 8 trillion more dollars in the world than there should be. And far more debt. But the United States was hardly alone. All the Organisation for Economic Co-operation and Development (OECD) nations have debt in excess of 250 percent GDP. Several—Britain, Japan, and the Netherlands—are twice that high.

This is the sort of out-of-whack situation that calls out for correction. Debt levels desperately needed to come down. That is the nature of the crisis that began in 2007 and continues today. Consumers in the United States—and elsewhere—borrowed too much money. They now needed to deleverage. They needed to pay down their debts.

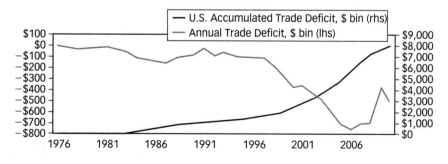

Figure 6.1 U.S. Trade Deficit

Source: Kevin Bambrough, "The Greatest Trade of All Time," *Markets at a Glance*, Sprott Asset Management, August 2011

They needed to get the burden off their backs so they could return to spending money again. This deleveraging spell was bound to lead to problems.

In a credit expansion, truly wonderful things happen. A bank takes $10 worth of capital and—thanks to the fractional reserve banking system—lends out $100 or more. Consumers spend money that they never actually earned. This, too, has a wonderful effect. Businesses typically pay out in wages much of what they take in in sales receipts. Labor is an expense. It is also their major source of sales. But when sales come from credit, there is no offsetting expense item. The money that would have been paid out in wages drops to the bottom line as profit.

In a credit contraction, however, less wonderful things happen. In fact, the cycles that were so beneficial become obnoxious. Consumers pay back $100 worth of loans and the money shrinks down to $10— or worse. Often, loans are not repaid at all. In this simplified example, if a single $10 loan is not repaid, the bank's capital is wiped out. It cannot loan any money to anyone. What happened to the $10? It disappeared.

In a contraction, sales disappear, too. Instead of spending more than he can afford, the consumer begins to spend less than he can afford. He withholds some spending in order to pay down debt. This has a knock-on effect that is even less wonderful. Businesses make fewer sales so they need fewer employees to make them. Joblessness increases, further reducing household incomes, sales, and profits.

These periods of deleveraging or credit contraction are so rare that economists can't study them. There aren't enough data points. The best we can hope to do is to understand them generally and theoretically. Probably the best recent example of a credit contraction—or a "balance sheet recession"—is in Japan over the last 21 years. A full analysis of that experience goes far beyond the scope of this book; still, it is worth looking at three implications:

- These things can last a long time.
- They are not susceptible to successful central planning intervention (although some would argue that Japan's two-decade slump would have been worse without determined, countercyclical fiscal stimulus).
- They can be brutal.

It's that last point that a long-term-oriented, macro-minded investor should keep in mind. And then, in the back of his mind should be
the American public's abhorrence of pain in all its forms.

So let us return to our gold bug. In 1998, gold hit its final low, at
$256 per ounce. The bear market had run its course. He could not
know it, but the major trends of the past two decades were getting
ready to turn around. The Nasdaq hit its high in January 2000. The
Dow, too, topped out. The feds came into the market with huge inputs
of cash and credit. They fought the downturn of the 2000s just as they
had every other one since World War II—just with much more fire-
power. But the story had changed in a dramatic way. They didn't get
the same results. Ten years and trillions of dollars later, the major indicators of the U.S. economy were in a slump again. It was obvious that
the countercyclical monetary and fiscal stimulus programs had reached
their limits. It should have been obvious, too, that the credit cycle had
reached its limit.

What would cause this? Well, we return to a well-worn idea: the
principle of declining marginal utility, applied to debt. As an economy
adds debt, each additional unit produces less and less incremental output. In the period of 1950–1980, more or less, additional debt paid off
at a rate of $1 of output for each $1.40 of debt. That rate began a steep
decline in the 1990s and ended up in 2007 at around $5 of additional
debt for every additional unit of GDP. Debt didn't pay.

This meant that you couldn't pull your way out of a slump simply by
offering more credit; the economy already had too much. Furthermore,
it meant that debt was no longer a boon to economic growth but
a drag on it. This was shown in the work of Carmen Reinhart and
Kenneth Rogoff. In their masterful study of government debt, they
illustrate how higher levels of debt are accompanied by lower levels
of growth. Roughly, when national debt equals 90 percent or more of
GDP, growth slows by 1 percent.[4]

It doesn't take much imagination to see how these trends become
self-exterminating. The higher debt grows, the less able the economy
is to support it. Debt must be paid down, not increased.

Markets generally eliminate debts quickly. Sometimes roughly.
When investors become concerned that a counterparty is no longer good for the money, they do not wait for Humpty to fall off
the wall—they push him. No one wants to be left holding the weak

debtor's paper. But more than that, they also try to figure out to whom the debtor owes money and sell his paper, too. And they sell even the debtor's solid assets, figuring that he will be forced to sell them himself, driving down the price. Lions show a wounded wildebeest more mercy. If the debtor is known to own shares in a small company, for example, they sell the shares. This reduces the value of the debtor's remaining good assets at the very moment he needs them most. And if he needs to borrow more money to stay afloat, his interest rates rise—making it harder than ever for him to make ends meet. In a matter of minutes, the poor fellow—be he an individual, a bank, a company, or an entire nation—is wiped out. His paper—his IOUs—are worthless.

That is the grim process that central financial planners seek to avoid. Not that there is a good reason, economically, to do so. On the contrary, the quick cleansing is probably the best way for the economy to get back on its feet as soon as possible. But voters don't like the feeling that the economy is out of control. And, of course, central banks look out for their member banks, which are the very banks the system usually needs to get rid of.

On the evidence, central financial authorities will go to almost any lengths to avoid letting nature take care of a debt problem. They will lend promiscuously. They will pass decrees and enact laws to prevent short-selling, bank runs, price increases, or whatever else they think will help. In the end, they will print money.

People rarely experimented with a pure paper money system. Their intuition told them it was a bad idea. So what happened when they tried it? Though the historical record is short, at least it is clear: No paper money system ever lasted through an entire credit cycle.

And so here we are. We have entered the challenging part of the credit cycle. We have a paper money system doomed largely by its own success. It has run for 40 years. It has allowed huge imbalances to build up, as well as the huge run-up in private- and public-sector debt. What will happen as the deleveraging downstroke runs its course?

No one knows. But the smart money knows how to bet. Looking at the big picture, the long-term picture—the part of the picture the efficient market hypothesis says is not worth looking at—tells us to bet against the dollar and against U.S. Treasury debt.

Maybe the central bankers have finally gotten the hang of running a paper money system without the discipline of gold behind it. Most likely, they have not. And if they have not, gold will be the ultimate victor. As paper money declines in value, gold—nature's own money—will rise.

The whole situation is one for the history books. Four decades of paper money—with effectively no limit on credit expansion—have created mountains of debt in all the developed countries. Now private sector debts are being sloughed off and asset prices wobble, making investors fearful and skittish. The more they sweat, the more they seek the safety of U.S. Treasuries and the lower interest rates go. Low rates delay Armageddon. If Japan is any indication, the final catastrophe maybe be put off almost indefinitely.

But the economy continues on the road to hell—and picks up speed. When it will finally arrive, we don't know. But we bet the price of gold will be higher when we find out.

CHAPTER 7

HARD STRUCTURES

"Hard structures" will be necessary to help your family money survive for generations. Without them, the fortune is not likely to last long.

We call them "hard structures" because they are expensive to put up. And they are hard like concrete or tempered steel; once in place, they're difficult to change. They are also expensive. You need lawyers, accountants, and tax experts to help you set them up.

Hard structures are the legal structures—trusts, tax and estate planning, and so on—that make having money a burden. It takes time and hard work to get them in place and to understand them. And then you must remember what you've done and why.

This, of course, is the way it has to work. It's a feature of the "zombification" of the U.S. and other advanced economies. You need to hire able, expensive professionals to help you do what you shouldn't have to do at all. Some of the best brains in the nation are put to work at things that do not add value; they just prevent a bigger loss of value. Trusts, corporate entities, partnerships, tax montages, insurance programs—they do not make the world a richer place; they just help prevent you from getting poorer. The whole idea is to stay ahead of the efforts of politicians (and others) to separate you from your money. And it becomes something of an arms race. The feds close one loophole. You have to find another one. The feds close one door, and you open up another one somewhere else.

We do not presume that the impositions—nor the attempts to avoid them—are efficient or fair. To the contrary, the whole system is twisted and grotesque. It is a very effective way of keeping lawyers and accountants employed and an especially effective way of transferring money from the pockets of the public into the pockets of the legal technicians. They write the laws, creating a minefield for taxpayers. Then they are paid high fees to help the wealthy get through it.

Yes, hard structures can be very complicated. You will often find yourself gazing far into the distance when someone is talking about them. You will hope your advisers and other family members are paying attention; you won't want to.

Often, these setups are so dense in technicalities and legal esoterica that you have no idea what is involved. Sometimes the complexity is just legal mumbo jumbo. Sometimes it is important. And you'll have to work hard to figure out which is which.

Many people find setting up these hard structures so costly and annoying that they don't bother with them at all. "Let the next generation sort it out," they say to themselves. Often, they dislike the implications of the hard structure systems, too—and the need to guess about things that won't happen for years—or they need to think about things they hope will never happen.

"Let's see, if you are killed in a car crash tomorrow, God forbid," the estate tax attorney begins, "what do you want to happen to your wealth?"

A lot of people don't want to hear the question, let alone answer it. Many others do not appreciate the suggestions that follow. In order to avoid a disaster after they are gone, they will be advised to give up control or ownership of assets during their lifetimes.

Successful estate planning/tax avoidance comes at a price. First, you have to be able to do the work. Paying someone else to do it isn't enough. You have to make sure it is done the way you want. And then you have to understand it well enough so you can stick to the plan. Finally, you have to follow through, often doing things that make you nervous, over a period of many years.

There are four key "hard structures" you need:

- A will and an estate plan
- A trust

- A tax strategy
- Investment/bank accounts

They are all connected. And all can take many, many different forms designed to fit an infinite variety of situations. And since people are generally fairly secretive about these things, it is impossible to pretend to know who's doing what or what works best.

If you are expecting a clear, detailed, and exhaustive survey of these things in this book, you will be disappointed. You could write a tome on each one. And still have enough left over for a sequel.

Also, please, keep in mind who is writing to you. The elder Bonner went to Georgetown University's Law Center in the 1970s. He never practiced law and has forgotten almost everything he learned. We are deliberately not trying to write a thorough, up-to-date guide to estate planning or tax avoidance. Nor are we trying to provide precise or practical advice.

Why?

Because we don't want you to make any important decisions based on this book alone. Setting up your own hard structures is much too complicated and too fraught with traps. This chapter simply lays out what we consider the main ideas involved, as understood by us, nonprofessionals with little patience for the details of estate planning or taxes. Our goal is merely to show you the kind of things you're going to have to deal with and to tell you a bit about our experience with them.

To those general warnings, we add two more:

First, you know what they say about the man who represents himself in a court case? He has a "fool for a lawyer." It's true of estate planning, too. If you try to do it yourself, your estate planner will be an idiot.

Second, we also want to alert you to the fact that there are, according to the old legal expression, many ways to skin this cat. We do not claim to be aware of all of them. And our approach may be very particular to us and our situation.

A WILL AND AN ESTATE PLAN

A colleague came up to me and said, "Why do you bother with all that complicated tax avoidance stuff? You can achieve the same thing with insurance."

This was not the first time we had heard about the insurance angle. The gist of it, as we understand it, is that certain life insurance payouts are not included in an estate, for estate tax purposes. So if you can convert wealth that you hold in a bank account or other assets to an insurance program, you may be able to avoid taxes.

May is a key word. Tax rules applying to insurance are complex. And they are subject to change.

We don't like using insurance in estate planning. First, because we always fall asleep when insurance agents begin to describe how their products work. And second, because much of the challenge of protecting wealth over generations is avoiding unnecessary costs. Over time, the fees and commissions in insurance programs tend to work against you. Insurance is big business. It is profitable because it gives itself a fat margin between what customers pay in and what it pays out.

Like almost everything else involved with multigenerational wealth planning, there's a big difference in how insurance works over a short term and how it works over a long term. Over a short term, you may protect yourself against a risk at reasonable cost. But over a long term, the risk is more likely to be realized as an event.

Over a long time, for example, death is not a risk; it's a certainty. The insurance companies know this. They price it in. You end up paying the cost of the loss, plus the cost of the insurance company's overhead and profits. In other words, you're not paying for insurance at all. You're just paying someone to mitigate and to help organize something that is bound to happen.

This comment applies to all insurance products. Taking your entire family and projecting it forward several generations, you are likely to suffer the calamities the insurance companies protect against. You will experience sickness, accidents, house fires, root canals, and other setbacks. The more the odds of these events approach 100 percent, the less sense it makes to pay an insurance company to cover them for you. You are not protecting yourself against risk; you are merely using insurance to finance the painful events of life. You could do so much more cheaply yourself by maintaining a family "emergency fund."

Insurance is expensive. It's a "high-friction" enterprise. Sales agents earn good livings. Actuaries and risk analysts are among the best-paid professionals in the financial sector. And then there are the inevitable lawyers who come along later to show why you shouldn't get the benefit the salesman promised you.

"Yes, all that is true," continued our colleague. "I hate insurance, too. But the difference between what you'll pay the IRS and what you'll pay the insurance industry can be huge.

"Let's say you've used up your exemptions. And the estate tax reverts back to its previous level, as scheduled. If you have a million dollars, the estate tax will cost you $550,000 in taxes to pass on $450,000 to your children. So there's plenty there for the insurance company. In this case, the insurance company takes a 10 percent commission right off the top. But who cares? You're going to lose $550,000, remember? Better to pay $100,000 to the insurance company than $550,000 to the IRS, right?

"Here's how it works. You just take your million and buy a life insurance product. Then you sell the death benefit to your heirs for peanuts—because who knows when you'll die? It's not worth very much. With this product, they end up getting a $1 million insurance payout—guaranteed."

"Yes," we replied. "If the insurance company is still in business. If the law hasn't changed. And let's hope the $1 million is still worth $1 million."

We didn't mention them, but there are other problems. The challenge to maintaining multigenerational wealth is not just getting money to the next generation without paying a hefty inheritance tax. The challenge is to put in place a system . . . an organization . . . a tradition . . . that allows wealth to be held, controlled, and managed over a long period of time. Part of that challenge is just to prevent letting it be chipped away by taxes, professional fees, or other charges. Insurance charges are to be avoided—if possible.

But there's another thing. As we've been pointing out, cash is a weak bungee cord for holding together a family fortune. It tends to stretch out . . . and disperse readily. A cash payment from an insurance company falls on most heirs like champagne. Within weeks, it is probably consumed.

You don't just want to get money from one generation to the next without paying the inheritance tax. That would be just a temporary solution. If it works at all, it leaves the next generation with the money and the problem of getting it to the following generation. It can save on taxes. But it does not create family money. That is something different.

We're not passing judgment on insurance products as a solution to the problem of estate planning. They could be a part of the hard structure that you put in place. That's entirely up to you. But keep in mind that the ultimate purpose of any hard structure is to be the shelter in which your family money lives. So you want to build that shelter very carefully. You want structures that will resist the storms that inevitably blow up. There will be challenges from the tax authorities, from your executors and trustees, and from trusted professionals.

There are market challenges, too. Suppose you set up a plan that gives your family a guaranteed return of 6 percent per year, locked in. And then suppose the inflation rate goes to 8 percent. Your family is guaranteed losses of 2 percent per year!

And then there are the heirs themselves. What will they want? Maybe not what you wanted for them.

Here's the point: You need carefully considered, thoughtfully put together structures that protect your family wealth. They must be rigid enough to hold up to the tempests that are surely coming. But they must be flexible enough to bend to the winds you can't possibly foresee. Locked into an insurance program, you may find yourself unable to shift your windscreen to face the challenges. Ideally, you do not want to have to depend on an insurance company—or any other company—to protect your family money.

In fact, the ideal estate plan is no plan at all. Or perhaps we should put that differently. The ideal thing is not to need an estate plan. Why? Because an estate is what you leave when you die. Ideally, you don't die. Of course, that is unlikely. But when you do die, you might still have organized your affairs so well that you leave no estate. So you don't need a plan for it. If you do it right, you will not own anything when you die. Now that we think about it, it's probably better to not own much of anything all your life. But that's a long discussion.

Why not own anything? So you won't have to pass along an estate—and especially not an estate that will draw the interest of the taxmen.

By the way, in much of the world, people pretend not to own anything. That is why diamonds, rare coins, and other forms of wealth that are hard to keep track of are so popular. This is tax evasion. It's completely illegal. It is not recommended. Certainly not by us! But it's what people do. We've heard of people showing up at a coin dealer with bags of coins left to them by their father. The coins never showed up on any balance sheet. They were never recorded in the man's estate.

As far as the children knew, the coins had little value. Here's the conversation, as reported by a friend:

The coin dealer examined one of the coins.

"Why did you come to see me?" the dealer asked.

"Because Dad left a note with your address."

"How many of these do you have?"

"I don't know. Dad left about 10 bags of them. We all thought he was a little nutty."

"Well . . . he was not nutty. Those coins are worth about $10,000 each."

A legal strategy would have been to give the coins to the kids while they were alive. The tax law allows for gifts of up to $13,000 per child per year. Then, there's the lifetime gift and estate tax exemption currently at $5 million per taxpayer.

The point is, the less you have left in your estate at the time of your death, the better. Give it away. Sell it. Spend it. But get rid of it.

BACK TO THE BEGINNING . . .

One of the first considerations of hard structures is an obvious one. Family money has to be owned by someone. You want it to be owned by someone who doesn't die, doesn't get drunk at parties, and doesn't run off with a buxom redhead.

If you merely pass your money down from one generation to the next, it will soon disappear. The tax collector will take a big chunk. And one generation—perhaps this one, perhaps the next—will turn out to be a bad steward. So you typically need a hard structure—usually a trust—to give wealth continuity.

"A family can stand one weak generation," says our friend Lord Rees-Mogg. "But not two."

The most suitable owner of family wealth that we know of is a trust. And the most suitable trust for this sort of thing is what is known as a "dynasty" or "perpetual" trust. A trust can last, in theory, forever.

English common law provided a "rule against perpetuities." A favorite question on bar exams and law school tests required students to figure out how long such a trust could last before it was stopped by the rule. The answer: the length of any life in being at the time the trust was begun, plus 21 years. States have generally modified the rule to make it more predictable. But a few states have eliminated the rule all together. This makes it possible for a trust to last, theoretically, forever.

What's the advantage? A trust is owned by no one. At least, if it is set up properly. So you eliminate the inheritance tax issue. No property passes from the dead to the living.

It simply stays in the trust.

We've already seen how the miracle of compound interest works. Put money in a trust. Let it compound year after year. You end up with a lot of money. The Standard & Poor's (S&P) 500 has returned (nominally) 9.6 percent a year over the past 50 years. Had you invested $10 million a half-century ago, it could be worth $975 million now. Before taxes, of course.

We've seen, too, how the miracle of compound interest works against you. The annual fees and charges on a mutual fund account of $100,000 can be as much as $2,500. Not a big deal in a single year, perhaps. But spread over a couple generations the fees compound, effectively transferring a large part of your fortune to the mutual fund company.

Same thing with taxes. It's all very well to want to pay your "fair share," but every 1 percent taken by the taxmen is magnified by time. On $1 million, 1 percent per year, compounded over 70 years—that's $1 million!

U.S. citizens cannot avoid federal income and capital gains taxes by using trusts. It's not that easy. But the avoidance of the inheritance taxes is a significant achievement. Put $10 million in a dynasty trust today. At a 6 percent annual rate of return (without capital gains or income taxes), it will grow to about $184 million in 50 years. But if the same money passes through two generations and is subject to a 55 percent inheritance tax, with a $1 million exemption, it will be worth only about $39 million at the end of the period.

Currently, there's a $5 million exemption. That is, an individual can put $5 million into a dynasty trust without paying a gift or inheritance tax. A typical strategy for increasing the transfer to the trust involves using the $5 million as a down payment so that additional assets can be bought.

If, for example, you have a business worth $10 million, you can give $5 million to the trust and then the trust gives you back the $5 million, along with a promissory note for another $5 million, in return for the business. Thereafter, the trust would have to pay off the note, but it would trigger no gift or inheritance tax in the process. Had the business been earning about $500,000 per year in profit, the numbers work easily. The owner of the business—the trust—uses the profits over a 10-year period to pay you off. At the end of the period, the trust is the full owner of the $10 million business. No estate or gift taxes due.

But the tricks do not end there. That's where they start. For example, a minority interest in a business is subject to a discount. A business is simply not worth as much if you do not control it. So, rather than sell the business to the trust at full market price all at once, you may sell it in pieces and reduce the price of each piece to reflect the minority discount. How much of a discount can you get? It depends. But we have seen some as high as 40 percent.

Another common way to reduce the value of the assets you put into a trust is to divide them into two parts. One part is the part you assign to the trust. The other part is a "life estate," giving you the right to the income from it while you are alive. Depending on how old you are, a "life estate" or a "life interest" should substantially reduce the value of the remainder of the asset.

Remember, the goal is to reduce the value of the asset as much as possible, pay the gift tax, as necessary, and get it into the trust. Thereafter, you will pay no further gift or inheritance taxes. This won't mean anything initially. But over a couple of generations, it will be very important to you.

You will notice, too, that it is best to put assets in a trust before they become valuable. If you are starting a business, for example, put it in the trust before it has succeeded. That way, the gift tax will be low, simply because the gift isn't worth very much. Often, families have some assets that they consider good bets for growth and others that are already fully mature. Put the growth assets in the family trust.

AN INTENTIONALLY DEFECTIVE TRUST

We're talking about ways to overcome the effect of estate taxes. It's bad enough that you have to give one-third to one-half of everything you earn to the government during your lifetime. You don't want to pay more when you finally adjourn.

This year is special. Congress extended a special estate tax break until the end of 2012. After January 1, 2013, the tax could go back up to 55 percent. This is a huge savings this year. It's tempting to trip mama at the top of the stairs. Or even fall down yourself. You could save a lot of money.

But unless you're sure you're going to enter the celestial choir before midnight on December 31, 2012, you need a strategy for moderating the effects of the death levy. You could try an insurance program. Or you could use something called an "intentionally defective trust."

Let's say you have a pawnshop. It produces $100,000 in net earnings per year. It is worth $1 million, if you were to sell it. But you want to pass it on to your heirs.

Here's what you do: You sell it to a trust with your children or grandchildren as beneficiaries. You retain a right to change the trustee. The trust is, therefore, defective. *For federal income tax purposes, it is as though it didn't exist.* But for estate tax purposes, it effectively transfers the asset into a trust for the benefit of those people you want to have it.

You sold the pawnshop. You didn't give it away. So far, so good. No gift taxes, either. But the buyer (the trust) needs to pay you for it. You have taken the asset and transferred it to the trust. So the trust takes the income—$100,000 per year—and pays it to you. Meanwhile, you use the money to pay the taxes on the earnings and to pocket what is left.

At the end of, say, 10 years, the trust owns the pawnshop free and clear. Then you give up the right to change the trustee. This perfects the trust: From this point on, the trust is viewed as the owner for U.S. federal income tax purposes, as well as for inheritance tax purposes. The asset has been transferred, free of death taxes.

We remind you that this explanation is complex trust law as fathomed by a poet with attention deficit disorder. Don't try this without competent, professional advice. But certainly consider it for your own purposes. It has the potential to save you a lot of money.

Trust law is extremely complicated, especially where it intersects with tax law. In America, as in many other places, the authorities will not let you escape taxes simply by setting up a trust. But we've just seen how you could save a bundle of money.

Trusts are useful—perhaps indispensable—if you're going to try to turn your personal money into "family money." Even if you weren't able to avoid inheritance/gift taxes on the first transfer to the trust, future generations could use it to escape death duties. The bottom line is that trusts are an important part of the "hard structures" you will have to master. The trust department of any major bank can help you set one up. Just be sure you know what you're trying to achieve and that you have a competent professional on the other side of the table.

When we started, we went to a bookstore and bought a book on international tax structures. We can't say that we were able to master the subject in this manner. But at least we could sound like we knew what we were talking about when we spoke to the trust lawyers.

EXPATRIATE YOURSELF

We tend to forget about state and local taxes. But they have gotten higher and higher. In Baltimore, for example, the combination of state and local taxes adds up to nearly 10 percent. And yet, these taxes can be escaped. A dynasty trust, created in the right place, in the right way, will not pay state and local taxes. Over time, this is a huge savings. If you can avoid a 10 percent tax hit each year, you must do it.

And while we are on the subject of locating your trust in a low-tax state, this is a good place to introduce a simple tax-saving angle that is the kind of thing family money must do. At the risk of repeating ourselves, a 10 percent tax may not make a huge difference in the average person's life, but over time it will destroy a family fortune. We can't say it often enough. Time is an ally of family money—but also an enemy. You have to do all you can to reduce the deleterious effects of time by cutting out any unnecessary, recurrent expenses.

So how do you avoid high state and local taxes? Easy. You move. You expatriate.

Expatriation is most frequently discussed in its more radical form: leaving the country. We'll get to that in a minute. In a word, we're in favor of it. Europeans and other nationalities do it all the time. But it's a bigger move for Americans because they can't just move out to avoid U.S. taxes. They also have to give up their U.S. citizenship. Not many people are willing to do that. And it's not a good idea—for most people.

But there's also unradical expatriation. You can simply move out of your high-tax state to a low-tax state. No law against it.

Fairly easy to do. No need to learn a foreign language or drive on the wrong side of the road. Heck, you might also get a lifestyle improvement.

For example, part of the reason tax rates in Baltimore are so high is that until 2010, the state had a special 6.25 percent tax on "millionaires." The tax was imposed for the usual reason. The spendthrifts in the state legislature ran over their budget. They decided that they could squeeze the rich who, according to the governor, were "willing and able to pay their fair share." The *Baltimore Sun* predicted that they would "grin and bear it."[1]

Interestingly, the state does have the second highest millionaire total in the nation. Which is not exactly surprising, considering that the federal government is the biggest, richest, highest-margin growth industry in the country and that Washington, D.C., is surrounded on three sides by Maryland.

In 2008, the first year the new tax was imposed, there were about 3,000 million-dollar tax returns filed in the state. The following year there were only about 2,000. The financial crisis surely knocked out some of them. But a few hundred probably decamped for less costly tax jurisdictions.

In our own family, for example, we now have three Florida residents. A few years ago, we had none. They get better weather. And they save nearly 10 percent on their taxes. We wouldn't be surprised to see a few more people move down there soon. Moving overseas works, too. You may not save on your U.S. federal taxes. But if you are not a resident of any state, you don't pay state taxes.

There—that takes care of local and state tax issues. And the inheritance/gift tax, too.

USING TAX HAVENS

But let's turn to federal taxes. You can't save federal taxes by moving to a different state. Or by moving out of the country. And a trust usually doesn't help, either. In the United States, you are generally considered the owner of the funds you put in a trust. You'll pay tax on them. Distributions are generally taxed, too—as though they were the products of an investment account.

However, a trust can be an exceptionally good way to avoid *all* taxes—including income and capital gain taxes—if you set it up the right way. Again, it may not matter to the ordinary person. He pays relatively little in taxes. And he figures, *grosso modo*, that he gets as much from the government as he contributes. But it's a very different calculation for family money. Income and capital gain taxes cut deeply into the rate at which you can accumulate wealth. As you can see from the compounding tables in Chapter 3, even relatively small differences in rates of return (net of taxes) make a dramatic difference to the results.

Some places—such as the Cayman Islands, the Channel Islands, and Cyprus—do a decent business helping out the "1 percent" of people who have enough money to make it worth trying to avoid taxes. These places are often islands, which is probably the source of the "offshore" designation. They provide rich people with a way to legally reduce their tax exposure. They also help people preserve their privacy. And they provide protection from financial predators.

Typically, they allow two kinds of tax reduction. First, they allow people to live in their jurisdictions at low—or no—tax rates. Sometimes you can negotiate a deal with a tax haven. Often, you don't have to. Tax havens typically do not tax income from a trade or business that is not done locally. As you can imagine, few people earn much money from local tax haven businesses. Instead, the typical tax haven exile has already made his money or has income from non-local sources.

Note that this opportunity does not apply to U.S. citizens. U.S. citizens pay U.S. taxes no matter where they live or where they put their money, which we'll discuss in a minute.

As attractive as it is to avoid taxes, few people really want to live in these tax haven places, so some of these residents are more residents *de jure* than *de facto*. Note that most people are taxed by the government of the place where they live. But rich people often have more than one house. So where do they live?

Where do you live?

We—the Bonner family—like living in different places. We like learning languages and local customs. And our business is global, with offices in at least 10 different countries. We move around, often trying just to keep up with business needs.

So where do we live? It is often a difficult question to answer.

The general rule is that residence is determined by a long list of interrogatories, beginning with where a person actually spends most of his time and ending with where he goes to church and with whom he plays bridge. Most countries claim anyone who stays more than half the year within their borders as a resident. And most then expect him to pay taxes like any other resident.

So you might think that someone who establishes an official residence in, say, Guernsey, and who does not stay anywhere else more than 182 days, is home free from a tax standpoint. That is basically correct, but not guaranteed. Any country can nab the fellow if they think they can make a sufficient case that he is in fact a resident. Or if they can grab his money, forcing him to make the case for why he is *not* a resident.

Imagine that you live officially in Jersey but nip across to France regularly. Imagine that you spend 180 days in France, and the rest of the time you spend only a couple of months in several different places. You have bank accounts in France. You have a house, friends, a business. The more contacts you have, the easier it will be for the French tax officials to say that you are a resident of France more than anywhere else.

And what are you going to say in your defense? And to whom? Fighting with tax officials is usually a losing battle. They often seize your assets first. Then you have the burden of proof, proving a negative, which is very heavy.

In the case of residence issues, you typically argue that you are not a resident of one country by proving that you are a resident of another. Not easy to do when you travel frequently. So what you want to do is to establish "permanent" residency somewhere, whether or not you actually ever live there.

Permanent residency gives you a plausible answer to the question about where you live. And it gives you a hub—in a legal or tax sense—around which your financial life can be organized. It is usually established by actual, physical residence, but it can later become rather abstract. The key is to fix a place where you keep a house, keep your records, pay your taxes, buy a burial plot, bank, have a passport, vote, be a member of churches and local organizations—all the things that residents normally do. Your physical whereabouts hardly matter if you move about and you've built your permanent residency correctly.

Naturally, the best place to be a permanent resident of is a place where you would plausibly be a real resident, where you are able to build the kind of connections you need and where tax rates are low. This, of course, depends on many different considerations. Family wealth is often low-income wealth, for example. You favor assets or organize your financial life so that you don't have much taxable income. So even if a place has high income tax rates, it may still be a nice place to live. And if you have your family wealth in a trust, inheritance taxes may not matter either.

It is a matter that requires careful planning. For most people, however, this kind of planning is impossible. Life goes on. It won't wait or conform readily to these considerations. You develop businesses, relationships, residences, careers, and so forth faster than you can plan for them. And since you don't usually know where you're going in life, it's impossible to plan for the future anyway—at least at this level.

But keep in mind that a family needs a permanent home. (We'll talk more about this later.) That permanent home should be in the "right" place. A place where it is safe, stable, and plausible.

By plausible we mean that it shouldn't raise eyebrows every time you cross a border. If you claim to be a permanent resident of a country, you should at least speak the local language.

Once you have your permanent residence established, you then can work on building out the structures that you need, depending on the laws of the resident country. That poses particular challenges for Americans, which we'll get to in a moment. But first a word about how the world actually works.

TAXES ARE LARGELY A MATTER OF CULTURE

We lived for many years in Europe. We paid taxes in the United States, France, and England simultaneously. Our businesses, meanwhile, paid taxes in the United States, France, Britain, Ireland, India, Spain, South Africa, and Australia. We were audited by several countries, often simultaneously. We were cross-referenced. We were studied, followed, tracked, and shaken down.

The experience showed us how the tax system really works. First, you have to understand, there is no real, single, clear tax law. There are lots of tax laws. Often, they are incomprehensible, mutually inconsistent, and almost impossible to apply in a rational, foreseeable way. Just how they are applied is as much a matter of culture, temperament, and fashion as it is of law.

Americans are particularly ill-prepared to deal with international taxation in an effective way. We Americans tend to try to obey the law.

When we first moved to France, we confronted a different type of tax system. We bought a house. Naturally, we hired lawyers to structure the purchase in a taxwise manner. And naturally, the lawyers failed to foresee what would happen. Within a few months, we got a notice telling us we owed a rather large amount of tax, the consequence of a detail we no longer recall.

What we do recall is that we went to see the local attorney we had used to set up the deal, who explained why it wasn't her fault. And when asked if we could contest the matter, she replied with something like, "The law is pretty clear on this point. You're supposed to pay."

We did.

Later, when we got to know people better, we realized that we had been fools. Lawyers in France—and other countries—typically give one kind of advice to Americans and another to their local clients. And when we described the transaction to an accountant a few years later, he looked horrified. Of the tax bill, he inquired in disbelief and amazement:

"You did what with it?"

"Well, we paid it. . . ."

"You paid it? You're not supposed to do that. The tax people must have been shocked. They were just negotiating with you. They didn't expect you to pay it."

The French tax system looks a lot like the U.S. system—on paper. The same concepts are there. Many of the same numbers, too. But the way it works is quite different. It is Anglo-Saxon—or perhaps European business school—on the outside. On the inside, it is Latin. It may appear clear and unambiguous, but there is always room for discussion.

Besides, most tax matters are not criminal. They are like disputes between a house owner and a plumber—or a man and his tailor. There is plenty of bluff and bluster on both sides and an inevitable settlement. Neither the taxpayer nor the tax collector is bound to tell the truth. Neither is particularly shocked or offended when he discovers the other is lying to him. And neither takes the tax law completely seriously.

Americans naively value "the truth" and "the law" much more than most foreigners. They also have some residual respect for the government. These are weaknesses in the American character that will probably be corrected in the years ahead. But readers should be aware that their own instincts and training are not always well suited to the circumstances in which they live.

There isn't anything especially uplifting or noble about submitting to governmental authority. Instead, treat it as it deserves to be treated— sometimes a protector, often a predator. It may be a sin to lie to your mother. But it is only a crime to lie to the government. And only a fool would tell the truth to a predator.

Tax havens have been used for many years to protect people from predatory governments. In World War II, for example, Switzerland was where wealthy German and Polish Jews put their money. Asked about it by the authorities, they surely lied. Under duress, many were forced to repatriate their wealth so that the Nazi government of the time could confiscate it. But if they could get away with it, they used the tax haven to protect their wealth. Those who survived were glad they did.

Tax havens are still useful, though less so. Governments all over the world have ganged up against them. In order to use the world's banking system and benefit from trade and travel agreements, the tax havens are being forced to open up their records and betray their clients.

Of course, many of the clients are probably rogues and rascals. Dictators use tax havens, too. So do drug dealers. And some of the money that ends up in tax havens may be "black" money, earned without the benefit of taxation. There may even be a "terrorist" with a bank account in the Cayman Islands or Luxembourg.

Be that as it may, our interest in tax havens is that they can provide low-cost (taxwise) jurisdictions for parking and managing family money. But there's another reason for holding money in tax havens. Remember that the best strategy for making money is to concentrate your forces on a narrow front, where you can make a competitive breakthrough. But the best way to protect money is to spread it out. You don't want all your eggs in one basket.

Typically, you will have your house and most of your assets in your home country. You may have investment property. You may have stocks, bonds, and cash, as well as business interests. These may be the elements of your family wealth. They may be only your personal wealth. But it's also a good idea to have some wealth outside the country where you live and work. Why? You never know.

Certainly, anyone who escaped from Nazi Germany in the 1930s could give you an answer. Here's one memoir that gives you a sense of how predatory governments can become:

GOLD AND MONEY IN EXTREMIS— ONE MAN'S STORY

By Rich Rabkin

My economic education was started as a child by my grandfather who was a living testimonial to the above. At 99 years of age, he felt there was simply too much debt and that the long downward spiral was underway with very difficult times ahead. Having lived through times of "extremis," his account of fiat money, war, gold, and survival serves as a reminder that those who chose to ignore history do so at their own peril.

On September 17, 1939, Russia invaded Poland, and over the next year over 1.7 million Poles were deported to labor camps or sent into exile into Kazakhstan and Siberia. Their only crime at the time was being Polish citizens. None of the lands and homes taken by the Russians was returned to the Poles after the war despite their release from the Gulag in 1942, and fighting with great distinction under the British army. Those who returned did so at their own risk. Per the 1943 treaty of Tehran, eastern Poland remained Russian. Winston Churchill said of Poland in 1946 in the House of Commons, "We who went to war on her behalf . . . watch with sorrow the strange outcome of our endeavors." Fiat money is particularly vulnerable during war and generally becomes rapidly worthless when countries fall. Such was the case for my grandparents, who in 1939 resided in eastern Poland. This is their story as told to me by my grandfather, Marion Szablicki:

> Early morning on September 18, 1939, I learned that the rumors of the Russian invasion of eastern Poland were true. Just three weeks before, we had been attacked from the south by Germany. Russia now attacked Poland from the east. In a matter of weeks, Poland was overrun. I reenlisted in the army after the Germans invaded, but upon hearing this news, those of us from the east were told to go home. I had a wife and a three-year-old daughter to protect. I left to go back to our village immediately, covering the 40-kilometer journey on foot in a day.
>
> We lived near the Russian border and I knew the soldiers would arrive soon. I was working class; however, my wife's family was better off, and

we had a very modest amount of gold and jewelry kept by her family since the Polish inflation 15 years prior. I hid it carefully in a hole in the ground. I knew our national currency (the zloty) would not last, and I knew that gold would be the only money I could use to try and save us.

Poland's inflation was concurrent with the Weimar in Germany. My father, brothers, and I bartered for food, goods, services, and gold. Gold was preferred to cash. My father was well versed in history, and he often he cited the great inflation of prerevolutionary France. It was he who taught me that gold was the only money with no sovereign borders.

Russian soldiers arrived at our village two days later.

Having been born in far eastern Siberia, and a boxer in Russia years earlier, I was fluent in Russian. I remembered their revolution; anyone who was not a peasant or was in any way educated was in danger. I spoke with many soldiers seeking clues about our fate.

Two weeks later, my wife's father, a recently retired Polish officer and landowner, was arrested and taken away by the NKVD [the secret police of the Soviet Union]. We never saw him again. He was likely executed at the Katyn massacre, where thousands of other Polish officers were later found to have been killed.

I immediately sent my wife's mother away. We would never see her again, either.

Winter came in earnest with a scarcity of goods and whisperings of mass deportations. In early February 1940, policemen and landowners and many educated people were arrested and deported along with their relatives. Late one night I received a knock on my door. In walked four armed Russian soldiers. One of them was a man I had spoken with several times over the previous months. I greeted them politely in Russian.

I was ordered to get my coat and accompany them.

I was taken to a station and asked many questions. It was a stroke of luck for me that the Russian soldier to whom I had spoken with in the past was present. After conferring with the others, he said, "because you were born in Siberia, speak Russian, and you're an uneducated worker—much like us, we will not detain you further, you may go for now." He then gently grabbed my elbow and said very quietly, "Go back to your family, Marion, get prepared for deportation to Siberia." I ran home.

At dawn the next morning I retrieved the gold and jewelry. I found my largest boots and heaviest jacket. I lined the bottom of my boots carefully with small coins and put leather over the insoles. I slit the heels, carefully hollowed out what I could, and stuffed larger gold coins inside the cavities. Finally, I opened up various parts of my jacket and distributed more gold chain and coins in it—with great care so they did not rattle and were hard to detect.

(Continued)

Just days later, we were awakened before dawn and told we were being deported to Siberia, with 15 minutes to gather any personal belongings needed for immediate use. Our land, homes, and possessions were now property of the Russian state. My wife, my three-year-old daughter, and I were put into a truck with a group of others and taken to a railroad station.

We would never see our parents or siblings again or set foot on Polish soil.

I was only relieved that they did not check my jacket or my shoes. My gold was going with me.

When the train arrived many hours later we were put into cattle cars. The trip to Siberia took almost 3 weeks. It was hellish, we were cramped in overcrowded cars with no toilet, and only a hole cut in the floor, with scarcely any food or water. We were given dark bread and water every few days. Many died, and they were simply thrown off the train, be they men women or children. I recall the last time I wept during those years: a baby had been born in our boxcar during the journey; it had died and was cast off the train by the soldiers like rubbish.

We finally arrived in northern Kazakhstan near the Siberian border. A ramshackle village was to be our new home. The Poles could not leave here under the penalty of death. It was freezing cold, 20 degrees below zero. The locals were told they must shelter us, but they were also very poor; the NKVD allocated three or four families to a house. The locals were as good as they could be to us under the circumstances.

Immediately that freezing winter, I needed to use my gold: I first bartered with a man to acquire better living quarters and then I exchanged with a local man some gold chain links and coins for a fair sum of rubles. I used these to get bread and food for the remainder of that winter, which was brutal. I also bought tools and worked cutting wood, fixing stairs, or other odd jobs for a few rubles or more often food. I sometimes went days without food so that my daughter and wife could eat. We managed to survive the first harsh winter and the following summer, and despite my coming down with malaria and my wife almost dying of typhus. We were able to get medicine and food from those who had it—as long as we had some gold. Zlotys (Polish currency) had never been accepted, rubles were, but gold was now preferred over anything.

Finally, one day in 1942, the exiled Poles were summoned by the local NKVD. We were being released, we suddenly were free to go—with no reason being given.

(Germany had attacked Russia on June 22, 1941, and the Poles, by agreement, were to be released from the gulag to form an army in Persia.)

I asked a Russian official. He said, "Marion, get to the train station and get on a train as fast as possible before they change their minds."

We left within hours. Many were simply too weak to go anywhere. Many simply remained. Upon arrival, we learned the Polish Army was being reformed, but the man in charge of the station was telling everyone that the trains were already overfull.

I very quietly made my way to the man in charge and offered him three gold coins, among my last, one for each of us—to get passage on the next train. He agreed. When the train arrived, he quietly motioned us around to the far side, spoke with another official, and they put us on the train, citing "special orders." We were finally on our way out of that terrible place and were now among thousands of exiled Poles all racing south as fast as possible to get into General Anders's Polish Army.

We crossed the Caspian Sea in a ship and arrived in Persia (Iran). We were lucky to be on that train, and on an early ship; later boats were turned back, the quota filled, they were sent back to Russia.

Most of us arrived in Persia emaciated. The local people took my family into their home those first weeks and nursed us back to health, and they were among the kindest people I have ever met.

I joined the Polish Second Corps under General Anders. Finally, there was hope for us. My wife and daughter were evacuated, though I thought they were on their way to South Africa, but instead they were sent to India. I didn't see them again for six years. For a long while, neither of us knew the whereabouts of one another, or if we were dead or alive.

I fought in Africa and Italy, and notably, Monte Cassino. Never have I seen so much blood and determination as there. We led the decisive final charge on the German-held Abbey. I was proud to be a Pole that day.

The war drew to a close, and I found out my wife and daughter were still in India, but that they would be moved somewhere near London. I would be going there, too, after my service.

When we were finally reunited in London two years later, it was like a miracle. Thankfully, Mr. Churchill did not force repatriation upon the Poles. All of my brothers had died in the war in the resistance. Without the knowledge my father imparted to me about money and history, we would not have made it.

I owe my life to a handful of gold coins and chains.

Several days before we were to leave for Australia to immigrate, I received a call. "Marion, we have an open slot for America—do you want it?" I told him yes.

He said to get here as soon as possible. I ran the entire way.

Victoria Szablicki passed away on June 5, 2011. Marion passed away on June 16, just 11 days later at 100 years of age and less than two years after receiving his last medal, the Siberian Cross, from the Polish government. They had been married for over 76 years.[2]

You never know.

You also never know what will happen to the currency in which your money is calibrated. The dollar, the pound, the euro, and other currencies are controlled by governments. And, occasionally, governments get themselves into a jam. When they do, they don't hesitate to destroy their own currencies.

We have a reminder of one of these events—a $100 trillion bill issued by Zimbabwe in 2009 (Figure 7.1).

You can imagine what happened to people who kept all their wealth in Zim dollars! An overseas account gives you some protection—against predatory governments, against incompetent monetary systems, against financial catastrophes, and against taxes.

There's nothing underhanded, illegal, immoral, or even shady about using offshore, foreign currency accounts. No need to lie about it, either. You can use accounts in tax havens legitimately to hold and invest wealth. Wealthy families typically do.

Remember, your family's wealth depends on two variables: its net (of costs/taxes) return per year and the number of years it continues. Taxes are the main cost. They need to be reduced so that your net rate of return will remain high. That is why one of your hard structures will ideally be located in a tax haven. Ideally, you will have a bank or

Figure 7.1 $100 Trillion Zimbabwe Bill

investment firm that you trust—with someone you know you can work with, with an unassailable reputation and an unleveraged balance sheet, and low fees. This is not going to be easy to find. Few institutions will match that description. And the best of them won't want you for a customer.

AN OVERSEAS ACCOUNT

Let us relate our experience. When we finally had made a little money, after 30 years of "busting our humps," we decided to find a private bank to hold it for us. We went around London, which was convenient for us at the time, talking to the leading "private client" departments at leading banks. Each one had a group of well-dressed, well-spoken business school graduates. And each group had the same palaver, referring to modern portfolio management theories, the "efficient frontier" of investment returns, and so forth. By then, we knew this talk was mostly gobbledygook. Then, we finally found one investment firm with its feet on the ground. Its analysts saw the world the way we did. The firm even specialized in family office clients. It seemed like a perfect fit. There was just one problem.

Sitting in the oak-paneled conference room, not far off Pall Mall, we saw a look of distress in the banker's eyes. We had been having a good conversation and were pleased to find that we were kindred spirits, at least in matters of economics. But we had just told him how much money we would like to place in the bank.

"I'm sorry, sir," said this very proper Englishman. "I don't know how to tell you this . . . so I'll just tell you. You don't have enough money to interest us. We only take accounts in excess of $200 million."

This came as a shock. We were surprised that there were enough clients with $200 million that the bank could make a business of managing them.

Later, we went to another country and found someone willing to take our piddling account. But most Americans face a further problem: Foreign banks don't want American clients. Why? Because the United States imposes such a burden of paperwork and menaces both clients and banks with such painful penalties, the banks have generally thrown up their hands and tossed out their U.S. clients.

This is a nuisance. But not an insurmountable obstacle. We'll tell you how we solved this problem in a minute. But a simple way to do it is to set up an account in a foreign country that is not perceived as a tax haven. Canada. Denmark. Britain. You will get most of the benefits of an "offshore" account in a major bank such as HSBC or Barclays, but without the problems.

You've heard the old saying: "Speak truth to power." You might prefer to give it the lies it deserves. But while there's no sin in lying to authority, there are a lot of inconveniences. Banks all are subject to international rules that require them to "know thy customer." Whenever we open an account we have to send proof of residence, not to mention passports and other identification. You could probably fabricate a whole separate non-U.S. identity in order to open a tax haven account, but God knows what would happen if you were discovered. You risk losing all the money you were so desperate to protect.

Not only that, but when you do squirrely things, you end up with a squirrely, difficult life. We had a friend who sold his business, made some money, and then sought professional help to lower the tax bill. He ended up with a foundation in Lichtenstein. The plan seemed to go okay at first. It looked like he saved a lot of money.

But it gradually became clear that he had made himself prisoner of his tax-saving strategy. We don't know the details of what he did. But it was evidently the idea of some bright lawyer or tax planner. On the surface, it was "legal" and permissible. But there are plenty of gray areas in and about the tax code. He had gotten himself into an area that was not only gray but dangerous. The IRS threatened to declare his tax-saving strategy not only ineffective but illegal. In theory, he could have been tried for a crime and put in jail.

As a precaution, our friend fled to Europe. Whether this was legally effective or not, we don't know. But having the Atlantic Ocean between him and the IRS made him feel safer. The trouble was it also put an ocean between his wife and her family. Living in Paris was fun—for a while. But the couple soon felt cut off from their own children and from the life they wanted to lead.

"I wish I had never tried to save on taxes. It's just not worth it," he told us.

Our friend contacted more lawyers. The new guys went to the IRS. They posed the situation as a hypothetical:" Suppose we had a client who . . .

Eventually, they were able to negotiate a settlement with the taxmen. Our friend gave up his foundation and his tax-saving plan. He paid the tax he would have paid had he not embarked on his tax adventure years earlier. He paid a modest fine and immodest legal fees. The deal was done.

There are a lot of tax strategies on offer. It is an arms race to find a loophole that the IRS has not noticed and then to use it before it is closed. One loophole tends to lead to another. Eventually, you have so many loopholes that your whole strategy gets a little loopy.

And, generally, the more complicated your strategy, the less effective it is. Lawyers and accountants get rich. You get poor, frustrated, and nervous. Many, maybe even most, are not worth the risk, the expense, and the familial wear and tear.

This is true not only of tax plans but also of trusts. You set something up. It sounds good. Then, conditions change and you find you are a prisoner of the system. You can't change it—not easily.

In the case of trusts, the key element is surrendering control of assets. If you give up control, the asset may be properly considered not yours. If it is not yours, the taxes that arise from it will no longer be your concern. At least that is the idea.

If you don't give up control, the tax authorities will generally consider that you are still the rightful owner. Gains will be attributed to you. Taxes will be expected from you.

But giving up control can be a frightening thing to do. You may have worked all your life to build up wealth. Then, by signing a document, you will no longer be able to decide what happens to it. Legal "ownership" could be in the hands of someone you don't even know: a trustee. What if the trustee stabs you in the back? How do you control the trustee? What can you do if the trustee absconds with your money?

The world of trusts is a scary world for many people. We wouldn't blame you if you didn't want to go there. But it seems to be the place to go if you want to preserve wealth over a long period of time.

A variant on the theme is the family corporation owned by a trust. This gives the family a greater measure of control over the source of its wealth. While the trustee may ultimately control the shares, at least the business can be directly controlled by the family.

Of course, there are many ways to secure your trust. There are trusts that give you the right to take back the assets you put in it. There are others that allow you to benefit from those assets; often, the trustee is instructed to provide you with an income from the assets.

AMERICANS' UNIQUE TAX PROBLEM

Which brings us back to the problem faced by Americans. The U.S. border police are essentially charged with a double mission: to keep poor people from getting into the United States and to keep rich people from getting out. Illegal immigration is a problem on one side; illegal emigration is a problem on the other.

Millions of people sneak into the United States. Millions sneak out. Those who come in do so to make their fortunes. Those who sneak out often do so to protect the fortunes that they created already. Even today, the United States is still a good place to make a fortune— though probably not as good as it was and probably not as good as the emerging economies. But when it comes to protecting and preserving a fortune, the United States is not a good place to be.

The world is a competitive place. Poor people compete with each other for jobs. Rich people compete, too. Wealth, beyond what is needed for survival, is relative. You have a certain amount. Someone else has more. Standards for being "wealthy" change with place and time. A person with very little money may still be considered wealthy in an African village. Put him in Zurich and the locals will put him on welfare.

In 1950, a "millionaire" was a very wealthy person in America. Now there's a millionaire next door and two down the street. If you own a house in a good neighborhood, you're likely to be a millionaire. The standards for what people consider wealthy have moved on. It takes a lot more money to be considered rich than it did a half-century ago.

If you want to be rich by U.S. standards, you can safely stay put in the United States. You'll be taxed like the rest of us. You'll get the asset growth, more or less, that everyone else gets.

But if you want to be rich by world standards, you probably need to move at least a portion of your financial life overseas. We have already looked at this from an investment perspective. Now we will see what it can do for your tax strategy.

Foreigners have a big advantage. They can compound their money at lower tax rates. Tax rates in the emerging markets, generally, are much lower. In Russia, for example, the top marginal tax rate is only 13 percent. In Europe, tax rates are higher than those in the United States. France even imposes a "wealth tax."

But this is misleading. Europeans have much more flexibility as to how they organize their financial lives. A Frenchman who has a fortune or wants to build one can move out of the country. He has only to move himself to Brussels, for example, to dodge the French tax *fisc*. Then, taking the TGV to Paris gives him less of a daily commute than many people who live and work in LA or New York. Also, Europeans have a long history of using trusts and other tax-reducing strategies. We don't know, but our guess is that the typical Old Money family figured these things out decades ago—or it wouldn't still be an Old Money family!

Nor did an effective tax strategy require the European to remove himself to a godforsaken island far from civilized life. Until recently, London was perhaps the world's largest and most important tax haven. The United Kingdom did not tax residents on income that they brought in from outside the country. This, of course, attracted rich people and helped create the most dynamic financial industry in the world.

Again, Americans could not benefit from this or from any other substantial tax-saving opportunity. The U.S. tax law reaches out and puts its hands on our shoulders no matter where we are. Many are the schemes and scams developed to get around this problem. Some are probably even legal. Many more are probably illegal or simply so confusing that nobody wants to invest the time and effort to figure out what is going on. If you could, for example, set up a business with foreign ownership, you could get out of the U.S. system. Foreign-owned companies are not taxed by the United States unless they are doing business in the United States and thus are able to accumulate profits free of U.S. tax.

We can imagine that the foreign owners give a contract to a U.S. citizen, which effectively gives him control over those profits—and perhaps envisions that they will be transferred to him at some point in the future. But since the money remains the legal property of the foreign-owned business, the American citizen is not taxed on it.

We can imagine that the foreigners might also put the money in a foreign-granted trust—and that perhaps the American's family might be among the list of potential beneficiaries. There is probably an unlimited number of confections that might be created. We can imagine that the IRS has a whole army of agents trying to figure out why the people who create these things should go to jail.

But we do not want to get involved with complicated confections. We are trying to build durable "family money." We can't afford the kind of risks and uncertainties that these structures entail. Ultimately, the United States maintains the right to tax the beneficial owners of any montage—if they are American citizens. You can put in as many layers of corporations and trusts as you want and set up blind alleys to lead the IRS astray, but as long as you are a U.S. citizen, you will never be completely in the clear.

FIVE-COUNTRY STRATEGY

A friend of ours counsels people to diversify across several different countries. He says you should put yourself in one country, your bank in another, your business in another, your income in another, and your investments in a fifth one. Each country should be selected on the basis of how well it functions for that particular purpose. You want to live, for example, where you will not pay estate taxes when you die. And you want your investment accounts in a country that doesn't tax capital gains.

While this strategy makes sense, it is very impractical for most people. Most of us just don't have the energy or attention span to work out so many complicated arrangements. What's more, if you are an American, you come back to the same problem. The U.S. government taxes you—personally. It doesn't care where you live or where you put your money.

The same logic applies if you were to start a business overseas. Let us say you are a . . . ahem . . . writer. And let us say you have a book contract that will pay you $100,000. Theoretically, you could assign the contract to a company in a tax haven. Instead of getting paid $100,000, the company could pay you $50,000. That would be obviously taxable income. But what about the other $50,000? You might think it is nontaxable because your company is not subject to taxes in the place it is located. But it's not that simple. If the tax haven company is a U.S.-controlled foreign company, the IRS reserves the right to look into the company and determine the real source of its earnings and the real beneficial owners of the money. On these facts, the income would be reassigned to you.

This is not true, however, of real earnings of a foreign-based but not U.S.-controlled business. Imagine a business that sells cigarettes on a street corner in the Cayman Islands. Such a business would pay taxes locally. If it paid you a salary, you would pay current taxes only on that.

To glide over millions of complications, generally, you can play games. But it's not worth it—at least to us. If you are an American, it is probably best to believe that you will be taxed like other Americans, no matter how many corporations and bank accounts you set up.

However, if you are not an American or if the businesses or trusts you set up are not controlled by or granted by U.S. taxpayers, it is a much different matter. There is the trick. There is the game. There is the goal. While there are many ways to reduce taxes, in our opinion, the family with long-term wealth ambitions should try to develop businesses, trusts, and assets outside the long reach of U.S. tax authorities.

Why? Are U.S. taxes really higher? No. Are U.S. tax collectors more aggressive? Not necessarily. The reason is that having wealth outside the United States gives you a little room to maneuver.

This may seem odd or even evil, but remember that the person who wants to conserve money over several generations—generally a person who might be considered "rich"—must try to pay less tax than people of more modest means. We have seen what time does to money. It wears it down. It wears it out. And it whacks it with unexpected losses. You protect yourself by having businesses and investments that make enough gains to offset the losses and by reducing the impact of fees, taxes, and inflation.

Naturally, you use all the angles your local tax guy can figure out. But a real tax strategy will involve some form of expatriation so that you will be able to use the opportunities that sophisticated international tax planning allows you.

PUTTING IT ALL TOGETHER

Now let's try to put the pieces of the hard structure together. This is a strategy developed for Americans. But there are elements to it that could be useful to almost anyone.

You can hardly mention the subject of expatriation in America without at least a few people getting hot under the collar. Some people—often members of Congress—think expatriation is "unpatriotic." They think it is a disloyal, even traitorous, act.

"After all the United States of America has done for you," they say, "you're turning your back on us!"

Well, there are probably many people who would like to turn their backs on America and stop being Americans. But that's not what this strategy is about. It's about a family's financial strategy. We're not talking about loyalties, fidelities, sentimentalities, or even nationalities.

If you are an American citizen, alas, you can benefit from this strategy only if one trusted member of the family is *not* American. For citizens of other countries, this is not a problem. But let's talk to Americans for a moment. We're not suggesting that anyone stop being an American. We're suggesting that someone in your family might want to give up his U.S. citizenship rights and responsibilities for the benefit of the family. He will still be an American; he will not be a U.S. citizen.

In fact, it's almost impossible for most of us to stop being Americans. Whether we were born into it or became American by choice, it's not something we can easily turn our backs on.

We are still proud to be Americans, but we are not necessarily proud of our current government.

Nationality is what you are: the product of education, birth, and experience. You can go and live wherever you want; if you are American now, you will still be an American. You can speak a foreign language; you will still be an American. You can pay taxes in another country; you will still be an American. It's what you are. It's not something you can change—or not easily. If you are an American now, you will remain an American—whether you like it or not.

In a sense, we Americans consider expatriation, not because we want to stop being Americans but because we are Americans and because we want to continue being Americans. We want to remain the people we were so proud of being 200 years ago.

"In the beginning, all the world was America," wrote John Locke. He meant there was a time when the entire world was like America in the early eighteenth century: open and free, an Eden waiting to be discovered.

Most Americans are Americans because some ancestor willingly chose to look for something better. America was a citizenship of choice, not of chance. The idea was that people should have the right and the opportunity to go where they want and shape their own lives as best they can.

We still believe in that idea of America. And that's why we are still searching for places where we can live freer and better. That's what makes us Americans. We're searching, yearning, exploring, and endlessly looking for America, all over the world.

Besides, citizenship is a political creation—the product of laws passed by politicians. Nationality—being an American—is something very different. It is the product of culture, attitude, and custom, which are natural things, almost antipolitical by nature.

HOW IT WORKS

The key to this approach is to recognize that it is a family solution, not an individual solution. And it is not an attempt to break off contacts with our home country. Instead, it allows a family to keep its ties with the United States (or other home country) while developing wealth independent of the home tax system.

Whether this approach will work for you depends on your own circumstances and your goals.

Here's the idea in a nutshell: The essential ingredient is that one member of the family must not be a U.S. citizen. This family member—preferably a young person—should have few appreciated assets at the time of expatriation. This means that the "exit tax" will be minimal.

The family member who is outside the U.S. system must then set up non-U.S. hard structures. These structures become the holder/controller of the family's non-U.S. assets. Sounds simple enough. Of course, it is not. How it works—or whether it would work for you—depends on the exact circumstances of the case. But here is an idealized example so you can see how it might work:

Let's go back to the fellow with the pawnshop. Let's imagine that the family owns a whole string of pawnshops and that it earns $1 million per year in posttax profits each year. The pawnshop chain has a total net value of $10 million. The couple is very well off. We will assume they are big spenders, using the entire $1 million per year for living expenses.

But this family wants to protect the source of its wealth. And it wants to keep the business in the family. Normally (we will keep this simple by ignoring exemptions and other complications), the tax cost of passing the assets to the children would be $5.5 million. To pay these taxes, the children would likely have to sell pawnshops or mortgage the operation.

To avoid this problem, the young man expatriates. He pays no exit tax because he has no appreciated assets. He then sets up an offshore structure—typically a trust, a corporation, a new will, and a bank/investment account. This structure buys the pawnshops from the parents at fair market value. He pays $10 million, making yearly payments of $1 million for 10 years (plus interest). The money still comes out of the business. It still goes to the parents. But the business, the profit-generating capital asset over time, is moved to a foreign entity, where it is free and clear of U.S. taxes.

Remember, we are not talking about the real property in the United States or even the corporate earnings of the business. Both are still subject to U.S. taxes, since they both are U.S.-based. The IRS has not lost a penny of revenue. Nor has your family gained a penny by avoiding taxes.

But the business itself, as a capital asset, may now be beyond the range of the U.S. taxman. It may be transferred—in the trust structure—to the next generation *without tax consequences*. Its after-tax earnings, too, are now the property of a non-U.S. owner.

Now the family has a financial structure—and assets—beyond the U.S. tax system. It can now organize itself in a way that allows those assets to grow in a tax-advantaged way. It can pass them from one generation to the next, also without being hammered by the taxman each time the baton is passed.

Now, in this example, the $1 million of *post-tax* tax earnings may now build up, with interest and capital gains, also free from U.S. taxes. Properly managed, they may grow free from any taxes.

But wait! Wouldn't, in the preceding example, the parents have to pay a capital gains tax on the appreciated value of the business? Well, maybe.

It depends on their basis in the property. And in any case, the capital gains tax rate is much, much lower. It is only 15 percent of the appreciation of the gain. That is not 55 percent of the value of the transfer.

Readers will notice that this idea is almost the mirror image of what ambitious immigrants have done for years. Typically, a young man from Asia comes to the United States to do his studies. He establishes a toehold in America that is then used by his family. Often, the immigrant family does not move over entirely to the United States. Instead, it uses its U.S. base to hedge itself against calamities at home and give itself more opportunities abroad.

The idea of the strategy is that it leaves a family with its attachment to the U.S. intact—and with assets inside and outside of the country. This gives a family much more flexibility. Ideally, the expatriate family member also establishes a toehold overseas. Perhaps the entire family will want to expatriate some day. Who knows what might happen?

Typically, the family will want to use up assets and income in the United States and leave assets to grow overseas. The reason is simple: Accumulated wealth in the U.S. structure is subject to complex and expensive inheritance and gift rules. Outside the United States, assuming you choose your jurisdiction carefully, wealth can be transferred to the next generation simply and with no tax. It can also build up, year after year, with zero income or capital gains taxes.

Broadly speaking, a better arrangement than the one presented in our example would involve an asset that is not fixed in the United States. Imagine that the business is Internet-based, instead of pawn-shop-based, for example. It could then be bought by a foreign entity and moved outside the United States, possibly giving much more in the way of benefits to the owners.

Or imagine the family asset is a portfolio of investments. Those could easily be moved outside the United States. Trouble is, the "outside" family member could not sensibly buy them. We haven't dealt with this issue. But even in this case, there is a variety of legal ways to transfer wealth from the U.S. structure to the non-U.S. structure. Gifts, fees, salaries—the range of possibilities is wide. Between spouses, for example, the tax law allows for a tax-free gift of $100,000 per year— from the U.S.-based spouse to the non-U.S.-based spouse.

But first you have to understand how the expatriation system works. Keep in mind that we're not recommending it. It's clearly not for everyone. Estate-planning lawyers refer to it as the "nuclear option" because it can be very troublesome. But we also believe that it can be very effective.

Also, it fits with two other "motifs" that we think are important to consider.

It puts the family in the position of an "outsider." Politics, power, and bureaucracy are the enemies of real wealth. It's easy to be drawn toward them because it is natural to want to use money to buy political muscle for the purpose of protecting wealth. But it is a trap. Better to keep a distance. This inside/outside strategy helps keep the family at arms' length from any political system.

It leaves the family free to select the places, laws, currencies, and tax systems that best suit it. Instead of being held hostage by a single political unit, the family can choose the most appropriate institutions for its own needs.

The developed world, generally, and the United States, in particular, do not seem to be the best bets for family wealth over the next few decades. Their costs are high. Their political and economic systems seem decadent, even degenerate.

The United States may be headed into an especially dark passage. In addition to the burdens imposed by an advanced welfare state, the United States has the singular burden of an aged empire. It is headed for bankruptcy—and perhaps worse—with a "military industrial complex" that needs to justify further wealth transfers to itself. In short, there are good times—and bad times—to be in certain places. This could be a bad time to have all your eggs in the U.S. basket.

To conclude this chapter: You need five hard structures in place. You need an owner of the family wealth, usually a trust. The owner needs an investment/bank account, usually in a place where you can trust the banks and the currency. You need a will and an estate plan. And you need a tax strategy that makes sense and connects these pieces with your family's wealth and financial goals.

It is a big job to put these hard structures in place. Our advice: Start early. Take your time. "Go nuclear" only if you have to.

CHAPTER 8

CREATING PROSPERITY FOR GENERATIONS

We have looked at how you get and keep money. And we've looked at how you get and keep a family, too. Now we consider how you get and keep the family and the money working together, helping each other to flourish. In order to turn your new money into Old Money, you will need a special kind of family, the kind that can handle family money through multiple generations.

How do you do that? Wish we knew! What we do know is that few families are able to pull it off. But some families are extremely successful at it.

Take the Kongo family of Japan.

Founded in 578, Japanese temple builder Kongo Gumi is a family business that has lasted for 14 centuries.[1] Its last president, Masakazu Kongo, was the 40th member of the family to lead the company.

This family business built Buddhist temples and many other famous buildings in Japan, for over 1,400 years. The Kongo family business has been around longer than most countries of the world. (For instance, modern-day Switzerland wasn't founded until 1291.)

The secret to this longevity is having secrets—valuable secrets.

Each generation passed on the traditions and secrets of temple building. The family also passed on a unique construction method called *kumiage koho*, a precision woodworking technique that is part of Japanese cultural heritage. They don't use any nails.

Each generation of Kongo children had to have a comprehensive knowledge of woods—right down to knowing how the temperature and humidity of various microclimates affect wood over time. These techniques allow wooden buildings to last for hundreds of years. (Some are designated as World Heritage sites.) And the Kongos are the only people who know how to repair these temples. Generations of the family have built and maintained each building.

The Kongos didn't have some sort of special carpentry gene. According to them, it takes 10 years of apprenticeship to become competent at this type of carpentry.

They also developed a successful leadership succession process. Instead of always handing the reins to the oldest son, Kongo Gumi chose the son (or son-in-law) who showed the most talent for the job.

The Kongos developed organized processes, what we call "soft structures," for succession and training each new generation.

SOFT STRUCTURES

Our family has put in place our own system of soft structures. They are soft because they are not legal entities but merely conventions and protocols that the family sets up for itself. These provide a structure, a system, for managing wealth and harmonizing relationships between family members.

Your family must sing together. These soft structures help get everyone on key. They provide instructions and rules for future generations of family members to follow.

Organizations need rules and structures in order to endure. Even bridge clubs have their rules. So do churches and empires. Families, too. More or less formal structures allow groups of people to get on with their work without having to constantly reinvent the rules.

Think of governments—the U.S. government, for example. It's a governance system of laws and agreements that has been around for over 200 years. It has a history. It has its foundational texts. It has a narrative. It has a governance or leadership structure. It has traditions and rituals, its dos and don'ts, its conventions and protocols. At least in theory, everyone knows how it works and all agree to work within the rules and guidelines it imposes.

Religions share many of these same elements. They have formal and informal structures that help them last for very long periods of time. Hinduism has been around for 5,000 years. These are living institutions that are rooted in tradition, but also are dynamic, changing slowly with the times.

Buddhism has been around for about 2,500 years. The Kongo Gumi family set up their family business right alongside the Buddhist religion, making themselves an institution by building temples for over 1,000 years. It shows you how effective these structures can be at preserving family wealth over the very long term.

Your family needs these structures, too, if you want it to last.

You want to turn your family money into an institution, rather than a temporary collection of people or the reflection of a single personality. Wikipedia defines an institution as "any structure or mechanism of social order and cooperation governing the behavior of a set of individuals within a given human community. Institutions are identified with a social purpose and permanence, transcending individual human lives and intentions, and with the making and enforcing of rules governing cooperative human behavior." Order, cooperation, permanence—these are the things that help families hold onto money.

When family fortunes are lost, it's usually the family that falls apart first. And it falls apart because it lacks organization and leadership. The problems are almost always family-centered, not money-centered.

And that's why the solutions can't come from outside the family. They need to come from inside it. Outside professionals can help temporarily, perhaps, but they can't solve family problems. And when a family turns to outside professionals, it is often too late.

As we discussed in Chapter 2, the family needs to create a well-developed culture, a shared sense of history, a common purpose, and so forth. These are essential. But there are also specific structures, such as a Family Council and a family investment committee, that help the family govern itself. Even a large, tax-advantaged family fortune will most likely disappear within three generations without the proper family governance system in place.

Good family governance allows a family to work out its problems, meet its challenges, and adapt to changes—without blowing up. And the easiest way to ensure good family governance is to build it around a series of soft structures. Unlike wills, trusts, and tax structures, soft structures aren't legally binding. They are much easier to set up and much less rigid. They should evolve with your family circumstances and help the family to continue to work out its problems together.

Soft structures help families do the following:

- Stay together in relative harmony for generations.
- All individual family members achieve all they can in life.
- Express and enrich the family identity.
- Preserve and grow wealth over generations.

The soft structures we recommend you use are not well known among estate planners. That shouldn't be surprising. There's not much money in soft structure planning. You don't have to be a licensed professional to do it. And setting up soft structures involves working with many family members other than just the patriarch. It can be too much of a hassle for the professionals, in other words.

Estate-planning lawyers tend to use "off-the-shelf" legal structures, in which the soft structures, if there are any, are perfunctory. These pre-prepared structures can be helpful in simplifying otherwise complex issues that concern family wealth. But they do not take into account many of the issues that ultimately determine whether a family will succeed over multiple generations.

This is a real pity because our research shows that families are much better off figuring out the family side of things first. The culture, the soft structures, are actually the most important part of your family wealth plan. You need to keep lines of communication open. Conflicts need to be resolved. Problems need to be solved. Family members need a structure in which they can work together. Taxes and trusts—the hard structures—should be built to house and protect the family's soft tissue. Most people start with the legal structures. And we did, too, at first, because we didn't know any better.

A family we grew up with had been in the boat business for generations. Its core asset, a boatyard on the shores of the Chesapeake Bay, had grown in value enormously as the area had developed.

Everything seemed to be going well until it came time to renegotiate a lease between cousins. Then and only then did family members discover how distant one group of cousins had grown from another, even though they lived barely a mile away from one another.

"I had no idea they felt so badly treated," said one of the cousins.

One part of the family had managed the boatyard for 30 years. Other parts felt left out. When it came time to renegotiate important leases, the cousins who had been out of the business took their opportunity. They seized control of the boatyard. The trouble was, after so many years away from it, they no longer had the skills or tools to operate it successfully. After a few years, the family business—which had never had a mortgage against it before—was deep in debt, while the cousins with the necessary expertise struggled to make a go of it in a new location.

This is the sort of situation soft structures are designed to prevent. Soft structures give family members a chance to talk. They force communication and conflict resolution. There are no guarantees. But at least soft structures give a family a place, time, and forum for confronting disagreements.

GETTING INVOLVED

But let's begin by asking: What sort of family do you have? What kind do you want? What are you trying to achieve? And how do you want to govern yourselves and manage your money? You really can't move ahead without answering these questions. You can answer them precisely, in writing. Or tacitly. But they must be answered. Otherwise, you won't know what kind of hard and soft structures you need.

This is the mistake most people make. Instead of addressing the hard questions about who they are and what they are trying to accomplish, they go to see a lawyer—an estate planner, for instance. The estate planner sends them in a direction, which may or may not be appropriate. He naturally favors measurable objectives and naturally guides the family toward solutions with the biggest payoff.

If one approach will save $100,000 in taxes, and another will save $200,000, he will—quite rightly—aim for the greatest savings. He has no way of knowing what the family is really trying to achieve. The family itself often doesn't know.

The matriarch and the patriarch, the founders of the family dynasty-to-be, should agree on a vision for the future. It doesn't have to be precise. It doesn't even have to be articulated. But they need to agree on the fundamentals: who they are, what they want, how the family is going to live, and what will happen to the family assets in the next 5, 10, 20, 100 years.

Then the second generation gets involved. The children need to contribute to the discussion (even if it is *sotto voce*), sign on to the project, and understand what will be required of them.

There's a lot of work and responsibility involved in preserving and growing family wealth. If the children don't want to do it, you're out of luck. Or if they are unwilling to share the founders' ideas about how wealth should be controlled and used, the family money project is not likely to go far. But assuming the children buy into the program, the family can move ahead. You can set up the soft structures you need. And you can get lawyers and other professionals to create the hard structures.

Once the family determines collectively what it wants to accomplish, as well as the groundwork it wants to lay for future generations, then the lawyers can find the most appropriate ways these goals can be achieved.

There are many different hard and soft structures you might use. We'll tell you about ours. After four years of studying conventional family office governance, we've created our own soft structures plan. It's called the "endowment model."

It consists of the following soft structures:

- The Family Council
- A mission statement and constitution
- The family bank
- The investment committee
- An education and mentorship program
- The family philanthropic committee

It's based, we believe, on the best practices of multigenerational business-owning families. That doesn't mean that your family needs to own a business to benefit from it. Instead, we found that the principles that helped business-owning families could be used by any family that wanted to preserve wealth.

The first step we took was to have a family meeting and set up the Family Council.

THE HEART OF THE FAMILY OFFICE SYSTEM: THE FAMILY COUNCIL

The Family Council is a group of family members who make executive decisions for the family as a whole. The Family Council determines the success or failure of your legacy over time. It creates and manages all the other soft structures that you will learn about in this chapter. Within the trust framework that we recommend, the Family Council also manages all distributions from family assets. As such, the Family Council is the linchpin of your family office structure.

If you are the person who created the family wealth, you may find the idea of a Family Council a little off-putting. It's your money, after all. Why bring others into the process of deciding what happens to it?

Successful leadership by a family wealth creator is what builds all great family legacies. And wealth creators—in addition to being lucky—tend to be hardheaded. They do not necessarily appreciate others meddling in "their" affairs. They do not necessarily like the windy democracy of family meetings. They may even question the judgment or competence of the people on the Family Council and wonder if they couldn't do better on their own.

You may be that person. You may be the son or the daughter, or the granddaughter or grandson, of that person. Or you may aspire to being a wealth creator yourself. It doesn't matter. What's important to grasp is that the wealth creator needs to set up a family decision-making process that can last longer than he does. And the sooner he begins, the better. He needs to give the rest of the family an opportunity to make decisions—and mistakes. More importantly, he has to encourage the family to work together by giving it something to work on.

Without a governing group in place, and a system of governance that works, family wealth is almost guaranteed to dissipate in the space of two generations.

As long as the wealth creator is in charge, things run smoothly. The decision-making process is clear. The rest of the family respects the wealth creator and gives him authority to lead the family. But when the wealth creator meets his own Creator, it can leave a dangerous hole in a family's decision-making process.

Succession struggles and power vacuums have always led to trouble. When kings or tyrants died, the insiders always tried to come up with a new ruler fast. Even a bad one. Otherwise, there could be civil war, fratricide, power struggles, and chaos. Peaceful succession is the goal of all enlightened government, including family government.

This is why setting up a well-run Family Council is a vital part of your wealth protection strategy. And it is why it is so important to start holding regular meetings as soon as possible to get the family used to group decision making.

WHAT THE FAMILY COUNCIL DOES

The responsibilities of the Family Council include:

- Drafting a family mission statement and family constitution.
- Overseeing the investment committee and monitoring performance of family investments.
- Managing and drafting legal documents concerning the family estate planning.
- Managing the family's philanthropy efforts.
- Overseeing family property management.
- Resolving family conflicts.
- Managing the strategic and tactical goals of the family enterprise.
- Organizing activities that strengthen family bonds.
- Formulating policies for family members working in the family business.
- Formulating policies regarding inclusion or exclusion of spouses.

Family Council meetings need to get "buy-in" from all of the members of your family. They must respect—and act on—its decisions. You need to make sure the decisions of the Family Council cannot be bypassed. That doesn't mean you need to have consensus on every issue. But important issues—such as the disposition of family wealth—should be based on persuasion and consensus, not a majority vote. This makes a Family Council, typically, a very conservative institution. Major changes should only be made slowly and reluctantly. Each one may require long periods of consensus building.

But that is as it should be. The role of the Family Council is to preserve the family and its money. It cannot afford to act hastily or to ignore the opinions of family members. It must move like a big ship: slowly, deliberately, and with all hands onboard.

Of course, the wealth creator—as long as he is alive—deserves special consideration. Family members should feel a sense of gratitude, if nothing else. But if the wealth creator is smart, he will treat his wealth as bounty from heaven, to be shared with the rest of the family, rather than his own personal property. That is, of course, the whole point: to transform personal money into family money.

The wealth creator should begin the process by sharing his wealth-management responsibilities with the Family Council. It will have to make important decisions after the wealth creator has passed on, anyway. Better to give it some practice while he is still on the job.

You should try to make the Family Council as "official" as possible. It should not be seen as just an artificial appendage of the wealth creator or a ruse by which he tries to get the rest of the family to do what he wants. Distribute an agenda ahead of meetings. Make sure council members have an opportunity to add to the agenda. Make sure they are prepared in advance, just as they would prepare for important business meetings. They should review the agenda ahead of time and be ready to ask questions and debate the topics.

It is also a good idea to have a family office staff member on hand at Family Council meetings to clarify issue or answer questions that council members might have. Typically, family offices, which manage the details of a family's wealth, have a bookkeeper or trustee who can be very helpful at family meetings. There may be important footnotes and elucidations that the family office person can provide.

Our family held our first official Family Council meeting during Thanksgiving 2010. This is when we "institutionalized" our family office. Our goals for this meeting were to:

- Introduce the family office concept to the family.
- Organize the family budgets.
- Get everyone thinking about how we can work together on family projects.
- Start to get the system of family governance working.

Up to this point, your authors had talked a little about the family office project to other family members. It was nothing more than a peculiar abstraction as far as the rest of the family was concerned.

Our Thanksgiving meeting made the family office more concrete. For the first time, it drew a clear distinction between family office projects and resources and the elder author's personal projects and resources.

This distinction (made official by legal documents) is what brings the family office into being. Certain assets are designated for the family. Others remain in individual hands. Until the wealth creator in your family does this, you don't have family money.

Leading up to our first family meeting, we worked hard on the agenda for the meeting. We tried to make the meeting as interesting and as accessible as possible for the other family members. And we limited the meeting to four hours.

Here's how we structured our first Family Council meeting:

THE FIRST BONNER FAMILY MEETING AGENDA

Family meeting called into session, acknowledgments of recent family accomplishments, events, and activities:

- Discussion leader: Bill
- Time allocation: 15 minutes
- Roll call and review of the family profiles*
- Discussion leader: Will
- Time allocation: 30 minutes
- Introduction of the family office and review of the family balance sheet
- Discussion leaders: Bill and Jean

Time allocation: 1 hour

—Break—

Review of the family office budgets, including:

- Allowances/support of children
- Maintenance of family properties
- Travel to family events (Thanksgiving, Christmas, etc.)
- Other items on Jean's list

Discussion leader: Jean

Time allocation: 1 hour

Official formation of the investment committee

Discussion leaders: Bill and Will

Time allocation: 30 minutes

—Break—

Review of family governance, how family office decisions are made

Discussion leaders: Bill and Will

Time allocation: 30 minutes

Closing remarks, summary of takeaways, and announcement of next
  meeting

Discussion leader: Bill

Time allocation: 15 minutes

---

*Children were to come to the meeting with a rough profile—a few sentences about
their backgrounds and a statement of where they would like to be in 10 years.

The meeting was a major leap forward. This was mainly thanks to Jean, who administers our family office in Baltimore. She came with a neatly organized binder that contained extensive data about our family office assets and liabilities.

Everyone came prepared, except for the youngest, who evidently hadn't gotten the e-mail! Other than that, we were surprised by the level of participation. There was a lot more interest in the family business than we were aware of. The family business is a big part of our family's identity and our only source of income. It is important to those of us who work in it and to those who don't. The children have grown up in and around the business. All have a keen attachment to it.

This was exactly the sort of "buy-in" for the family office that we were looking for. There are six children in the family. They have very different interests and professions—physical therapy, acting, medical school, geology, and music. We had been concerned that it would be difficult to get them all involved in our family office project. It turned out not to be difficult at all.

During the meeting, we also talked about the family properties, family budgets, our schedule for the year ahead, charities, cost control, and a number of other issues. At the end of the meeting, we went around the room and asked everyone for his "takeaway." Everyone seemed to have learned something; the family office was on its way.

WHO SHOULD SIT ON THE FAMILY COUNCIL?

Filling your Family Council with capable family members will be a huge help in preserving your family's legacy. The selection process depends on your family culture. Typically, in the first and second generations, all family members are part of the Family Council. Everyone is expected to familiarize himself with the issues affecting the family and to participate in the decision-making process. Young family members can start participating in the Family Council in their early teens.

But when your Family Council reaches 15 to 20 people, it is best to switch to a representative system. Under this system, an elected senior family member will represent different family branches to avoid the Family Council becoming unwieldy.

Most American and European families include spouses in their meetings. Excluding people who play such an important role in the family can breed ill will toward the Family Council. Spouses are influential over the lives of current and future family members. It would be a mistake to alienate them.

But bringing in spouses is not risk free. Spouses do not necessarily share the family's culture or its goals. And in today's world, divorce is common. You wouldn't want to bring a spouse into the inner sanctum of your family wealth, only to have him or her leave on bitter terms 12 months later.

Think 100 years into the future. You will be long gone. And your family office will be made up of people you don't know. You want your Family Council and its system of governance to last for a long time. That means it will need to function with the participation of a diverse group of people, not just the group currently involved. Including spouses can help make your family office's governance process more robust. It can bring more capable people into the Family Council. And it can help reveal—and perhaps resolve—problems arising within your family's marriages, at least insofar as they are connected to the family money.

But what if your son or daughter married a gold digger? (Not likely. But you have to think of all the possibilities.) What if one married someone who was either uninterested in or opposed to the family's goals? What can you do?

You'd want to keep a close eye on a potentially troublesome spouse. It may be better to engage this person in the controlled environment of the Family Council, rather than leave them on the outside. A Family Council meeting is a great place to gauge whether the person is trouble—or not. You can't pretend this person won't be a major influence over his or her spouse, and therefore your brother or sister, son or daughter. It's better to confront these issues head-on. After all, it's these unspoken conflicts—many involving spouses—that cause so many families to fail.

THE FAMILY COUNCIL'S ROLE IN TRUSTS

As part of our family endowment model, we recommend you put in place a special kind of trust: a perpetual trust, also called a "dynasty trust." We discussed trusts in the previous chapter. A perpetual trust, as the name indicates, holds assets on behalf of beneficiaries in perpetuity. In our version of it, trust beneficiaries must be engaged in "productive behavior" to be eligible for distributions, and then only for education, business, and career advancement. It's the role of the Family Council to make these distributions. It is also the job of the Family Council to determine that beneficiaries are abiding by the terms of the trust.

If members of the Family Council are also beneficiaries of the trust, they need to fully understand their role as beneficiaries. They should also understand the role of the trustee and meet with him.

Let's back up for a moment and explain the big-picture strategy behind the endowment model.

HOW MULTIGENERATIONAL FAMILIES GROW THEIR WEALTH

The endowment model is a family office organizational structure in which family assets are held in a perpetual trust. Assets are distributed by the Family Council only for the purpose of funding productive family-member projects. The model helps hold and preserve the family wealth, instead of distributing it. This, in turn, helps hold the family together by keeping their financial interests united. And the model helps future generations be more successful by making resources available, while neither undermining them nor robbing them of their own need to work and support themselves. Only family members engaged in "productive behavior" are eligible to sit on the Family Council.

Of course, the council will make mistakes. And there will be conflicts. But in regularly coming together to make decisions and discuss problems, the council helps preserve family unity for the long term.

It's not easy. Preserving family wealth for multiple generations is not a science. It's an art. You're dealing with dozens of people with all kinds of complex psychological issues, relationships, and agendas. It's critical that you get everyone organized and on the same page. You need a self-perpetuating culture of prosperity. Or, to put it another way, you need to create such an extraordinary system for holding onto old wealth and for building new wealth that even ordinary people can keep it going.

Ours is a perpetual trust with no built-in disbursements. Beneficiaries don't receive any money at a certain age.

The purpose of our trust is to:

- Give support for family members starting new careers.
- Fund family member educations.
- Help support family members in the arts or humanitarian work.
- Fund family member business ventures and start-ups.
- Assist in emergencies.

In return for these benefits, beneficiaries have the following responsibilities:

- Helping guide the investments in the family portfolio as a member of the investment committee.
- Participating as a member of the Family Council.
- Helping manage the family property.
- Helping protect and grow the family business grow in a manner consistent with family values.
- Helping manage any family philanthropy.

Family members have to earn their way as beneficiaries. And they have to make their own way in life and in their careers—just like everyone else. Different family members will play greater or lesser roles in each of these things, depending on their inclinations and abilities. And these responsibilities will become more significant and complex down the road.

We think the endowment model is the best structure for our family. The perpetual trust protects our wealth from taxes and legal threats. But, more important, it emphasizes self-reliance and individual achievement, while at the same time providing support for family member ventures. We want to be a family of producers, not consumers.

But we're still a young family. Only one member of the second generation is married with a family of his own. Most members of the second generation are just starting their careers. They don't yet have the pressures of supporting a family and of competing in the business world. Those things will put more pressure on the family office. We have a long way to go, with many challenges ahead.

Let's move onto the next step: writing a family mission statement.

SET YOUR PRIORITIES WITH A FAMILY MISSION STATEMENT

The elder Bonner thinks this may be a waste of time. Still, following the advice in the guidebooks, this is what we've done: written a mission statement. The idea is that successful families need a simple statement of purpose that everyone can get behind. Drafting the family mission statement is one of the first tasks of your Family Council. The family mission statement should motivate your family members to want to be a part of the family office project. All the other soft structures you put in place should center on this document.

The family mission statement is supposed to give your family a shared sense of direction. (Of course, if it doesn't have a shared sense of direction already, writing out something is probably not going to help.) More important than the mission statement itself may be the act of trying to write one. It may show you that you don't really have a mission or a unified idea about what you're trying to do.

Aim to draft your family mission statement at your first Family Council meeting. Then take it to the rest of your family. It is crucial that your family mission statement sound right to everyone. Make sure it reflects the genuine values of the family and makes clear the benefits of a family office structure for each family member. If there is disagreement about the mission statement—or if you are unable to come up with a statement that satisfies your family—you are probably doomed.

The first meeting is especially important because it sets the tone for all that comes after it. During this process, it is important to remember that disagreements can be healthy. Issues are coming to the surface, and opinions are being expressed. Remember: *For your family mission statement to bring your family together, it has to include everyone—even family members who appear not to "fit in." Try to bring all family members into the process.*

If you can come away from your first Family Council meeting with a rough draft of your mission statement, approved by a consensus of the family members, it will be a significant breakthrough.

THE FAMILY CONSTITUTION

Small, first-generation families may not need a family constitution. But as your family grows and circumstances become more complicated, a family constitution can clarify issues and provide more structure to keep your family together. The family constitution provides a mechanism for realizing the goals spelled out in the mission statement. It is usually prefaced with a statement of your family's core beliefs, its values, and its more practical considerations, such as how the family aims to manage its wealth and run its business, if it has one.

Subsequent generations will reassess and amend the constitution. But if you give it plenty of time and thought to begin with, and base it around a genuinely shared family mission statement, most of what you draft will last for decades.

The Family Council drafts the family constitution. It typically explains:

- Who makes up the family.
- Who makes up the Family Council.
- How the family is governed.
- How family money is managed (for example, choosing an investment director and the members of the investment committee).
- How family assets (for example, real estate) are managed and used.
- When the Family Council meets and how it communicates.
- The family's code of ethics.
- How family conflicts are resolved within the family and how family members can avoid litigation.
- A plan for changing the constitution, as necessary.

The family constitution does not need to be a formal document. It might even be better that it isn't. It needs to evolve—but slowly. But to start out, it doesn't hurt to have a rough version signed by all family members.

Our family has not yet drafted our own constitution. We are still a young family, and things are not yet that complicated. We don't need a full-blown constitution yet. But we *will* need one. Around the time of the transition between the second and third generations is when families tend to need a constitution.

SETTING UP THE FAMILY BANK

We don't want family money to fund lifestyles. But at the same time, we want to be able to financially support family members' productive pursuits. That's why we set up a family bank.

The "family bank" is where your family can go for funding for entrepreneurial ventures, education, buying a home, or health care needs. These can be outright disbursements, or they can be loans. Loans typically don't carry interest. But borrowers are required to pay them back in full.

The family bank is not a real bank. It has no teller, no ATM cards, and no banking license. It is just a convenient way of describing another Family Council function: running a lending program for the benefit of family members.

These loans can be a huge advantage for your family. They give them access to cheap funding. And they reduce the amount of costly outside debt family members need to take on. Banks make money by charging interest on loans and collecting various fees. They have expensive offices to maintain and big bonuses to pay out. A family bank is another way to lower the cost of operating a family and ultimately protect the family fortune.

It helps you eliminate banking fees and also insurance charges. For instance, if you don't have a mortgage or a car loan, you save a lot on the ancillary costs of those loans, not to mention the interest payments. Likewise, you can use the family bank in the place of an insurance fund, lending money to family members to cover setbacks that would otherwise be covered by insurance. These savings allow family members to live better on less money.

The Family Council also makes disbursements for family members' educations. It supports them when they're getting started in new careers and new business ventures.

The aim of the endowment model is not just to help family members alive today but also to help future generations. So the purpose of distributions from the Family Council must be the financial stability of family members *and* the sustainability of the family bank itself.

There are no handouts. No bailouts. Family members must pay their own debts. In our family's case, we expect each family member to live on what he earns. But we don't mind helping him get started.

CREATING PERMANENT LEADERSHIP

As your family grows, there are more people involved in the family leadership. The leadership must be balanced and spread across each generation—or the family enterprise topples over.

That doesn't mean that everyone is a leader. It means your family needs to make decisions collectively. But be warned: consensus becomes increasingly difficult as the family expands.

Some family members will be more suited to leadership roles than others. But a brother, sister, or cousin does not usually command the respect and authority that the patriarch does. After he goes, governance will be harder. You'll hope you find a strong leader in each generation. And work hard to build consensus for key moves. The system takes practice. The best you can do is to start early, include everyone, and be consistent. Permanent leadership is one of the great secrets to preserving a family fortune over generations.

Leaders and individual family members will come and go. But an enduring leadership system will keep your family, and your family legacy, together for generations.

HOW TO HANDLE THE TRANSITION

The best way for a wealth creator to successfully transfer the reins of power is to oversee that transition himself while he still has his wits about him. That means making the transition sooner rather than later. For the wealth creator, it means a transition from being the "commander-in-chief" of the family to an elder.

The role of the elder is a critical one for a successful multigenerational family. Elders serve as a sort of judicial branch of the family. Elders can also help resolve family disputes and make sure the family is following its stated values and goals.

Each elder will have his preferences about where he wants to be and what he wants to do. It's a personal matter. The important thing is to make sure you don't sideline him and that you show the respect for the position as an elder and encourage him to perform that role.

If you set things up right, the wealth creator will be happy to take on the role of elder at the right time. Beyond settling disputes, elders should transmit the family culture from generation to generation by telling the family stories and being the family history. The elders also help with the spiritual development of the family, religious or otherwise. They also help preserve family ethics.

FAMILY COUNCIL LEADERSHIP

In each generation, there needs to be a leader of the council, someone who takes a little more responsibility for making sure things stay on track.

Centuries ago, the Irish clans had a system called *tanistry*, wherein a successor to the chief was chosen from a group of eligible males who were related, via the male line, within four generations of the chief. This group of eligibles was called the *roydammna* (meaning, "those of kingly material"). The *tanist* was the heir to the monarchy and immediately took the throne when the king died. He was, essentially, the chief's right-hand man. He was elected for life and considered the most worthy of the same male-line blood of the clan. The deputy prime minister of modern-day Ireland is called the *tanaiste* in Irish.

A modern version of this *tanist* model might be a good one for multigenerational family offices. While members of the Family Council are equal, someone in the second generation needs to fill a leadership role.

We would be reluctant to give him a formal role with a title like "chairman" of the Family Council. Such a perceived inequality could breed contempt. And, obviously, this person in the second generation, and onward, does not occupy the same role that the wealth creator of the first generation does. Instead, the *tanist* would be a protégé of the wealth creator. He would be more focused on family office issues than the other members of the Family Council. Let's face it, not everyone is going to have high levels of interest and understanding of family office matters.

Someone needs to understand all the issues that the family office faces and set the agenda for family meetings. The family office *tanist* needs to help the discussion by introducing important information that might affect Family Council decisions. He needs to make sure that the Family Council discussions stay on track, that they focus on business issues and do not try to deal with personal issues, for example.

The *tanist* should be apprenticed to the current leader. The *tanist* should not receive special treatment or privileges not agreed upon by the Family Council. The Family Council is a collective decision-making body. It shouldn't have a president, but there should be a respectful and capable leader who can help keep things on track. Each generation needs a *tanist*.

DISPUTES: WHY THEY'RE NORMAL AND HOW TO SETTLE THEM

The lack of family disputes can mean issues are simmering below the surface. These unspoken issues have a nasty habit of coming to the surface when there is a major family event, such as a death, a wealth transfer or the sale of the family business. It is best to have the most senior members of the family (of course, still of sound mind), the elders, settle disputes. It is the role of the elders to find the consensus-building solution to family conflicts.

But if, for whatever reason, there are no elders to resolve disputes, the Family Council must act as moderator. Family Council members must understand that deeply rooted biases often fuel sibling rivalries and that these biases can factor heavily into any conflict. The key here is to separate the people from the problem. There are relationships—and there is the problem. Moderators should emphasize the importance of maintaining healthy relationships and then deal with the problem based on its own merits.

It is natural for family members to take opposing positions based on different interests in the outcome. The challenge of the moderators is to find the common ground and build on it. They can do this by first clearly identifying the problem and the conflicting interests. Then they can brainstorm to identify the joint interests and options for resolution. They should set a tangible, mutually beneficial objective that can be reached by the most desirable option of resolution for both parties.

If a resolution is not forthcoming, it may become necessary to bring in a trusted outside mediator. It is crucial not to let family conflicts fester. Unresolved disputes break up families and destroy wealth.

HOW TO DEAL WITH PROBLEM FAMILY MEMBERS

It is the job of the Family Council to protect the family and the family wealth from threats. It should avoid judging individual family members on moral issues. For instance, the Family Council may decide that a family member who is a known drug addict may not be eligible to receive any funds from the family bank. It should try to keep its position as businesslike as possible. It needs to avoid "getting personal."

Instead, it should elaborate and enforce policies believed, by consensus, to be fair.

Families with a history of substance abuse may want to consider a clause in their trust that disqualifies family members from the benefits of the trust if there is evidence of drug or alcohol abuse.

CREATING A "FAMILY REPUBLIC"

During the life of the wealth creator, he is more often than not "the decider": a kind of compassionate oligarch. All family members of a certain age and in sound mind get a vote on the Family Council. But the founder typically retains the right of veto.

When the next generation takes charge, it typically functions as a representative democracy. Each council member gets an equal vote. But this is a majority of, usually, brothers and sisters—still very close to one another and not far from the source of the family's wealth and its culture. We urge you to operate on the basis of consensus, and universal consent, rather than majority rule. But it's up to you.

Beyond the third generation, there is a big change. People know each other less well. The family culture tends to be more diffuse and indistinct. At this stage, most families choose a representative democracy—a sort of "family republic." The Family Council becomes more representative of various wings of the family. There are too many family members (usually more than 30) for everyone to be a part of the council.

When a family reaches the family republic stage, it is a good idea for individual family units to meet separately to discuss the issue at hand before sending their representatives to meet with the Family Council.

PRESERVING YOUR FINANCIAL LEGACY: HOW TO ESTABLISH YOUR INVESTMENT COMMITTEE

This is a common narrative among wealthy families: The wealth creator dies and leaves the money to his family. But he takes his wealth creation and investing skills with him. Family wealth is then transferred from the widow and her children to the children of investment managers and estate planners.

Wall Street brokerages sometimes have what is effectively a "sucker's list." Often, it is composed of the names of widows and children who were left sizable estates without the ability to competently manage that wealth. You don't want your family on the sucker's list.

A well-functioning investment committee can prevent that from happening. Here's how it works:

The committee stays in regular communication and shares investment ideas. But with such an ultra-long-term time horizon, the committee does not do a lot of buying and selling. New investment committee members from each generation are trained and groomed from a young age. They learn about investing through educational programs and direct experience. They deliberate long and hard. They study. They think. There is no need to make quick decisions in family money investing. There is plenty of time to learn. Just relax and take your time.

Every family member should understand how money works—how you earn it, save it, and manage it. Investing in financial education is another crucial step toward successfully preserving wealth.

This is very different, however, from formal college training in economics or finance. Instead, get your family together often. And get it to pay attention to the investment performance of your funds. The members should take an interest—and, hopefully, satisfaction—from your investment progress. This will focus their attention on what you're doing and give them a sense of purpose.

So how do you get future generations to learn about managing money?

- You give them a baseline education in personal finance and investing through courses, books, and web sites.
- You give them responsibility, such as a role in the family office or as a member of the investment committee.
- You bring them into the picture of family finances—as early as possible.

The best time to take these steps is when your children are in their early teens. It sounds strange, but you want to give them responsibility earlier than you think they are ready for it. Plus, take your children to investment programs. Read and discuss investment books. Critique popular theories and fads. Do not invest in what Wall Street considers "conservative." But operate your investment committee very conservatively.

THE WEALTH STRATEGIST IN EACH GENERATION LEADS THE COMMITTEE

Just like the Family Council, the investment committee needs a leader. Usually, the wealth creator of the first generation becomes the wealth strategist for the investment committee. Someone in each subsequent generation must take over that role.

The *tanist* to the wealth strategist needs to have a thorough understanding of investment strategy and years of direct experience in investing. The *tanist* apprentices with the current wealth strategist. It's part of the wealth strategist's job to educate the other members of the investment committee and to train his successor.

Some of the other duties of the wealth strategist are:

- To hold brokers, wealth managers, and everyone involved with the family portfolio accountable for performance.
- To establish clear investment objectives and goals.
- To have a big-picture outlook that translates into simple and manageable investments.

The wealth strategist leads the investment committee team to create an asset allocation model and the follow-through for implementing the model. He should also act as chairman of the investment committee. He should have the most investing experience and be capable of directing the overall strategy. He should understand asset allocation and risk management (deep value investing, diversification, and position sizing).

A key function of your family office is to professionalize the asset management of your family over multiple generations. You can't do this without having a capable investment committee in current and future generations.

A TRAINING GROUND FOR THE NEXT
GENERATION: A FAMILY PHILANTHROPY

The elder of your authors doesn't believe in philanthropy. He thinks it is throwing money away, at best. At worst, he thinks it hurts the beneficiaries.

He may be right. Our family saw up close what happened to the inner city. We lived in the Baltimore ghetto when the family was young. Welfare payments ruined the poor families who lived there. They stopped working. Families broke up. Unearned money turned the place into a living hell.

But philanthropy is a major component of most successful families and successful family offices. It is important for family members. It gives them a unified purpose and builds the family culture. It also helps them focus on properly administering wealth . . . and getting results.

In the *Palm Beach Post*, there are often pictures of photogenic wealthy people attending local fundraising events. Many families enjoy the social component of philanthropy. This is not something that appeals to us. But there may be some causes that would actually do some good . . . as well as making the family feel good about itself.

Our advice: Make it as personal and direct as possible. Control the spending carefully. See the results for yourself. Take responsibility for the outcome. For example, while we have serious doubts about giving money to people for "education" and about education itself, we nevertheless provide scholarships for the children of the people who live on our ranch. We get to know the recipients personally and monitor their progress. And while we have mixed feelings about religion, we still built a wing on the local church so the itinerant priest would have a place to stay. And though we suspect that government-administered health care is inefficient and often ineffective, we also are building a clinic on the ranch—staffed and furnished by the local government— so the families there will have somewhere to go to get medical help.

CHAPTER 9

FAMILIES WITH MONEY

We've already shared a number of stories about wealthy families in this book. However, there's much to learn from families that have succeeded, as well as from the ones that failed.

And most families do fail. Ninety percent of family-owned businesses do not last past three generations of ownership. And the ones that do succeed for longer can still have a dramatic falling out when things go bad. That's why you can read about so many scandals about wealthy families in the newspapers.

The reasons why they fail are as numerous as raindrops in a downpour.

There are so many things that can go wrong. After all, we're dealing with human beings and the complicated relationships that can develop among family members.

Sometimes there are deeply rooted biases that fuel family fights.

These biases develop over time between siblings who grow up together. Lee Hausner and Douglas K. Freeman, the authors of the book *The Legacy Family*, call these biases "headsets."[1]

These headsets, or biases, tend to muddy the waters of family conflicts. They blend multiple issues and emotions.

Family mediators, the family elders, and/or the matriarch need to untangle this mess and deal with one issue at a time.

They can do this by, first, clearly identifying the problem and the conflicting interests. Then they can brainstorm to identify the joint interests and options for resolution. They should set a tangible, mutually beneficial objective that can be reached by the most desirable option of resolution for both parties.

But what often happens is that, in later generations, there are no moderators with authority in the family to help settle disputes.

The next thing you know, you have siblings and cousins feuding against each other.

A BROTHER'S BETRAYAL AND THE LIQUIDATION OF THE WAXMAN FAMILY BUSINESS

Sometimes conflicting personalities can, eventually, cause a shocking betrayal among family members. This is what led to the unfortunate demise of the Waxman family business.

Isaac Waxman was a Jewish Polish immigrant to Ontario, Canada, in 1911. He was fired from his first job for refusing to work on the Sabbath. So he bought a horse and carriage and started collecting bottles, cans, and scrap metal for recycling. He worked for 11 years before he had earned enough to bring his wife and five children from Poland. He and his wife then had four more children, two of whom, Morris and Chester, joined their father's business.

They were able to grow I. Waxman and Sons into a successful recycling company, selling scrap to the city's booming steel mills.[2]

The brothers worked well together. Chester was the more outgoing of the two, and he handled sales and the financial side of the business. The elder brother, Morris, ran the yard, managing the large volume of business that Chester brought in.

They won contracts with large manufacturers such as Firestone. And the brothers built up a good reputation in the city.

The brothers bought matching Cadillacs for themselves and lavish gifts for their wives.

But trouble was brewing.

Chester was more ambitious, charismatic, and aggressive than Morris. He felt that he was mainly responsible for the success of the business and deserved a larger share of it.

Also, he had three sons, whereas Morris had only two. So Chester feared his family's stake would be diluted when it came time for his ownership stake to be passed to the next generation.

To counter this, Chester and his accountant proposed an "estate freeze" in which Chester's three sons and Morris's two sons would each inherit an equal 20 percent of the company. Morris realized that this proposal gave control of the company to Chester's sons, since three could outvote two. And he rejected the scheme.

At this point, Chester realized that he and his sons could bilk compensation out of the business in various ways. They formed side businesses that provided services to the company at inflated prices.

In 1983, Morris was having heart problems and was to undergo open-heart surgery. At that point, Chester got him to sign some documents that essentially gave away Morris's half of the business to Chester. Morris pleaded with his brother to destroy the documents after he realized what had happened.

For five years, Morris continued to demand that his brother return his rightful share of the business.

As a last resort, Morris and his sons filed suit against Chester's side of the family. The lawsuit dragged on for 14 years.

During that time, Chester and his family sold off the business's assets, and in 1993, they sold the core business for $30 million. And they secured long-term contracts for themselves with the new owner.

In her 440-page ruling, the Ontario Superior Court's Madame Justice Mary Anne Sanderson decided in favor of Morris in the case of *Waxman vs. Waxman*.

The judge ruled that Chester had "duped" Morris out of his 50 percent share of the family business.

The ruling reinstated Morris as half-owner of the company and ordered Chester and his family to return his share of profit and bonuses pocketed since 1984.[3]

In March 2007, the family business and Chester's family holdings were ordered into liquidation. Chester Waxman died of lung cancer in 2008.

The trial became the longest civil suit in Ontario history and racked up $5 million in legal fees.

The fallout from the trial continued until October 2011, when Chester's son Robert (Bobby) Waxman was sentenced to eight years in prison for stealing almost $18 million from Philip Services Corp., one of the spinoffs from the family business.

Bobby Waxman bought copper on delayed payment terms from a supplier and then immediately sold the copper at a loss to companies he controlled that in turn sold it at a profit, often back to the original supplier.

Like father, like son.

Bobby wasn't able to pay the legal bills for his defense because he had been bankrupted by the ruling against his family in the civil suit.[4]

It's too bad there wasn't a matriarch or another elder family member to keep members of the Waxman family in check.

BROTHERS' PROMISE TURNS INTO A FAMILY FEUD

Other times, it's not so clear that a family member's intentions are malicious. Take, for example, the case of the Demoulas family.

There could be a simple misunderstanding that boils over and becomes a family feud.

Two brothers, Mike (Telemachus) and George Demoulas, the children of Greek immigrants, bought their parents' deli and transformed it into a modern supermarket chain. They made a promise to each other that if one of them died the surviving brother would provide for the other's family. In 1971 George died of a heart attack while vacationing in Greece.

Mike provided for his brother's family, buying them luxury condos, and a new income-generating business by selling out their share of the supermarket chain. The supermarket business kept growing, but Mike launched a new chain called Market Basket that did even better.

In 1990 George's heirs filed a lawsuit against their uncle, alleging that he had defrauded them out of all but 8 percent of the company stock. They also accused Mike of diverting profits into a new chain of grocery stores owned only by his side of the family.[5]

The courts agreed with George's family and returned the controlling interest to the widow and sons and ordered Mike to return $1 billion to the business.[6]

The ruling escalated the feud to extraordinary levels. There were fistfights in court and an attempt to trick a law clerk into revealing evidence of judicial misconduct via a phony job interview.[7]

If the brothers had only defined what "take care of my family" meant, it may have saved the family a lot of grief and a fortune in legal fees.

Sometimes it's a simple thing. The family is just asleep at the wheel when it comes to basic estate planning. They wait until it's too late, for which they pay dearly.

PAY TWO ESTATE TAX BILLS AT ONCE?

That's what happened to the Leverett family.

Clayton and Will Leverett come from a long line of cattlemen. Their great-great grandfather, the son of an English immigrant, moved from Virginia to Texas in the 1860s. He leased land and grazed cattle. He saved his money and bought small tracts from the people he was leasing from. He was able to put together a ranch of several thousand acres through hard work and frugal living.

The ranch was passed down from generation to generation. Then, in 1997, upon the death of Clayton and Will's grandmother, the IRS came knocking.

The old saying goes, "Nothing's sure except death and taxes." And like it or not, the two go hand in hand. When a relative dies and leaves assets to you, the IRS sends its condolences in the form of a big bill: the estate tax.

The Leverett family was suddenly forced to pay 38.5 percent tax on the appraised value of the land that their ancestors had purchased and worked on for over 100 years.

They weren't prepared. They didn't know the value of the land. And the estate didn't have much in the way of liquid assets to pay this debt to the IRS. So their father set up a payment plan and began working to pay it off.

But their father fell ill in the middle of 2006. The family got together a team of lawyers and accountants to try to defend themselves from the dreaded estate tax should something happen to their father. But they didn't act fast enough. Their father passed away just a few months later, before the structures that had been created went into effect. Again, they had to face the full brunt of the estate tax.

The family ranch passed to Clayton and his brother Will, the fifth generation to own and work the land. But they had to pay the government to transfer the ranch again! And, once again, they didn't have much cash saved up. And what they did have was quickly spent on lawyers and accountants, just to determine what they owed the IRS.

So they had to set up another payment plan with the IRS!

Now they have to make two estate tax payments every year. One for the grandmother's estate, and the other for the father's estate a decade later.

They will be making these payments for the next 15 years.

Five generations of the family have worked the land. But they didn't prepare to pay off their silent partner, the U.S. government, to allow them to keep family property in the family. According to Clayton, they will probably have to sell off more land to pay the government. The more land they sell, the more it hurts the profitability of their cattle-ranching operation.

Not preparing for the estate tax is the most basic family wealth blunder you can make. It destroys thousands of otherwise prosperous family businesses.

"PRINCESS TNT" SAVES THE ROYAL ESTATE

Albert von Thurn und Taxis has $2.3 billion. The 28-year-old is considered one of the most eligible bachelors in Europe. He's a billionaire prince after all.

In 1490, his ancestors organized a postal line connecting Europe's capital cities. They eventually became the postmasters general for the Holy Roman Empire. Emperors, popes, and the Prussian kings awarded the family with titles and landed estates, and from then onward his family amassed fortunes. Albert, along with his mother and sister, still lives in the 500-room castle in Regensburg, Bavaria, that his family acquired in 1812.[8]

His father was German's richest aristocrat, Prince Johannes von Thurn und Taxis. The family goes back to twelfth-century Lombardy. He was the largest landowner in Germany. He owned a bank, breweries, metallurgical companies, 10 other palaces and castles, and extensive properties in Brazil, inherited from the Portuguese royal family.

The marriage of his father, Johannes, and his mother, Gloria, came to massive media attention during the late 1970s through mid-1980s. She was 20 and he was 53. They lived a wild, jet-set lifestyle. He was openly bisexual and frequented gay clubs. Princess Gloria wore "punk"-style clothes with brightly colored hairdos, earning her the nickname "Princess TNT." She famously barked like a dog on David Letterman's show.

The couple spent lavishly. One 210,000-square-foot palace contained 400 clocks—and 72,000 square feet of glass, which required weekly cleaning. They retained 70 liveried footmen. They had dozens of cars and limousines.

Overspending and bad investments took a toll on the family's great wealth. When Prince Johannes died in December 1990, following two unsuccessful heart transplants, he left debts totaling more than $500 million. Just months before his death, the prince had fired his management consortium because of their poor performance.

His 30-year-old widow was left to sort out their complicated financial situation. For her part, she dramatically changed her lifestyle. She gave up most of her social life to spend time with her children and educate herself about her husband's financial affairs. She studied tax law, economics, and financial management with private tutors. She got to know the companies that the family owned so that she could make competent decisions.

She sold off a large portion of the family silver and jewelry, and two auctions in the early 1990s brought in about $24 million. She sold the metallurgical companies and the bank. She trimmed the palace staff and gave up all but three of her cars. She donated family heirlooms and properties to the German government in exchange for a reduced tax bill.[9]

Through her diligence, she was able to preserve the family wealth as a trustee on behalf of her young son. At age 18, Prince Albert inherited the family fortune, which had endured thanks to the efforts of his mother.

THE PUBLIC SPECTACLE

A bad marriage is another way to lose a fortune. That's why the heirs of the Spanish House of Alba forced their mother to take legal precautions before her recent marriage to a much younger man.

Spain's 85-year-old Duchess of Alba has more royal titles than anyone else in the world—40 of them. Her full name is Maria del Rosario Cayetana Alfonsa Victoria Eugenia Francisca Fitz-James Stuart y de Silva. She's distantly related to Queen Elizabeth and Winston Churchill.

She's known for her flamboyant style and frizzy hair and for having received extensive plastic surgery.

Her wealth is estimated in the range of $800 million to $5 billion. She owns estates all around Spain. The 500-year-old House of Alba owns paintings by Goya and Velazquez, a first-edition copy of Cervantes's Don Quixote and letters written by Christopher Columbus. Much of this is classified as part of Spain's national heritage and cannot be sold without government permission.

In August 2011, she married Alfonso Diez, a 60-year-old civil servant from Madrid earning $2,000 per month. He had to sign away his claim to the wealth of the House of Alba and any title. But he's planning to quit his job and live the lifestyle of a duke.[10]

The duchess's six children balked at the idea of their mother marrying this man. So the month before the wedding, the duchess signed over vast chunks of her estate to them and her grandchildren, to essentially buy their support of her marriage.

She was quoted in the Spanish press saying, "I have been alone in this project, and got nothing but negative opinions until they realized what kind of man he is."

The wedding itself was a spectacle. A crowd of several hundred clapped and cheered as the duchess kicked off her shoes and danced the flamenco on a red carpet following her wedding at Palacio de las Duenas, her opulent fifteenth-century residence in the cobblestoned old quarter of Seville. Her new husband stood by, ready to catch her if she were to fall over.

Perhaps the duchess is entitled to her fun. But this is the sort of thing that makes a wealthy aristocratic family nervous, and for good reason. It could have gone very wrong.

BEWARE OF PARASITES

Tulip. Armchair. Duck.

The second richest woman in the world was unable to remember these three words for more than a few seconds, according to experts who performed a court-ordered mental health test on her. She was also incapable of telling them where she was, what day it was, and her age.

Liliane Bettencourt, who is now 90 years old and one of France's wealthiest citizens, is the heiress to the $23.5 billion L'Oréal fortune.

The mental health experts concluded that the cosmetics billionaire suffers from "mixed dementia" and "moderately severe" Alzheimer's disease and that she was in the midst of a "slow and progressive process of cerebral degeneration."[11]

As a result, in October 2011, a French judge placed her physical well-being under the guardianship of her grandson. And her estranged daughter, Françoise Bettencourt Meyers, together with her grandsons are ordered to look after her wealth and property.

We don't have all the evidence in the case. But we think it is certainly very possible that Liliane Bettencourt has been the victim of parasitic advisers, who have been lining their own pockets at the expense of her estate.

For years, details of this mother-daughter feud have filled the French papers. Bettencourt Meyers has been filing court appeals since 2008 to have her mother made a ward of the court because of mental incapacity. But her mother's lawyers were able to successfully block her attempts in the courts.

The new evidence of Bettencourt's mental state suggests that her lawyer and legal "protector," Pascal Wilhelm, and the head of her family office, Patrice de Maistre, may have played a role in engineering this "feud."

In her latest ruling, the judge in the case condemned Wilhelm for paying himself €200,000 ($275,000) a month to represent Bettencourt. And that's probably just the tip of the iceberg.

There's also the case of the society photographer François-Marie Banier. Mr. Banier was accused of taking advantage of Bettencourt's weak mental state to get her to hand over €1.3 billion worth of old-master paintings, cash—and even a private island in the Seychelles!

Bettencourt's butler was so distressed by the conversations between Bettencourt, de Maistre, and Banier that he recorded them for 21 hours. The butler's tapes created a public scandal. They revealed that Bettencourt had €78 million hidden from the French tax authorities in Switzerland. Evidently, that was an arrangement her father had set up a long time ago. Her estate quickly settled the matter with the French government.

But it was also revealed that Clymene, the family office, was employing Florence Woerth, the wife of employment minister Éric Woerth. This revelation dovetailed with a political finance scandal: Woerth is said to have channeled Bettencourt's money into his party—and the party of French president Sarkozy, the UMP.[12]

It seems unlikely that Bettencourt, suffering as she is from "moderately severe" Alzheimer's, was the architect of this political finance scheme. Instead, what's much more likely is that de Maistre wanted to gain political influence for himself, and he made use of Mrs. Bettencourt's estate to do it.

There's a clear takeaway message from all of this: You have to keep your family close. You also have to keep a close eye on your family office advisers and their intentions.

THE END OF AN AMERICAN DYNASTY

Other times, a family breakdown can be subtler and take a lot more time, as in the case of the Busch family.

Budweiser is one of America's most iconic brands. And the family behind Budweiser was once one of America's most celebrated success stories. Until recently . . .

In 1860, a German immigrant called Eberhard Anheuser took over the St. Louis brewery that would become Anheuser-Busch. It was on the brink of bankruptcy. Four years later, his son-in-law Adolphus Busch joined him as a business partner. When Anheuser died in 1880, Busch became the company's president.

Busch introduced pasteurization to bottled beer and invested in railroad cars cooled by manufactured ice. His company introduced Budweiser in 1876 and was soon shipping it along St. Louis's extensive network of rail connections. Busch was first to bottle beer on a large scale. This helped make Budweiser America's first national beer.

Adolphus and his wife, Lily, had 13 children. Nine survived to adulthood. The Busch family lived in a Victorian mansion next to the brewery. And they were wildly successful.

When Adolphus traveled, he did so by private railcar, and a cannon blast would announce his return from a long trip. To celebrate their 50th wedding anniversary in 1911, Adolphus and Lily held a party for 13,000 people at the St. Louis Coliseum.[13]

Adolphus looked after his children well, famously giving each of them $1 million to build a home. His oldest son, August A. Busch, Sr., took over the company upon his father's death in Germany in 1913. August lived at the French-style mansion on Grant's Farm that his father had paid for.

As well as beer, the company made submarine engines in the Great War. In 1920, Prohibition put many of America's breweries out of business. But Anheuser-Busch kept afloat by selling yeast and barley malt syrup for home brewers.

August's son, August A. "Gussie" Busch Jr., said the company survived as the "biggest bootlegging supply house in the United States." This allowed the Busch family to keep their workforce and factory going. And it gave them a jump on the competition when Prohibition ended in 1933.

The company philosophy was "Spend money to make money and make friends." But perhaps the Busch family spent too much money and made too many friends.

Gussie Busch took over the company in 1946 after the death of his older brother, Adolphus Busch III. Gussie was a rough-around-the-edges character who married four times. (This was a trend followed by many Busch men.) He bought the St. Louis Cardinals in 1953 and built the first and second Busch stadiums for them to play in.

He also restored Anheuser-Busch as the nation's number one brewer. And in 1959, Anheuser-Busch opened the Busch Gardens amusement park in Tampa, Florida.

In 1975, Gussie Busch's eldest son, August "Auggie" Busch III, forced his father's resignation as chief executive. Auggie accused his father of ignoring the growth of the competition. Auggie wanted to fight an advertising war against their largest rival, the Miller Brewing Company.

The problem was that all this spending whittled down the family's ownership of Anheuser-Busch to just 12.5 percent at the time of Gussie's death. Worse, his death unlocked trusts that allowed family members to sell off even more stock over the coming years.

When Auggie took over the reins at Anheuser-Busch, he took the company public. He used the proceeds to build 11 new breweries and support one of the biggest advertising budgets in the country. By the 1990s, Anheuser-Busch sold one of every two beers in the United States.

But this growth had come at great expense. The Busch family's ownership stake shrank to only 4 percent of the company. But in St. Louis they were still treated as if they owned the place. And Auggie's eldest son, August Busch IV, was born the scion of an American business dynasty.

But by most accounts, he was a reckless party boy. As a college student at the University of Arizona, he left the scene of an accident that left a 22-year-old girl dead. His father splurged on a team of lawyers and private investigators to extricate him. After an eight-month investigation, the authorities declined to press charges.

In 1985, while at St. Louis University, he had a run-in with police. And officers shot out a tire on his Mercedes. When they found out who he was, they ended up changing his tire. They did arrest him on assault charges. But a jury acquitted him.

August IV started as an assistant to the brewmaster at Anheuser-Busch and climbed through the ranks. He had some success in the marketing department, putting together some successful advertising campaigns for Budweiser in the 1990s. And in 2002 the board of directors named him CEO of the company.

In 2007 Anheuser-Busch turned a $2.1 billion dollar profit on $16.7 billion in sales. But the company failed to expand internationally. And consolidation in the brewing industry meant it was just a matter of time before the company became a takeover target. Rival brewer InBev made a series of unsolicited bids, with a final offer of $70 a share—$20 over the share price at the time. It was irresistible for the Anheuser-Busch shareholders and its board.

August IV tried to resist the takeover. He said he would have given his life to keep the company from merging. But he was powerless.

But that misses the point. The demise of the Busch dynasty began years earlier when the family sold its controlling ownership stake. August IV made $100 million from the sale. But despite the cash, he is reported to have become depressed and reclusive after the deal. After all, his family legacy—his very identity—had been lost.

In December 2010, a staff member made a 911 call from August IV's mansion in Missouri. August IV's 27-year-old girlfriend was found dead of a drug overdose—a combination of the opioid oxycodone and cocaine. The windows of that wing of the house were blacked out, and loaded guns were found in the bathroom. The police declined to press charges. But there is an ongoing civil suit against August IV.

This is clearly a sad story. But it contains an important message. And it is this: Once the focus of your family's productive life is gone, the demons start to come out.

Never sell controlling ownership of the family business unless there are no other options.

A GREAT FAMILY BUSINESS LOST

Maybe it's something about the alcohol business, but the famous Guinness family of Ireland lost ownership, after seven generations, in a similar way to the Busches.

Arthur Guinness founded the family brewery in Dublin in 1759. He and his wife had 21 children, 10 of whom lived to adulthood.

He signed a 9,000-year lease for the brewery at St. James's Gate in Dublin at an annual rent of £45.

Guinness first brewed porter in 1778 and stopped brewing ale by 1799. The dark brew was a favorite drink among the street porters of Covent Garden, London. Guinness developed several types of porter, eventually using the word *stout* to describe it.

The brewery's water came from an illegal pipe hooked up to the city's water supply. Guinness fought the city for 20 years over having to pay for the water and a subsequent fine.

The next three generations of Guinesses to inherit the brewery were not the eldest sons. Instead, the most able son did, and he was also put in charge of managing the family fortune.

They were a pro–English Protestant family selling beer to Catholics, but they were good self-promoters. And they used whatever means or connections they had, in the religion or politics, to grow the family business and their wealth.

Arthur Guinness's grandson caused scandal by having a gay relationship with a clerk in the brewery. He was banished to a family estate in Stillorgan.

The next generation's Arthur, Lord Ardilaun, was also probably gay. He married out of convenience and left the family business to enter politics. He sold his half share of the brewery for £600,000 to his younger brother Edward Cecil.

Edward grew Guinness to be the largest brewery in the world. And he floated the business on the London stock exchange in 1886, generating £4.25 million, a huge fortune in those days. But he retained only 35 percent ownership.

While highly lucrative, this event ultimately doomed family ownership of the business.

Edward moved to England and bought a title, Lord Iveagh. He was considered the second richest man in England, at a time when England was a global empire.

Two of his sons became active in English politics. They won a seat that the family held for 85 years, from 1912 to 1997. It was known in the House of Commons as Guinness-on-Sea.

Walter Guinness was Britain's agriculture minister during the 1920s.

The family members were active philanthropists. They donated estates to the Irish and English governments and gave generously to charitable foundations.

But they were becoming increasingly disconnected from the business.

Edward's three granddaughters, the "Golden Guinness Girls," who came of age in the late 1920s and early 1930s, were the Paris Hiltons of their generation. They were spoiled rich girls who became involved in various public scandals. They also had a tragic streak: each had a child who died from an illness or accident.

In the early twentieth century, the board of directors was still filled with Guinness family members. But they became increasingly insular and lacked sufficient knowledge and experience to competently lead the business. The shares were being divided between the sons of each generation. And family ownership was being diluted by mergers and expansion.

Rupert Guinness successfully led the company for 35 years. The *Guinness Book of World Records* was launched under his management. Rupert was chairman until 1962, at age 88. His younger brother and his son had been killed in World War II. So Rupert waited for his grandson, Benjamin Guinness, to reach an age at which he could take over the reins of the company. He was appointed chairman at 25, just four years after joining the business. He was a shy man who evidently wanted to become a farmer. He was not a shrewd businessman.

He tried to diversify the company outside of alcoholic beverages, which was a big mistake.

By the 1970s, the business was in bad shape, and profits were collapsing.

Since going public, management of the brewery had been passed down from father to son(s) for 100 years. Then, in 1986, Benjamin hired an outsider, Ernest Saunders, to be CEO. Saunders was an experienced executive from Nestle.

Saunders did turn the business around. He focused on selling the core stout beer.

He also pursued a bold acquisition strategy, consolidating the spirits industry. Guinness acquired Distillers Co. in 1986 for $4 billion. Distillers was bigger than Guinness. This single acquisition reduced the Guinness family's ownership from 22 percent to 4.5 percent.

And it turned out that Saunders had illegally pumped up Guinness's share price to make the stock-and-cash offer to Distillers.

The scandal sullied the Guinness name, even though the family was not involved in the stock scheme. Saunders went to jail.

To avoid a possible takeover, Guinness merged with Grand Metropolitan to form Diageo in 1997.[14]

The Guinness family still owns 51 percent of the Dublin brewery, but less than 3 percent of the company that bears their name. No Guinness family members sit on the board or have a role in the management of the business.

The Guinnesses still have plenty of money. Edward Guinness, the fourth Earl of Iveagh, is reportedly worth around $3 billion. He's a farmer and an alternative energy investor.

In 2006, the family set up a multifamily office—the Iveagh Wealth Fund. They now make a business out of managing their own wealth and offering family office services to other families.

Perhaps the Guinnesses can be as successful in this new business as they were in brewing. But it's awfully hard to generate the same returns from investing as you can get from a growing a profitable business.

Unless there is a very good reason, don't dilute ownership of the family business. And don't bring in outside management. Keep the family active and in control of the business. It's often at the core of your family's identity and its wealth-building strategy. Generally, it's better to have control of a smaller business that you know than it is to have shares in a bigger business you neither understand nor control.

INTRODUCING THE HÉNOKIENS

We're talking about the Club des Hénokiens.

The name comes from Henok, or Enoch, one of the great patriarchs of the Bible. Henok was Methuselah's father and Noah's grandfather. He was said to have lived to be 365 years old.

The family businesses that are invited to join this group have been in business for at least 200 years. (For this reason, it's also known as *l'Association d'Entreprises Familiales et Bicentenaires*.) Other membership criteria include:

- The family must be the owner or majority shareholder of a company.
- One member of the founding family must still manage the company or be a member of the board.
- The company must be financially successful, with annual revenues of more than $2 million.

There are currently 38 members from around the world. The oldest member is a Japanese family business called Hoshi Ryokan, a traditional Japanese inn founded beside a hot spring in 718.

The northern Italian Beretta family is also a member. The family has been making guns since 1526. Everyone knows the name.

The Mellerio family has been making jewelry since the early 1600s. The Barovier family has been blowing glass on the Venetian island of Murano since the 1400s. And one French winemaking member family also makes their own oak casks. (One of their casks dates from 1715 and is still in daily use.)

Every member family has a story—and an amazing history. Think of the change that has happened over the past 200 years. These businesses have survived every calamity you can imagine.

Having read all their profiles and a number of interviews with the current managers, a few things jumped out at us.

First, the managers of these businesses, rooted in history and tradition, saw entrepreneurship and innovation as key to their success. For the business to last, there has to be a wealth creator in each generation.

Incredibly, most of the families still own 100 percent of their companies. They are extremely protective of the family equity. And some had established restrictions on family members selling out of the business.

This is contrary to what you might read in family wealth books, in which they tell you to let family members be able to sell out. To preserve ownership for centuries you have to maintain your equity.

But there's one thing above all else that bound these families together. They all developed strategies to preserve and enhance their family assets. That is, they all transferred their history, their legacy, and their values down through the generations.

This has meant that each successive generation is ready to take on the challenges of the day and contribute to the success of the family enterprise. That contribution changes over time. But something of the family values and business ethos remain remarkably constant.

The Henokiens will tell you that succession planning is critical.

A PATRIARCH'S IRON GRIP SPELLS TROUBLE FOR A FAMILY BUSINESS

Trying to hold on to control of the family wealth for too long without working out a succession plan with the rest of the family is a recipe for trouble. This often happens when the patriarch of the family wealth is a hard-charging type-A personality. Sumner Redstone matches this profile to a T.

He controls the majority voting stock in Viacom and CBS. He also owns National Amusements, a theater chain that his father started and that became the foundation for the family wealth.

Redstone is a gifted entrepreneur with a laser focus on his work. His life revolves around his businesses, to the detriment of his relationships.

While successful at vanquishing his business rivals, he's also a difficult and combative person by all accounts. He's short with his subordinates.

His estranged son, Brent, filed a lawsuit against him to force the liquidation of his share of the business, worth $1 billion. He ended up taking a $240 million buyout. He now lives on a 625-acre ranch in the mountains west of Denver.[15]

Sumner and Brent had a falling out over Sumner's divorce from his wife, Brent's mother, after a 52-year marriage. (Sumner remarried a few years later, to a woman over 40 years his junior. They divorced in 2009.)

Sumner expected Brent to take his side and help with a scheme to protect Sumner's assets during the divorce proceedings. But Brent supported his mother instead. Sumner found this unacceptable and cut Brent out as a successor in retaliation.

Sumner's daughter, Shari, did support her father through the divorce. Her loyalty earned her the position of heir apparent. But he has since undermined her in public comments that he made. In a speech at Boston University, he said, "I'm in control now, and I'll be in control after I die."[16]

Sumner set up an irrevocable trust holding 80 percent of National Amusement for the benefit of his grandchildren. But it's not clear who will actually be in charge of these assets. The trust names Shari as chairperson if he quits or dies. Sumner has reportedly been trying to convince Shari to give up her rights to the chairperson role. And in July 2008 Sumner said, "The boards [of Viacom and CBS] should decide who succeeds me. I'm not worried about it 'cause it's going to be another 20, 30 years." He was 85 years old.[17]

Sumner and Shari have been quietly battling over the last few years. She has challenged him over his salary and charitable giving, while he has questioned her abilities.

Sumner, in a letter to *Forbes* magazine in 2007, disparaged Shari as having made "little or no contribution" to the entertainment empire he built.

It turned out that the catalyst for the spats was $1.6 billion in debt, which came due in December 2010.[18] Within days of the announcement about the debt, Shari and Sumner were pointing fingers at each other. Shari took some of the blame as she had been expanding the movie theater business aggressively.

Another recent scandal involved Sumner reportedly giving away $100,000 in Viacom stock to a singer. There were also reports that he ordered MTV to start developing a reality TV show for her all-girl rock group, the Electric Barbarellas. Redstone then supposedly tried to bribe a reporter to find out who snitched on him about the stock payouts.[19]

Sumner Redstone's combative, relentless business style helped him reach the top of the entertainment world. But these same traits are making succession and the future of his estate highly uncertain.

CHAPTER 10

THE FAMILY STRONGHOLD

The big news on February 11, 2011, was that Hosni Mubarak had called it quits. After supporting him for three decades, the United States threw him under a tank. Almost everywhere except in the Mubarak household, people rejoiced. We were surprised they had an opinion, one way or the other.

We got e-mails from strangers telling us what a "hopeful" development this was . . . or how "free elections" might be coming next.

Typical was the report in the *Washington Post*: "Mubarak became the second Arab leader in a month to succumb to his people's powerful thirst for freedom."[1]

"Thirst for freedom"? If Egyptians were thirsty for freedom, they must be like camels. They need a drink of it only once every 30 years. Mubarak ruled for three decades. Egyptians went without quenching their "powerful thirst for freedom" through the 1980s, 1990s, and 2000s. Apparently, they needed to bring the cup to their lips only in 2011.

Many spoke of the "jubilant crowds" and the "idealistic youth" behind the peaceful revolution.

We were tempted to mention the jubilant crowds that attended the execution of Louis XVI, or the idealistic youth who gathered to jeer at Nicholas II when he and his family were shipped off to

Yekaterinburg, where they would be murdered, along with their valet and even the cook.

Mubarak left office on Friday. The army took control on Saturday. On Sunday, the generals dissolved parliament.

Revolutions don't always turn out well. The French Revolution was a good time to be in England. The Russian Revolution was a good time to be almost anywhere other than Russia. Even the American Revolution was a good time to be elsewhere, too. And then, when Americans finally got their freedom from Britain, they almost immediately began shackling one another. Tax rates had been only about 3 percent when the English ran the colonies. Now the federal rate alone is more than 11 times as much. And for every injustice done to Americans by the English, there must be 100 Americans have done to themselves.

But revolutions happen.

Where should you be now? We don't know. But we suggest that you have a bolt-hole somewhere—a refuge, a getaway, a family stronghold.

Many things could go wrong. Earthquakes. Plagues. Volcanic eruptions. Wars. Bankruptcies. Hyperinflations. And—we wouldn't rule it out—invasions from space.

These events are hard to predict. Even something as obvious as the revolution in Egypt was unforeseen by almost everyone. We pay the CIA hundreds of billions to keep on top of things like this, but as one journal put it, sarcastically, CIA forecasts "kind of suck."[2]

However, we take up for the CIA, just as we would stand up for any drunk or half-wit. The CIA's work is at least on par with the Securities and Exchange Commission or Amtrak. We have no doubt about it. It is at least as efficient as the post office. It is as necessary as the Transportation Security Administration. And it is as competent and effective as the Congressional Ethics Committee.

But we do not take up the pen to criticize America's intelligence agencies. Instead, we merely point out that bad stuff happens.

What kind of bad stuff? All kinds. Kinds you expect. And kinds you don't.

The problem with bad stuff is that it often comes as a counterfeit, pretending to be something it is not. A "peaceful revolution," for example, can turn bloody mighty fast. And no one gives you advance notice.

Real trouble comes unannounced. If you knew that the dollar would collapse on June 3, for example, you could switch your money into euros. If the Irish prime minister called you on the phone and tipped you off—"Hey, we're going to default next Thursday"—you'd know what to do. You'd short the euro and make a bundle. Or if you intercepted a secret cable—"Nuclear Attack on Washington, D.C., 4 p.m., October 13"—you'd get out of town as soon as possible.

But black swans do not honk before they appear. They just appear.

We've spent a lot of time anticipating disaster. We expect a collapse of the international monetary system, for example. It is almost inevitable, but it is still unpredictable. We can't say when or how it will come about.

Likewise, much higher inflation rates are coming, as well as a huge sell-off in government bond markets. Those things will provoke widespread financial disasters, possibly leading to riots, revolutions, and other bad stuff.

It is possible that these financial calamities will cause a major economic disruption, like the collapse of the Roman Empire. In the chaos, trading networks could fall apart and take many decades to be rebuilt. Gross domestic product growth could turn negative and remain in the red for years. Developed regions could slide backward for generations. Emerging markets could explode. Who knows what would happen?

And then, there are the disasters that are impossible to see coming at all. For example, our old friend Marc Faber recently included an essay on "cyber security" by William S. Leavitt in his newsletter: "Whether we acquiesce or not, our lives are determined by technology and computer systems. Our electric grids, nuclear systems, water supplies, financial institutions, fuel systems, communication systems, as well as our governments, are directed by technological systems, which are subject to attack or disruption."[3]

Apparently, the cyber attackers are well-funded, very sophisticated groups engaged in serious warfare all the time. For the moment, they are outgunned by the forces of law and order—led by the United States. But imagine what happens when the United States runs out of money? How long will it take the attackers to get ahead technologically? With all the billions and billions of dollars' worth of capital in the world and the millions of people with high-tech computer skills, it seems like a matter of time before a serious black swan event occurs.

One thing about cyber war makes it especially attractive to low-budget terrorists: It costs relatively little to maintain a serious threat. No battleships necessary. No billion-dollar fighter jets. No nuclear deterrent. In fact, with the right team of software geniuses, it may be possible to turn a nation's own nuclear capability against itself.

In other words, when it comes to bad stuff, the sky's the limit. It's gonna happen eventually, one way or another. And it could be real bad.

And when bad stuff happens, you're better off being somewhere else. And being prepared.

WHERE TO GO?

Generally, bad stuff seems to happen most often in cities. Why is that? Cities are where most people live. It is where governments are. And it is where the labor force is most specialized.

There are no subsistence farmers living in cities. Nor do urban populations "live off the land." Instead, they depend on complex networks of commerce. The typical city dweller produces neither food nor energy. He sits all day in an office, completely dependent on others to provide power and food. Then he goes home, still completely dependent on the division of labor for his most important needs.

Progress can be described as the elaboration of the division of labor. In man's most primitive state, specialization is extremely limited. From what we've been told, the early man was the hunter. Early woman gathered. That's about the extent of it.

As the tribe grows larger, specialization increases. One person might tend the fire. Another might be in charge of making clothes or arrows.

The advent of sedentary agriculture and towns caused a big leap forward in human progress and, not coincidentally, the division of labor. Some townspeople went out to tend the fields. Others began to focus on woodworking or iron mongering or making weapons or clothes. Some played cards and hung around at bars. There was soon a homebuilding industry and, not long after, merchants, prostitutes, and bankers and even shyster lawyers and tax collectors.

As the division of labor expanded, the average person became richer and more dependent on others. In order to eat, someone else had to plant and till and harvest and hunt and gather. And then, when agriculture became mechanized, he depended on faraway people who produced oil and gasoline and people who built tractors and combines and bankers who financed industries and factories. And, of course, he was more dependent on money, too. In the days when he bartered, money was no threat. Then, when he traded only with gold and silver coins, there were no monetary breakdowns, no hyperinflations, and no financial crises.

As the twentieth century progressed, more and more people gave up agriculture, moved to cities, and took part in other industries. Today, cities may have millions of residents—like Bombay with 14 million or Sao Paulo with 20 million, or Mexico City with even more. All of these people are dependent on vast, stretched lines of communication and commerce.

Even the farmers themselves are now dependent on these sophisticated networks of commerce. They depend on money and what it will buy. Agriculture has become monocultural. That is, a farmer is likely to produce only wheat. Or only rapeseed. Or only barley. Or only cattle. Gone are the chickens around the farmhouse and the pig in the back pen. If the system of transport and trade breaks down—or if the money itself goes bad—thousands of farmers could go hungry, too.

There are black swans all over the place, waiting to be discovered. And when a black swan appears, people in the cities seem to suffer most.

In the hyperinflation in Germany in 1923, for example, farmers had so much food they ran out of storage space. But they wouldn't sell it to city slickers. The mark was losing value so fast, farmers preferred to hold their crops off the market, knowing that the price was soaring and that if they sold, the money they got would soon be worthless.

People in the cities, meanwhile, were starving. Soon, gangs roved the countryside, raiding rural barns and houses and occasionally killing farmers who tried to resist.

Plagues hit city dwellers hard, too. Proximity seems to be a curse when an infectious disease appears.

And, of course, in time of war and revolution, cities tend to be the battlegrounds. Advancing armies are rarely polite. Even if they are advancing through the countryside, they are usually advancing toward cities, which they attack. In the old days, cities were besieged, starved out, and then, when they were taken, the attacking soldiers were given three days in which to sack the cities. In other words, they had three days to commit whatever mischief and mayhem their imaginations suggested.

When bad stuff happens, progress goes into reverse, and so does the division of labor. When an economy goes backward, much of the specialization that developed during the boom years turns out to be uneconomic, unaffordable, or unwanted. People may be willing to pay someone to park their car when they are flush. But when they are broke, they will park their own cars.

As the division of labor goes backward, people also find they must tend to their own food and energy needs. Here is where it gets very tough for people who live in cities. They have no stores of Mason jars with food from their own gardens that they have canned themselves. They have no hams hanging in the barn or stocked away in the larder. They have no animals on the hoof that they can slaughter. They get no eggs from the chickens they don't have, and they can hardly go into the local park and shoot squirrels to make a pie.

Instead, they are out of luck.

Generally, when the black swans come out, you are better off in the country—with country-boy skills, real friends and family close at hand, and old-time farm supplies.

We once met a fellow who had a keen appreciation for apocalypse. He was sure it was coming. So he moved to Arkansas where, he said, "I'm protected by 300 miles of armed hillbillies."

That's something else to think about. Not only do you have to worry about food and energy, you also have to worry about your neighbors. If you have a nice little vegetable garden next to a large apartment complex, for example, you might have a hard time protecting your crops. And don't count on fattening a calf in Central Park during a famine.

You need to be somewhere else. Where?

"Little electricity or gasoline," reports an eyewitness from the *Washington Post*, visiting Sendai, Japan, in March 2011. "Nearly all restaurants and shops are closed . . . roads blocked, supplies depleted . . . the devastation . . . is catastrophic."[4]

We are elaborating on the benefits of having a family stronghold . . . a retreat . . . a bolt-hole somewhere. When the going gets tough, you need a tough place to go to.

In 2011, we saw two big blow-ups: one in the Arab countries, the other in Japan.

Neither was expected. What's next? Obviously, we don't know. If it's a big, nasty surprise, we're hope we're not in Bethesda, Maryland, when it comes.

Why? Because the supermarkets would be cleaned out in minutes, the gas stations would run dry, and we'd be trapped in a hostile environment, depending on the kindness of strangers and the competence of government officials.

What do you need to survive a disaster? First, you need access to water. As we've seen in Japan, even the most developed and sophisticated infrastructure in the world can collapse when it is struck by an earthquake and a tsunami. Public water pipes break. It can take weeks or months to replace them, assuming the government and local utilities are still functioning.

That's why it's a good idea to have your own private source of water: a spring; a well; a small, clean stream. Failing that, you should have enough water stocked up to last at least a couple of weeks.

Then you need to worry about food. How long could you live on what is in your refrigerator? We could make it for about 24 hours. Then it would be slim pickings. And what if the supermarket were closed? What if the 7–11 were stripped bare? What if trucks couldn't make deliveries?

Well, surely the president would call out the National Guard. Yes, if everything is working as it should, and the National Guard doesn't have more important things to worry about.

Just as a precaution, you should maintain a stock of canned goods and dried food. Enough to last two weeks is the minimum. A month is better. Then, rotate your stock—don't leave it untouched for so long it goes bad.

Having an inventory of basic foodstuffs and water is essential. It will keep you calm. You won't be in desperate straits. It will give you time to carefully assess the situation and choose your best option. You won't do something rash.

But what if the breakdown stays broken down for months? War . . . hyperinflation . . . a full collapse of the financial or political system . . . the crisis could take many months to run its course. In the meantime, supply and distribution systems may be severely or completely interrupted. You need a strategy.

A PLACE OF YOUR OWN

And that's where the family stronghold comes into play. First, you must be able to get there. When we were confronted with the Y2K crisis more than a decade ago, we lived in Paris. Maybe the French bureaucrats would be able to maintain order, and maybe they wouldn't. We kept our tank full of gas, just in case. It took only one tank of gas to get out to our country house. We figured we'd wait for the desperate mobs to leave the streets. Then we'd drive out of the city and make our way to the country. Once there, we had food stockpiled in the pantry and firewood ricked up to the eaves in the barn. There were cattle on the hoof in the fields and chickens in the henhouse.

Your stronghold should be a place where you can live almost indefinitely on local resources. It doesn't mean you have to have everything you need on your own property. But you have what it takes to trade with your friends and neighbors to get what you need. You may have to barter for a cow or vegetables with the local farmers, for example. You may have to improvise with tools and machinery. You will almost certainly get your hands dirty. And you should keep on hand some small gold and silver coins. They could be useful.

Of course, your standard of living will surely go down, at least in money terms. But it could be fun. Some people actually yearn for simpler, more "authentic" lives. Some find genuine satisfaction in small community life, with heavy emphasis on self-sufficiency and survival skills. As for us, we're never happier than when we're cutting firewood or planting a garden. Keep your laptops and your hard drives. Give us a wrench and a hammer! Dining *al fresco* on *dinde aux groseilles* at a fancy restaurant is fine, but we're just as happy eating a turkey sandwich outside in the yard.

A breakdown in complex civilization? Bring it on!

Since the beginning of the twentieth century, many people have gone to bed hungry. Tens of millions have died of starvation. But almost all the deaths can be traced to the murderous intentions or incompetent administration of governments. In this regard, as in many others, the Soviet Union and China were world leaders. Goofy theories and bad policies reduced the amount of food available. Then communist governments used food shortages as a weapon against their internal enemies.

Obviously, the first protection against famine is wealth. There is almost always food available at some price. Generally, but not always, it goes to the highest bidder. So having some money is in itself a measure of safety. Always has been.

But people with wealth can also be popular scapegoats when times get tough. The easy money policies of the Fed during the last two decades have made America's rich richer than ever, while the incomes and wealth of 99 percent of the population have barely risen at all. If food supplies were short, it wouldn't be at all surprising if the mobs turned against "the rich," intentionally withholding food from them.

Hunger was largely responsible for the French Revolution. Mobs gathered in front the Tuileries Palace, protesting the high cost of food. Inflation and bad weather had driven up the price of a loaf of bread to almost an entire day's wages by an ordinary laborer.

Marie Antoinette, wife of Louis XVI, is said to have asked:

"What are they complaining about?"

"They have no bread," came the answer.

"Well, let them eat cake," was her witty, but ultimately fatal, reply.

She lost her head in the Revolution. So did thousands of others.

Mobs need scapegoats. And hungry mobs are not particularly careful about whom they choose.

"That's one of the big differences between the French and British aristocracy," our family matriarch, Elizabeth, enlightened us:

The French aristocrats were encouraged to move to Versailles and take part in the life of the central government. They may have owned vast estates in Normandy or Aquitaine. But the real action—social, as well as political—took place in and near Paris. So they lost contact with their sources of power, their *terres*, their family strongholds. When the revolution came, they had no local support. Their peasants turned against them. Many lost their estates and their heads.

The English aristocracy, on the other hand, tended to be jealous of its local rights and privileges and stuck close to its land. They were never so cut off from the local people and never so dependent on the court of St. James in London. That was part of the reason they evolved a different, more decentralized system of government with more emphasis on individual rights and limited central power. And it's probably why there was never any popular uprising against them.

Lesson? If you want to keep your head, keep your feet on the ground. Stay close to your roots, your base, and your family stronghold.

You need roots, a sense of being connected, a refuge from the outside world, a place where your family is safe and sure of itself. As our old friend Gary North says, you need a place where you can "dig in."

Today, very few families can survive on their own. In developed countries, there are few subsistence farmers left. Very few people could live for more than just a few days if the sophisticated system of production and distribution were interrupted. Yet it seems very unlikely that the system won't be disrupted.

War, revolution, Internet bugs, real bugs, bankruptcy, hyperinflation—there are so many things that could go wrong, it is hard to believe that at least one of them won't.

In light of this, you should have a place where the family can run, hide, and survive. Where? The best place is a farm—a place not too far from where you usually are, easy to get to, and stocked with enough food and water to keep you going for a few months. Best bet is an old-fashioned pantry full of canned goods, chickens in the hen house, and a pig or two in the sty.

Here in Maryland, your editors have not completely followed their own advice. They have a country house in Maryland, for example. But they have no animals. And they have never gotten around to stocking anything more than firewood and wine. How long can you survive on Bordeaux? We don't know, but in case of a total breakdown, we intend to find out.

Does this sound alarmist? Paranoid? Nutty?

Maybe. We are so accustomed to thinking that everything will work out fine. It always has, at least in our lifetimes. But everything doesn't always work out fine. There are, remember, a few black swans as well as many white ones. Those black swans can be nasty. And it takes only one to wipe you out.

Here's one way to look at it: A bolt-hole of your own is like an insurance policy. Maybe you won't need it. But if you do need it, you'll need it very, very badly.

Of course, if an asteroid strikes the Earth or if the Yellowstone volcano blows up or if government goons go through the countryside, as the Soviets did in the Ukraine, torturing peasants to find out where they had hidden grain, even a family farm of your own may not save you. But in the case of many other calamities, it might make the difference between life and death.

"You're just looking at the negative side of it," adds Elizabeth. On the positive side, a family stronghold can give you a richer family life. You need a place that gives your family a sense of identity, unity, and stability. Generations come and go. But places last. A place gives a family a sense of permanence, too:

> Family strongholds help families develop their own culture . . . their own resources . . . their own histories. They are good places to get the family together for holidays, for reunions and to help family members learn to work together. They're places that you remember, no matter where you go or where you live. They're places where grandparents live. Where family portraits and family papers are stored. Places you think about. Places where you bury your gold.
>
> A family stronghold or a refuge is also a good place to retreat to, to recover and to think. It should be fully paid for, of course. You don't want to have to worry about it. It should be a real stronghold where you're safe. And where you're happy. So if you lose your job, for example, it's a place where you go back to, to take time to think about your next move. Or if you want to write a book or invent a new computer app or just try to figure out what's going on in your life, a family stronghold is a good place to do it. It should be quiet, tranquil, and protective.

We recovered the family farm in Maryland last year, after spending 15 years in Europe. The place was a mess: overgrown with trees and bushes, with fallen-down fences and grown-up fields, cracked and rotting shutters on the house, and barn roofs that you could see daylight through.

Almost every weekend since, we've spent fixing the place up. Sometimes just Edward (the last child still living with us) would be available to help. Sometimes one of the other boys would come home for the weekend. Occasionally, the girls would be able to help out, too. And sometimes—such as Thanksgiving weekend—we had the whole family outside—pruning, clipping, digging, raking, nailing.

It is a great thing when you can get the children to help. There's nothing quiet or tranquil about it. The noise of chainsaws and old diesel tractors. Hammering. Sawing. Clipping. Sweating. Swearing.

Working together as a family is probably the best way to build a family and to hold onto family wealth.

NOTES

PREFACE

1. Yuichi Shoda, Walter Mischel, et al., "Predicting Adolescent Cognitive and Self-Regulatory Competencies From Preschool Delay of Gratification: Identifying Diagnostic Conditions," *Developmental Psychology*, 26(6) (1990): 978–986.
2. Jonah Lehrer, "Don't!: The Secret of Self-Control," *The New Yorker*, May 18, 2009.

CHAPTER 1

1. Denise H. Kenyon-Rouvinez, Gordon Adler, et al., *Sharing Wisdom, Building Values: Letters From Family Business Owners to Their Successors* (Marietta, GA: Family Enterprise Publishers, 2002), 137.
2. Michael Snyder, "19 Statistics about the Poor that Will Absolutely Astound You," *The Economic Collapse* (blog), Nov. 4, 2011, http://theeconomic collapseblog.com/archives/extreme-poverty-is-now-at-record-levels-19-statistics-about-the-poor-that-will-absolutely-astound-you.
3. Douglas Holtz-Eakin, David Joulfaian, et al., "The Carnegie Conjecture: Some Empirical Evidence," *Quarterly Journal of Economics*, May 1993.
4. Thomas J. Stanley and William D. Danko, *The Millionaire Next Door: The Surprising Secrets of America's Wealthy* (New York: Pocket Books, 1996).

5. Robert Cottrell, "Danger: Riches Ahead," *Intelligent Life*, September 2007.

6. Gareth Davies, "Stop Cruising and Start Supporting," Letter, *Financial Times*, March 5, 2011.

7. Laurence Kotlikoff, "Some Deficit Magic for the Supercommittee," Bloomberg, Nov. 28, 2011.

8. Robert J. Samuelson, "Who Will Stand up to AARP?" *Orange County Register*, Feb. 21, 2011.

9. James E. Hughes Jr., *Family Wealth: Keeping It in the Family—How Family Members and Their Advisers Preserve Human, Intellectual, and Financial Assets for Generations* (New York: Bloomberg Press, 2004), 35.

CHAPTER 2

1. "Iphigene Ochs Is Dead; Central Figure in Times's History," *New York Times*, Feb. 27, 1990.

2. Niall Ferguson, *The House of Rothschild, Vol. 1: Money's Prophets, 1798–1848* (New York: Penguin Books, 1998).

3. Miriam Rothschild, "The Silent Members of the First EEC: Family Reflections. II: The Women," *The Rothschilds: Essays on the History of a European Family* (ed. Georg Heuberger) (Woodbridge, England: Boydell & Brewer), 155–164.

4. Ferguson.

CHAPTER 3

1. Jeff E. Biddle and Daniel S. Hamermesh, "Beauty, Productivity and Discrimination: Lawyers' Looks and Lucre," *Journal of Labor Economics* 16(1) (1998): 172–201.

2. Richard J. Herrnstein and Charles A. Murray, *The Bell Curve: Intelligence and Class Structure in American Life* (New York: Simon & Schuster, 1996).

3. "Doug Casey on Charities," www.caseyresearch.com/cwc/doug-casey-charities.

4. Jonathan Davis, "Secrets of Success: Compounding Is the Road to Riches," *Independent*, Sept. 16, 2006.

5. Mike Tierney, "With Nine Mouths to Feed, Travis Henry Says He's Broke," *New York Times*, March 11, 2009.

6. Ellen Goodstein, "Unlucky Lottery Winners Who Lost Their Money," *Bankrate* (blog), March 29, 2006, www.bankrate.com/brm/news/advice/20041108a3.asp.

7. Brandon Schmid, "The Lottery Is Not the Solution: Lottery Winners Who Have Lost Their Millions," *How to Manage Money Tips* (blog),

http://howtomanagemoneytips.com/the-lottery-is-not-the-solution-lottery-winners-who-have-lost-their-millions/.
8. Goodstein.

CHAPTER 4

1. "Doug Casey on Fresh Starts," www.caseyresearch.com/cwc/doug-casey-fresh-starts.
2. "William C. Weldon Profile," Forbes.com, http://people.forbes.com/profile/william-c-weldon/46484.
3. Abbigail J. Chiodo and Michael T. Owyang, "For Love or Money: Why Married Men Make More," *Regional Economist*, April 2002.

CHAPTER 5

1. Tyler Cowen, "The Inequality that Matters," *American Interest*, January/February 2011.
2. Gary P. Brinson, L. Randolph Hood, et al. "Determinants of Portfolio Performance," *Financial Analysts Journal*, July/August 1986.
3. Roger G. Ibbotson and Paul D. Kaplan, "Does Asset Allocation Policy Explain 40%, 90%, or 100% of Performance?" *Financial Analysts Journal*, January/February 2000.
4. Jeffrey Snider, "Wall Street's Random Walk Doesn't Exist," *Real Clear Markets* (blog), June 3, 2011, www.realclearmarkets.com/articles/2011/06/03/wall_streets_random_walk_doesnt_exist_99056.html.
5. Martin Conrad, "The Money Paradox," *Barron's*, December 31, 2011.
6. Kevin Bambrough, "Oil or Not, Here They Come," *Markets at a Glance*, Sprott Asset Management, October 2011.

CHAPTER 6

1. Text of Bush's speech at West Point, *New York Times*, June 1, 2002.
2. Detlev S. Schlichter, "Forty Years of Paper Money," *Wall Street Journal*, Aug. 15, 2011.
3. "Remarks by Governor Ben S. Bernanke before the National Economists Club," Nov. 21, 2002, www.federalreserve.gov/boarddocs/speeches/2002/20021121/default.htm.
4. Carmen M. Reinhart and Kenneth S. Rogoff, "Growth in a Time of Debt," *American Economic Review Papers and Proceedings*, January 2010.

CHAPTER 7

1. "Millionaires Go Missing," *Wall Street Journal*, May 27, 2009.
2. Rich Rabkin, "Gold and Money in Extremis . . . One Man's Story," *The Gloom, Boom and Doom Report* (Marc Faber, ed.), November 2011.

CHAPTER 8

1. James Olan Hutcheson, "The End of a 1,400-Year-Old Business," *BusinessWeek Special Report*, April 16, 2007.

CHAPTER 9

1. Lee Hausner and Douglas K. Freeman, *The Legacy Family: The Definitive Guide to Creating a Successful Multigenerational Family* (New York: Palgrave Macmillan, 2009), 28–29.
2. Steve Arnold, "Tough, Honest Business Grew From Junk Buyer to Scrap Empire," *Hamilton Spectator*, Dec. 15, 2008.
3. Guy Crittenden, "The Waxman Decision," *Solid Waste & Recycling*, Aug. 1, 2002.
4. "Bobby Waxman Sentenced to 8 Years in Prison," *Solid Waste & Recycling*, Oct. 31, 2011. www.solidwastemag.com/news/bobby-waxman-sentenced-to-8-years-in-prison/1000653208/
5. "The 50 Wealthiest Greeks in America List," *National Herald*, Feb. 19, 2011.
6. Tere D'Amato, "Family Feuds: Part 1," *Private Wealth*, December 2008.
7. Gerard O'Neill, "The Demoulas Trap," *Boston*, December 2006.
8. Andrew Farell, "The World's Richest People: Dynasties of the Billionaires," *Forbes*, Oct. 29, 2008.
9. Bob Colacello, "The Conversion of Gloria TNT," *Vanity Fair*, June 2006.
10. Tom Worden, "Spanish Duchess Marries Toyboy in Lavish Wedding Ceremony," *Mail* Online, Oct. 6, 2011.
11. Henry Samuel, "L'Oréal Heiress Liliane Bettencourt 'Unable to Remember Three Words,'" *The Telegraph*, Oct. 18, 2011.
12. Peter Allen, "Office of Financial Advisor to L'Oréal Heiress Raided in Sarkozy Funding Investigation," *The Telegraph*, July 10, 2010.
13. Susan Berfield, "The Fall of the House of Busch," *Bloomberg Businessweek*, July 17, 2011.
14. Bill Yenne, *Guinness: The 250-Year Quest for the Perfect Pint* (Hoboken, NJ: John Wiley & Sons, Inc., 2007).
15. Claudia Eller and Meg James, "Redstone Files for Divorce," *Los Angeles Times*, Oct. 22, 2008.

16. Robert Lenzer and Devon Pendleton, "Family Feud," *Forbes*, Nov. 12, 2007.
17. D'Amato.
18. "National Amusements to Sell CBS and Viacom Shares," *New York Times Dealbook*, Oct. 14, 2009.
19. Peter Lauria, "Sumner's Witch Hunt," *Daily Beast*, July 20, 2010.

CHAPTER 10

1. Craig Whitlock, "Mubarak Steps Down; Egypt Exults," *Washington Post*, Feb. 12, 2011.
2. Spencer Ackerman, "CIA: Our Mideast Forecasts Kind of Suck," *Wired Danger Room* (blog), Feb. 10, 2011.
3. William S. Leavitt, "Cyber Security," *The Gloom, Boom & Doom Report* (Mark Faber, ed.), February 2011.
4. Andrew Higgins, "In Sendai, Long Lines of Quiet Desperation," *Washington Post*, March 15, 2011.

ABOUT THE AUTHORS

Bill Bonner is president and CEO of Agora Publishing, one of the world's largest financial newsletter companies. He is the creator of the *Daily Reckoning*, a financial newsletter with more than 540,760 readers of six different global daily editions, including French and German. Bonner coauthored with Addison Wiggin the international bestsellers *Financial Reckoning Day* (John Wiley & Sons, 2003) and *Empire of Debt* (Wiley, 2006) and coauthored his third *New York Times* bestselling book, *Mobs, Messiahs, and Markets* (Wiley, 2009) *with Lila Rajiva*. In 2011, he authored *Dice Have No Memory: Big Bets and Bad Economics from Paris to the Pampas* (Wiley). He files his *Daily Reckoning* dispatches from a ranch in Argentina, the home office in Maryland, various joint ventures, and other hot spots around the globe.

Will Bonner is executive director of the Bonner & Partners Family Office, an independent estate-planning and investment research group. Will got his start working in the mailroom of the family business, Agora, at age 11. Later, he helped launch, and served as CEO of, Early to Rise, a leading self-improvement publishing business. In 2007, he opened Agora's South American office in Buenos Aires, Argentina, and set up a successful business partnership that is one of the largest investment research and education companies publishing in Spanish. He is a graduate of St. John's College's Great Books program, earning a double major in philosophy and mathematics. He lives with his wife and two children in Delray Beach, Florida. He's the eldest of Bill's six children.

INDEX

BONNER & PARTNERS
Family Office

Is Your Family Prepared to Pass on Wealth?

Take the complimentary Family Wealth Survey to find out: www.bonnerfamilyoffice.com/wealth

Bonner & Partners Family Office helps members setup their own family office structure within 12 months.

Managed by authors Bill and Will Bonner, it provides daily guidance in the markets, a weekly family wealth-building report, a model asset allocation, monthly legacy investing recommendations, a comprehensive guide to family governance, and advice on legal structures and tax avoidance.

To find out more about applying for membership, please contact our Member Liaison, Emma Walsh, at 1-855-849-2885. You can also reach Emma by email at: ewalsh@bonnerfamilyoffice.com.

The Family Wealth Survey is the best way to get started in setting up your own family office structure. You can find out more at: www.bonnerfamilyoffice.com/wealth